THE MEANINGS *of* "BEAUTY AND THE BEAST"

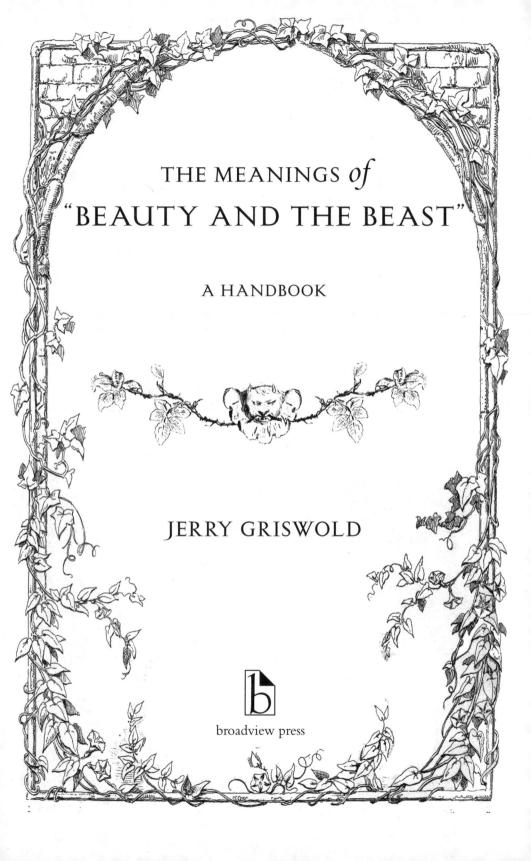

THE MEANINGS *of*
"BEAUTY AND THE BEAST"

A HANDBOOK

JERRY GRISWOLD

broadview press

National Library of Canada Cataloguing in Publication

Griswold, Jerome
    The meanings of "Beauty and the Beast": a handbook / Jerry Griswold.

Includes bibliographical references.
ISBN 1-55111-563-8

1. Beauty and the beast (Tale)—History and criticism. 2. Leprince de Beaumont, Madame (Jeanne-Marie), 1711-1780. Belle et la bête. 3. Fairy tales—History and criticism.I. Title.

PQ1995.L75B343 2004   398.21   C2003-906408-5

Broadview Press Ltd. is an independent, international publishing house, incorporated in 1985. Broadview believes in shared ownership, both with its employees and with the general public; since the year 2000 Broadview shares have traded publicly on the Toronto Venture Exchange under the symbol BDP.

We welcome comments and suggestions regarding any aspect of our publications—please feel free to contact us at the addresses below or at broadview@broadviewpress.com.

North America:

PO Box 1243, Peterborough, Ontario, Canada K9J 7H5

3576 California Road, Orchard Park, NY, USA 14127

Tel: (705) 743-8990; Fax: (705) 743-8353
E-mail: customerservice@broadviewpress.com

UK, Ireland, and continental Europe:

NBN Plymbridge
Estover Road
Plymouth PL6 7PY UK

Tel: 44 (0) 1752 202301;
Fax: 44 (0) 1752 202331
Fax Order Line: 44 (0) 1752 202333
Customer Service:
cservs@nbnplymbridge.com
Orders:
orders@nbnplymbridge.com

Australia and New Zealand:

UNIREPS,
University of New South Wales
Sydney, NSW, 2052

Tel: 61 2 9664 0999;
Fax: 61 2 9664 5420
E-mail:
info.press@unsw.edu.au

www.broadviewpress.com

Broadview Press Ltd. gratefully acknowledges the financial support of the Government of Canada through the Book Publishing Industry Development Program for our publishing activities.

Book design and composition by George Kirkpatrick

PRINTED IN CANADA

WHAT COUNTS FOR US in a work of literature is the possibility of being able to continue to unpeel it like a never-ending artichoke, discovering more and more new dimensions in reading.

—ITALO CALVINO, *Why Read the Classics*

CONTENTS

INTRODUCTION

THIS BOOK IS THE HISTORY of an obsession. Over the years, I have asked my students to identify their favorite fairy tale and then to consider why that is so, since answering that question will tell them things about themselves. In my own case, for quite some time, "Beauty and the Beast" has been my favorite fairy tale. For more than ten years now, like a Zen student with a koan, I have thought and thought about this story; and I am only now beginning to understand some of the reasons of its appeal to me.

In examining that story here, I am "beating around the bush." At the center of this study is the most well-known version of the story: Madame LePrince de Beaumont's "Beauty and the Beast." That text serves as a touchstone; and I circle around it, investigating it this way and that, returning to it time and time again. My aim in all this has been to enter the very heart of this story; after all, the point of beating around the bush is to finally be *in* the bush. In this book, I invite students of the fairy tale and general readers to do the same.

In these pages will be found many possible ways of understanding "Beauty and the Beast." I look at the work biographically, coming to understand how this story about a difficult courtship between a beautiful virgin and her beastly suitor reflects the problems of arranged marriages, a custom which led to Beaumont's own disastrous marriage and divorce. And I look at the work historically, noting how the account of Beauty's merchant family and the aristocratic Beast might be seen against the backdrop of the eighteenth-century clash between the rising mercantile class and the bluebloods of the *ancien regime*.

Turning to illustrated versions of the text, this work examines how the story became a kind of reverse Rorschach test for artists, an occasion to reveal themselves in deciding what a woman named "Beauty" looks like and how a man might be made into a beast. Approaching from a different direction, I also examine the sources of the story; I point out that in its ancient antecedents "Beauty and the Beast" tells of the problems of "marrying out" (the difficulties of a maiden leaving her family and tribe and joining her husband's family and tribe), and I show how Beaumont rewrote another's version, changing an erotic story told in adult circles into one of the very first works of Children's Literature.

Coming at the tale in yet another way, I examine how contemporary authors have rewritten the story: how feminist Angela Carter made it into an account of a liberated woman's "walk on the wild side" and how science-fiction writer Tanith Lee turned it into a racial allegory where Beauty is undone by her encounter with a strikingly beautiful black male. And looking at film versions by Jean Cocteau and Disney Studios, I discuss still other ways of accessing meaning in the tale by observing how gay writers have used "Beauty and the Beast" as an occasion to talk about intolerance towards "difference."

As varied as my methods are, even these do not exhaust the richness and depth of this remarkable story. Pamela Travers—the author of the Mary Poppins books and a great student of fairy tales—once said, "The fairy tale is like a prism in the window. It reflects *many* meanings."[1] In a similar way, Italo Calvino observed in his *Why Read the Classics?* "What counts for us in a work of literature is the possibility of being able to continue to unpeel it like a never-ending artichoke, discovering more and more new dimensions in reading."[2]

"Beauty and the Beast" has that gem-like or prism-like perfection and, to mix metaphors, the unpeeling of that artichoke is my endeavor here. Still, one cannot go very far in that direction without encountering a problem with traditional techniques of *explication de texte*. "We go to the fairy tales not so much for *their* meanings as *our* meanings," Pamela Travers said. Echoing that sentiment,

---

1 I quote Pamela Travers several times in this Introduction. All her remarks were made to me in conversations. Some of her ideas about fairy tales can, however, be found in *About the Sleeping Beauty* (New York: McGraw-Hill, 1975) and *What the Bee Knows: Reflections on Myth, Symbol and Story* (London: Penguin, 1993). Some of my conversations with Travers appear in my interview: "P.L. Travers: The Art of Fiction LXIII," *The Paris Review* 24,85 (Winter 1982): 210-29; rptd. in *Writers at Work, Ninth Series*, ed. George Plimpton (New York: Penguin, 1992) 37-53, and in *Women Writers at Work*, rev. ed., ed. George Plimpton (New York: Penguin, 1998). After her death, I published a remembrance of Travers ("Revealing Herself to Herself") in the *Los Angeles Times Book Review* 16 June 1996: 2.

2 Italo Calvino, *Why Read the Classics?*, trans. Martin McLaughlin (New York: Pantheon Books, 1999) 197.

Northrop Frye once observed: "Since myths can be made to mean an indefinite number of things, it is more fruitful to study what in fact myths have been made to mean."[1]

As a result, the subject of this book is not only the meanings that can be discovered *in* "Beauty and the Beast," but also the meanings that have been imposed *upon* "Beauty and the Beast." So, this study presents Bruno Bettelheim's "Beauty and the Beast," and Jean Cocteau's, and Angela Carter's, and that of dozens of others.

In a fashion, I am considering different translations of the same story. In itself, Beaumont's "Beauty and the Beast" is a description of experience in the dream language of story. To offer, say, a psychoanalytic interpretation is to translate the story into a different language. Illustrated versions of the story, or revisions of the tale by contemporary writers, are also translations into still other languages, as are the additional translations of the story into films. My endeavor, then, is to point to these various translations of the tale into different languages — the equivalent of Spanish, Latin, Russian, Japanese, and dozens of other tongues. My hope is that by reading this story in multiple translations, the reader will suddenly — like the moment in a cartoon when a light bulb suddenly appears above a character's head — "get" what "Beauty and the Beast" is about: that through a growing understanding of the story, something will finally "click," and the reader will intuit the experience described there.

I offer here no apology for my obsession and sole-minded attention to a single story, as opposed to my writing another kind of book concerned with many works. What is the use, I have sometimes wondered, of many shallow wells if you don't reach water. Instead, I have found (as I hope readers of this book will find) that sole-mindedness and the experience of depth, when it is thorough and genuine, does eventually give way to an awakened breadth.

ACKNOWLEDGMENTS

In writing this work, I owe a great debt to Betsy Hearne. Her *Beauty and the Beast: Visions and Revisions of an Old Tale* (1989) is

---

1 Northrop Frye, *Anatomy of Criticism* (Princeton, NJ: Princeton University Press, 1957) 204.

the only other monograph exclusively devoted to this story, and from it I have learned much. Organizing her work in a chronological fashion, Hearne (quite literally and quite usefully) shows how the tale has changed over the years. Suspicious of discussions of meaning, however, she advises us that her book deliberately avoids literary interpretation: "This is a study of the art and artifice of the story rather than an analysis of its meaning. In this introspective era, the study of a story's meaning sometimes overshadows the story itself. We must remember that the story is fundamental and irrepressible, the meaning secondary and chameleon in that it shifts with time and culture."[1]

In this book, I am wandering in that very realm Hearne avoids. I am primarily concerned with the meanings of "Beauty and the Beast," and, as that plural suggests, I am not troubled by shifting meanings. In fact, because I welcome multiple meanings, instead of Hearne's chronological approach, I organize my work in terms of the story's appearance in various genres (from story to film) in order to explore meaning from deliberately different points of view. Finally, I do not reckon multiple meanings as *prima facie* evidence of the dubiousness of literary criticism. Instead, I take this versatility as one measure of the tale's potency and prism-like perfection.

Besides Hearne, I owe debts of gratitude to others. Over the years, knowing of my obsession, friends and acquaintances have sent me clippings, ideas, and comments that have served as clues that sent me in new directions or encouraged me to go deeper; they are too numerous to mention or remember. More than any others, however, it has been my students who, for more than ten years, explored with me the varied meanings of this tale and its reincarnations; and from them, in the give-and-take of discussion, I have learned much that shaped the manuscript of this work. In bringing this manuscript to press, I wish to thank my editors Julia Gaunce and Betsy Struthers, as well as the staff at Broadview Press, for their aid and guidance.

This book also reprints some work by others. Let me also acknowledge the permissions granted to do so:

1 Betsy Hearne, *Beauty and the Beast: Visions and Revisions of an Old Tale* (Chicago, IL: University of Chicago Press, 1989) iv. Subsequent references to this text designated as *Visions and Revisions*.

ONE

THE IMPORTANCE OF "BEAUTY AND THE BEAST"

WHILE AUTHORS SOMETIMES have to make the case for the significance of their subject, the situation is considerably easier when their topic is a literary work which has itself touched many people in some deep way. In that regard, the facts suggest that "Beauty and the Beast" is a story especially worthy of contemplation.

The popularity of this tale over time suggests its importance. The oldest version in print, most scholars would say, is the story of "Cupid and Psyche" in *The Golden Ass*, a work by the Roman writer Apuleius that appeared around 150 A.D. Even so, Apuleius probably drew on earlier, oral renditions of the tale from Greek versions; and the Greeks, in turn, may have derived their story from Asian sources since "Cupid and Psyche" resembles the story of "The Woman Who Married a Snake" which appears in the Indian classic *The Panchatantra*, a work known to have existed in oral form well before its appearance in print in 500 A.D. For more than two millennia, then, through the Middle Ages and the Renaissance, the eighteenth and nineteenth centuries, up to our own time, "Beauty and the Beast" has been told and retold. As the song in the Disney film suggests, "Beauty and the Beast" is a "tale as old as time," and its endurance is one measure of the story's significance and power.

Besides its appearance over the ages, another measure of this story's importance is its wide geographical distribution. Folklorists have tracked variants of "Beauty and the Beast" in a geographical fashion, and one scholar has offered his own census:

Finnish 12, Finnish-Swedish 3, Estonian 3, Lithuanian 30, Swedish 2, Spanish 3, Catalan 2, Dutch 1, Flemish 8, German 24, Italian 12 (incl. Tuscan and Sicilian), Rumanian 1, Hungarian 7, Czech 10, Slovenian 1, Serbo-Croatian 1, Polish

15, Russian 8, Greek 13, Indian 1, Franco-American 3, English-American 4, West Indies (Negro) 5.[1]

But even this does not exhaust the list of peoples among whom the story has been found. To be sure, these tales differ with different circumstances; in some, for example, the Beast is a snake (Roman, Chinese), a pig (Turkish), a monkey (Japanese, Filipino), a bear (Norwegian, Appalachian), a lion (Singhalese, Tibetan), a bull (Scottish, Jamaican), a lizard (Indonesian), and even a small-toothed dog (English). Despite these differences, what folklorists have identified as the same basic story appears among the French and the Irish, among Spanish Americans and Native Americans, among Israelis and Africans.[2]

Besides its wide appeal over time and space, we might note *who* this story especially speaks to. Over the years, I have asked people from all walks of life to identify their favorite works of literature; I've taken surveys, and some of the results have appeared in print.[3] When I've asked people about their favorite fairy tale, one story consistently emerges as the most popular: "Cinderella." But when the answers are divided by the gender of the respondents, after "Cinderella," the second most popular fairy tale among women is "Beauty and the Beast." Women tell me they love the tale because of its vision of feminine empowerment in the way Beauty tames the huge and formidable Beast and changes him into a gentleman, because it offers them the hope that in their own love lives they might be able to do the same, and because (they sometimes reluctantly admit) they are drawn to the erotic notion of the beastly lover.

But that's not to suggest that men don't find "Beauty and the Beast" an appealing tale. In my own experience, however, men have been less candid in describing the story's attraction to them,

1 Antii Aarne, *The Types of the Folktale: A Classification and Bibliography*, trans. and rev. by Stith Thompson, Folklore Fellows Communications 184 (Helsinki: Academia Scientarium Fennica, 1961) 143; cited in *Visions and Revisions* 10.

2 Cf. Betsy Hearne, *Beauties and Beasts* (Phoenix, Arizona: The Oryx Press, 1993) and W.R.S. Ralston, "Beauty and the Beast," *The Nineteenth Century* (December 1878): 990-1012.

3 Cf. Jerry Griswold and Amy Wallace, "What Famous People Read," *Parade Magazine* 13 March 1983: 21-25.

but part of the reason may be, as W.R. Ralston has observed, that "many a plain man has been secretly consoled by the favorable impression produced upon [the story's heroine] by its unprepossessing hero."[1]

But adding women and certain men to the category of the story's partisans does not exhaust the list of constituencies for "Beauty and the Beast." We should mention children, as well. When Beaumont published her version of the tale in the 1750s, the story was, for the first time, directly addressed to juveniles. And ever since then, right through to the Disney film, the story has been considered a special property of the young.

In charting the story's demographics, we should also not overlook the obvious: the tale has been popular among heterosexuals. "Beauty and the Beast" is a great romantic story about courtship, about differences overcome and the rise of love; indeed, if we recall that the meaning of "hetero" is "other," then the striking inequality between the title characters makes even more emphatic that this is a story about heterosexuality. But, as has already been suggested, "Beauty and the Beast" has also been a favorite among men and women in the gay community as well. Behind the well-known Cocteau and Disney films are gay men who have invited audiences to consider their reluctance to accept "difference"; lesbian writers have also been drawn to the story and rewritten it because—as one author explained—those who do not conform to the "mainstream's sexual mores are also seen as monsters."[2]

A timeless tale, then, and one that can be found all over the world, popular among women and men and children, finding its audience among heterosexuals and homosexuals alike—few other stories have this kind of wide appeal and so commend themselves to study as does "Beauty and the Beast." We might also consider its special significance for our own time.

1   Ralston 990.
2   Pat Calafia, "St. George and the Dragon," *Once Upon a Time: Erotic Fairy Tales for Women*, ed. Michael Ford and Mike Ford (New York: Masquerade Books, 1996) 123.

"Beauty and the Beast": The Dominant Myth of Our Times

Do certain fairy tales speak to certain times? In 1933, Disney Studios won an Academy Award for "The Three Little Pigs"; during the Depression, when impoverished Americans were trying to "keep the wolf from the door," they were whistling the film's tune "Who's Afraid of the Big Bad Wolf?" In the 1970s, we seemed to need "Cinderella" stories: in "Rocky," Sylvester Stallone's character goes from rags to riches; in "Saturday Night Fever," working-class John Travolta goes to the ball. In fact, if we recall both Cinderella's godmother and the film "The Godfather," we might say that in some quarters during the 1970s there seemed to be a special hunger for the Italian-male Cinderella story.[1]

Be that as it may, in the last two decades or so, the fairy tale that has most spoken to us has not been "Little Red Riding Hood" or "Hansel and Gretel" or dozens of other possibilities. Instead, our dominant myth seems to be "Beauty and the Beast."

Consider films. If movies are our shared dreams projected on to the Big Screen—our culture or our times "dreaming out loud"—then a psychologist sitting in a theater for the last few years might observe that we seem obsessed with incarnations of that story: not just Disney's "Beauty and the Beast," but "Elephant Man" (David Lynch's film about a severely deformed man in Victorian England, with its haunting line "I am not an animal. I am a human being"), "Man Without a Face" (where the handsome Mel Gibson plays, incredibly, an ugly tutor to a young boy), "Mask" (where Cher is the mother of a boy afflicted with elephantiasis), "Edward Scissorhands" (where Johnny Depp plays a monstrously scarred and lovelorn boy)—these are not even the beginnings of a list.

Or consider events on stage. The Disney film has been converted into a popular musical that has had a long run in theaters. Robert Moran created an opera ("Desert of Roses") based on "Beauty and the Beast," which premiered in 1992 at the Houston Grand Opera, and Philip Glass has created a touring opera based on Cocteau's "Beauty and the Beast" in which Cocteau's film plays in

---

1 I rehearsed these ideas in an essay ("Wild at Heart") in the *Los Angeles Times Book Review* 6 December 1992: 14, 34.

the background. More revealing, perhaps, is the extraordinary popularity of that play which has been performed for more than a decade now: Andrew Lloyd Webber's "Phantom of the Opera."

"Phantom of the Opera" is, of course, a revival; and what is interesting is that in choosing which works should be revived, we have been drawn to Beauty-and-the-Beast stories. "Hunchback of Notre Dame" was brought out by Disney Studios once again. Jeff Goldblum appeared in a remake of "The Fly." Jessica Lange starred in a new version of "King Kong" — a film best remembered for its famous line "It wasn't the airplanes. It was beauty that killed the beast." And Gerard Depardieu reprised the long-nosed cavalier in a new version of "Cyrano de Bergerac."

Actually, "Cyrano" was brought back twice. In "Roxanne," a contemporary adaptation of the story, Steve Martin plays an unbecoming and long-nosed fireman in Colorado who woos his lady love played by Daryl Hannah. A few years before, Hannah appeared in "Splash," a movie that must be reckoned a cross-gender version of "Beauty and the Beast" with its story of a mermaid who is in love with a human. And if the vision of Hannah as a mermaid recalls how the Beast in the fairy tale is half human and half animal, we might also think of the image of Val Kilmer in his Batman suit — another vision of a man behind his animal form. In fact, echoes of "Beauty and the Beast" can be seen in all its story cousins that tell tales about quasi-humans whether they be werewolves (e.g., Jack Nicholson in "Wolf"), vampires (e.g., Tom Cruise in "Interview with a Vampire"), or others of Frankenstein's tribe.

These same motifs appear in music videos. In what is still the most famous music video ever made, "Thriller," Michael Jackson transforms into a beast and — perhaps needlessly and revealingly — points out to his startled date that "I'm not like other guys." Madonna, in the video "Cherish," speaks of love while a merman arcs in the waves behind her. And in Snoop Doggy Dogg's "Who Am I (What's My Name)?" when a father pounds on his daughter's bedroom door, her male visitor turns into a doberman pinscher — recalling, in a way, the Korean expression that "the son-in-law is always a dog."

Movies, theatricals, revivals, music videos — these are just a few places where our era's obsession with this fairy tale can be seen. Other avatars can be seen on television. For three seasons (from

1987 to 1990), the series "Beauty and the Beast" was a popular television program. It tells the story of Catherine (played by Linda Hamilton) who is a Manhattan business executive who sometimes consorts with her beastly and leonine lover, Vincent (played by Ron Perlman).

Catherine's world is divided into two realms. Above ground, in Manhattan, she lives with slick and ambitious urban professionals who lack emotional and spiritual lives. Below ground, in Vincent's world, are a group of refugees who have formed a community of outsiders. They live in a kind of cultural museum, surrounded by Tiffany lamps and books by Shakespeare and Dickens, and they dress in medieval clothing that seem cast-offs from a gathering of the Creative Anachronism Society. In this regard, the program presents a haunting allegory and picture of our times.

Perhaps the most important fact about television's "Beauty and the Beast" is the fact that Catherine is a single career woman in her thirties—a good description of the program's target audience, its Ally McBeal demographic. The television series presents a problem similar women face these days: feminism may have got them into the board room, but what has been the price of success and what is still missing? In that regard, Vincent, the Beast, is the ideal soulmate; indeed, explaining the bags of fan mail he received from women every day, actor Ron Perlman observed that Vincent makes no demands on Catherine, gives 110 per cent, and is so attentive to her and her needs that he is able to read her thoughts.[1] Moreover, we might add, Vincent is a stay-at-home spouse.

But even more importantly, the television series makes use of the story of "Beauty and the Beast" to discuss a missing wildness. Above ground, in Manhattan, Catherine wears her hair in a tight bun, carries a briefcase, and dresses in a businesswoman's suit. Below ground, when she consorts with Vincent, she lets her hair down, discards her briefcase, unbuttons the top button of her

---

1 Commenting on the huge volume of fan mail he received, Ron Perlman observed: "Women say that Vincent is the ultimate fantasy lover, someone who asks nothing in return but gives 110 percent.... He evokes deep unconscious feelings of longing for connection to someone who understands things on a very emotional level." Associated Press, *Chicago Sun-Times* 5 July 1988; cited in *Visions and Revisions* 220.

blouse. In her popular book *Women Who Run With the Wolves: Myths and Stories of the Wild Woman Archetype*, feminist Clarissa Pinkola Estés argues that the success of the women's movement has come at the cost of forfeiting an essential wildness, and Estés argues that women need to recover that.[1]

More typically, in cross-gender versions of "Beauty and the Beast," the female is beastly or unattractive because of issues of class; then, instead of the female rescuing the male (as is the case in "Beauty and the Beast"), the male rescues the female by "raising her up" to social acceptability. We might call this the "Pygmalion" variant since it appears not only in George Bernard Shaw's play and its later incarnation in "My Fair Lady," but also in such films as "Pretty Woman" (where Julia Roberts's character goes from the streets to the mansion with the help of a wealthy gent played by Richard Gere), "Flashdance" (where welder/dancer Jennifer Beal is raised up thanks to the factory owner's son), "Working Girl" (where a lower-class secretary from Brooklyn played by Melanie Griffith becomes a Manhattan exec with the assistance of her lover, Harrison Ford), "Pretty in Pink" (where poor girl Molly Ringwald finally goes to the prom or ball with rich boy Andrew McCarthy), as well as others. In cross-gender versions of "Beauty and the Beast," in other words, our culture turns more often to its story cousin of "Cinderella." The television series suggests the same.

But it is not just women. Robert Bly argues in another best-selling book, *Iron John: A Book About Men*, that men have lost their wildness. In his meditations on the figure of the Wild Man, Bly

---

1   Supporting Estés's observation that the lack of wildness in the lives of contemporary women may be the general absence of cross-gender versions of "Beauty and the Beast." While our own culture has had little difficulty in imagining beastly males — i.e., males who are animal like or ugly — there are relatively few stories of their female counterparts. In this regard, we are different from other eras; apart from our own times, there is a long tradition in folklore of animal-like females (in "Swan Maiden" stories) and of ugly females (in stories of "The Loathly Lady," so named because of her appearance in Chaucer's story of Gawain). In our own time, however, there are only a few stories of animal females (e.g., "Company of Wolves," "Splash") and even fewer stories of ugly females (e.g., "Muriel's Wedding"). See Clarissa Pinkola Estés, *Women Who Run With the Wolves: Myths and Stories of the Wild Woman Archetype* (New York: Ballantine Books, 1992).

lays out a similar project of recovery for men. Again, "Beauty and the Beast" has provided a tool for this project. An announcement of a 1995 meeting of a Men's Council in San Diego—following "concepts taught by Robert Bly, James Hillman, and Michael Meade"—took as its theme "Beauties & Beasts," adding that participants can "experience the old ways of learning the masculine path using the traditions of drumming, poetry, and storytelling.... Extra drums will be available."

If this desire for a missing wildness is not gender specific— whether it takes the form of, say, "Thelma and Louise" or "City Slickers"—its coupling with the story of "Beauty and the Beast" has meant our era's rewriting the fairy tale in a specific manner. The traditional story is evolutionary in the way the Beast changes into a man, but our own revisions of the tale have often moved in the opposite direction and towards an atavistic conclusion. Consider three examples.

Edgar Rice Burroughs' famous novel *Tarzan of the Apes* is unabashedly inspired by the work of Darwin and a paean to evolution; in its conclusion, Tarzan has left the jungle and his ape family and entered society, become a gentleman wearing clothes and courting Jane. However, in the recent film version, "Greystoke, the Legend of Tarzan," the story heads in another, regressive direction: in the end, Tarzan abandons Jane and society, sheds his clothes, and returns to his ape brothers in the jungle. In a similar way, the traditional story of the mermaid is evolutionary; in Hans Christian Andersen's famous tale, for example, the mermaid eventually changes into a human. But in the conclusion of "Splash," Daryl Hannah's mermaid does not become human; instead, the film ends with her lover (Tom Hanks) diving into the water and becoming a merman. This same regressiveness appears in the movie "Wolf" where Jack Nicholson plays a book editor who is described as "the last civilized man"; after a car accident when he is bitten by a wolf, Nicholson's character begins to change, so that by the end of the film he has become a werewolf who runs away with Michelle Pfeiffer who has become a she-wolf. The movie "Wolf" is the story of "Beauty and the Beast" on rewind.

Our favorite fairy tale, in other words, not only provides the figure and occasion for considerations of what it means to be a woman or a man in our own era, but (as the way we have been rewriting the story suggests) it also serves as a site to take up the issues of Freud's *Civilization and Its Discontents*. Freud argues that the more we become civilized, the more we have to surrender an essential wildness; the more we become civilized, the more we miss an essential wildness.

In a hyper-civilized society like our own, this theme of Missing Wildness is omnipresent and being a beast is not such a bad thing.[1] For children, this vision of wildness is often associated with stories of the feral child: "The Jungle Book," "Nell" (where Jodie Foster's character has grown up alone in the woods of North Carolina), "Emerald Forest" (where a white boy has been kidnapped and raised by a jungle tribe in the Amazon), "Teen Wolf" (where Michael J. Fox suffers from the hairiness of puberty in a dramatic way), "Where the River Runs Black" (where a latter-day Mowgli is not raised by wolves but by freshwater dolphins in the Brazilian jungle), and, of course, Truffaut's and Herzog's stories about the Wild Child ("L'Enfant Sauvage" and "Kaspar Hauser," respectively). Related to these are visions where suburbia is invaded by a monstrous reminder of wildness, whether that comes in the form of a comic visitation by Bigfoot ("Harry and the Hendersons") or the tragic stay of a beastly boy with the Avon Lady and her suburban neighbors ("Edward Scissorhands"). Other stories tell us this. The animated feature "Shrek" tells of a kindly but unattractive ogre who is in love with the Princess Fiona, and in the conclusion we expect

1 This theme of a hunger for a "missing wildness" not only appears in "Thelma and Louise" and "City Slickers," but in numerous other works and configurations. With men, it varies from Lester Burnham (played by Kevin Spacey), who throws over his old life in "American Beauty," to a film like "Never Cry Wolf," where a scientist studying wolves begins to imitate them and by the end is naked and running with the pack as they hunt caribou. For women, the hunger for a missing wildness often appears in the twin-brother motif and the woman's attraction to the dangerous and wild brother: in "Moonstruck" Cher's character abandons her fiancé (Danny Aiello) and falls in love with his tormented, younger brother (Nicholas Cage), the Beast, a one-handed opera lover and baker; in "Piano," Holly Hunter's character abandons her insensitive husband (Sam Neill) and turns to the barbaric and heavily tattooed white man (Harvey Keitel) who has gone native, exchanging underwear for music lessons; indeed, we might call all this the "Brad Pitt Phenomenon" since Pitt has played the role of the dangerous and attractive brother in several films, including "A River Runs Through It" and "Legends of the Fall."

his transformation into a handsome prince. Instead, in a wonderful surprise and moment of beastly magic, Fiona is transformed into this ogre's match and the same kind of zoological creature.

Claude Levi-Strauss is generally credited with the saying that "animals are good to think with" and with that observation, our attention is directed to the way we smear human qualities on animals and anthropomorphize them, so that, for example, certain animals are rendered "good creatures" while others are made "bad" — "Gorillas in the Mist" and "Free Willy," on the one hand, and "Jaws," say, on the other. With "Beauty and the Beast," however, our imaginative process is the opposite, and we smear animal qualities on humans. This slight shift is distracting and permits, under this ruse, the allegorizing of certain social issues too sensitive or volatile to be addressed directly.

Take "Planet of the Apes." Knowing that its author, Pierre Boulle, was a prisoner in a Japanese prisoner of war camp during World War II and that he also wrote "Bridge Over the River Kwai" makes more obvious that this story of a human underclass and their ape overlords is a racial allegory. In the same way, our stories about beastly visitors from outer space in science-fiction films can be seen as reflecting our anxiety about immigrants and other "aliens" — E.T. with a green card.[1]

Here, then, is another reason for our era's fascination with "Beauty and the Beast" and our use of it as a convenient site to work out cultural issues. In a fundamental way, "Beauty and the Beast" is about Otherness, and the story permits an investigation of our own reactions to Otherness in all its various forms. Imagine, if you can, a different conclusion to the Disney film where the Beast doesn't change into Disney's brunette and Fabio-look-alike Prince, but into a handsome black male along the lines of Denzel

---

1   A link between the motifs of "Beauty and the Beast" and immigrant issues is suggested by the curious fact that in 1990 Gerard Depardieu appeared in two films, playing the unbecoming "Cyrano de Begerac" and an immigrant in search of legal status in "Green Card." Just as American policy towards Mexico, for example, vacillates between a borderless openness (e.g., the NAFTA treaty) and a reinforcement of the border to exclude the Other (e.g., Operation Gatekeeper), science-fiction films waver between welcoming the aliens (e.g., "Close Encounters of the Third Kind") and sending them packing (e.g., "E.T.").

Washington; if the mind boggles for a moment at such a possibility, then the Beast is still a beast and has to undergo yet further transformation to please us. Or imagine the Disney film concludes, instead, with the Beast's transformation into a beautiful lesbian along the lines of Ellen DeGeneres; if such a change seems humorous, then the Beast is still a beast and must undergo yet further transformation. Beauty, in other words, is not the only thing that lies in the eyes of the beholder. Beastliness lies there as well.

Tanith Lee, Emma Donaghue, and the creators of Cocteau's and Disney's movies make use of "Beauty and the Beast" in this way, as a figure to examine and question our reactions to Otherness. In the same manner in 1996, while controversy was raging about the entertainment industry's presentation of alternate lifestyles and unconventional families, Mike Geletoz drew a two-panel cartoon for the *Dayton Daily News*. In one panel, a dark-suited gentleman with a bow-tie (identified as "Southern Baptists") declaims: "Disney condones marriages that are unhealthy, unnatural and against traditional family values!" In the next panel, Belle is seen holding hands with Disney's Beast.[1]

As a tool, then, to consider what it is to be a man or a woman in our own times, as a means to reckon how our hyper-civilized society has come into being at the cost of wildness, as a site for examining our troubled reactions to Otherness in all its varied forms — in these and additional ways, our era's fascination with this fairy tale suggests that "Beauty and the Beast" is what Joseph Campbell called a "living myth." It is a story that is still alive and informs the way we live: the way we recoil, for example, from the ugly woman or homeless man begging for a hand-out, and how we feel guilty in the next heartbeat; the way we encounter a couple in the aisle of a store and then wonder, "What does she see in him?"[2]

---

1   Reprinted in *Time Magazine* 24 June 1996: 20.
2   The question "What does she see in him?" is also provoked by certain celebrity weddings; recall, for example, the catty comments provoked by Julia Roberts's marriage to Lyle Lovett.
    Sometimes the answer to this question is similar to the one Dear Abby provided to "On the Fence" when she wrote about her love interest "Dan," who was a kind and perfect gentleman, but also overweight and wore extremely thick glasses. Responding to her reader's query about whether she should listen to her friends' advice that she was too pretty to settle for such an unattrac-

Another answer to the question "What does she see in him?" is suggested by a celebrity like Mick Jagger. In himself, it would have to be said, Jagger is not particularly handsome. Nonetheless, there is something else that has made him immensely attractive. Mindful of "Beauty and the Beast," we might call that something else his "animal magnetism."

"Beauty and the Beast," our era has found, is good to think with.

tive partner, Abby advised in 1997: "An average-looking man who is kind and caring will become more attractive with time, just as a handsome man will become less appealing if his behavior does not match his appearance" —*North County Times* (Escondido, California).

TWO

THE TALE AND ITS AUTHOR

Numerous authors have told the story of "Beauty and the Beast," and variants of this tale can be found all over the world, but the version of the story that is generally considered to be the definitive and most influential one was penned by a Frenchwoman, Madame Jeanne-Marie LePrince de Beaumont.

Beaumont's "Beauty and the Beast" first appeared in French in her book Le Magasin des enfans, ou dialogues entre une sage gouvernante et plusieurs de ses élèves de la première distinction, *published in London in 1756. This tale first appeared in English in 1759 when Beaumont translated it in her* The Young Misses Magazine, Containing Dialogues between a Governess and Several Young Ladies of Quality, Her Scholars.[1] *Since then, other writers have been dissatisfied with Beaumont's English version and modified it to make the story more understandable, often taking great liberties with it.[2]*

The version of Beaumont's story that appears here is my own. In creating it, I have aimed to fashion a story that can be easily understood by contemporary readers and one that more closely resembles Beaumont's original intentions in both her English and French versions.

ONCE UPON A TIME there was a very rich merchant who had six children, three sons and three daughters. He was a sensible man and spared no expense for his children's education, and he hired all kinds of tutors. His daughters were very pretty, especially the youngest. When she was a child, everyone called her "The Little

1 A facsimile copy of Beaumont's story in English, as it appeared in the fourth edition (1783) of *The Young Misses Magazine*, is printed in *Visions and Revisions*. Iona and Peter Opie also publish Beaumont's English version of the tale in their *The Classic Fairy Tales* (New York: Oxford University Press, 1974).

2 Among the most popular early translations of the French tale was one done by Dinah Maria Mulock Craig in her *The Fairy Book* (1863). Among the best contemporary translations is one by Jack Zipes in his *Beauty and the Beast and Other Classic French Fairy Tales* (New York: Dutton Signet, 1997).

Beauty." As she grew up, she still went by that nickname and was called "Beauty." This made her sisters very jealous.

Besides being prettier, Beauty was also better than her sisters in other ways. The older two were proud because they were rich. They put on airs, refused to associate with other merchants' daughters, and kept company only with high-class people. Every day they went out to parties, balls, plays, and concerts; and they laughed at their youngest sister because she spent her time reading good books.

Since these young women were known to be wealthy, several prominent merchants asked for their hands in marriage. But the older sisters said they would never marry unless they could make a match with a duke or with an earl, at the very least. On her part, Beauty politely thanked those who courted her but told them that she was too young to marry and that she preferred to stay with her father for a few years more.

Then the merchant suddenly lost his whole fortune, except for a small country house quite far from town. With tears in his eyes, he told his children they must go there and work for a living. The two oldest answered that they wouldn't leave town because they had several suitors who would marry them even if they didn't have a fortune. They were mistaken. Their suitors didn't want anything to do with them once they were poor. Moreover, people didn't like them because of their arrogance and said, "They don't deserve to be pitied. We're very glad to see their pride humbled. Let them go and put on airs while milking the cows."

But the same people also said, "We feel sorry, however, for Beauty. She is such a charming, sweet-tempered creature. She speaks kindly to poor people and has an agreeable nature." In fact, several gentlemen would have married her even though she didn't have a cent. But when they asked, she said she could not think of leaving her poor father in his misfortunes and was determined to go along with him to the country in order to comfort and care for him. At first, she was saddened by the loss of her fortune. Then she said to herself, "If I were to cry, that wouldn't make things better, so I must try to be happy without a fortune."

When they came to their country home, the merchant and his three sons became farmers and worked the land. Beauty rose at four in the morning, cleaned the house, and got dinner ready for the family. In the beginning, she found it very difficult because she had not been used to working as a servant, but in less than two months she grew stronger and healthier than ever. And after she finished her housework, she read or played the harpsichord or sang while she sat at the spinning wheel.

Her sisters, on the other hand, did not know how to spend their time. They got up at ten and wandered around all day, lamenting the loss of their fine clothes and acquaintances. "Just look at our youngest sister," they said. "What a poor, stupid peasant she is— happy and content in this dismal situation."

The good merchant did not agree with them. He knew that Beauty was better than her sisters in virtue as well as looks. She was humble and hardworking, but her father especially admired her patience because her sisters not only left her all the work, but insulted her every chance they got.

The family had lived about a year in this remote vicinity when the merchant received a letter saying that one of his ships had safely arrived in the harbor. Thinking that the family might now recover some of its wealth, the two oldest daughters were delighted; they hoped to return to town because they were quite weary of country life. When they saw their father getting ready to set out on his journey, they begged him to buy them new gowns, head-dresses, ribbons, and all kinds of finery. But Beauty asked for nothing for herself because she thought that the money her father was going to receive would scarcely pay for all the things her sisters wanted.

"What will you have, Beauty?" asked her father.

"Since you are kind enough to think of me," she answered, "please bring me a rose since none grow in these parts." It wasn't that Beauty really wanted a rose. She asked for something only because if she hadn't, it would have seemed as if she were trying to make her sisters look bad and they would have criticized her for it.

So, the merchant set off on his journey. But when he got to the harbor, there was a lawsuit over his debts and his merchandise was seized. After a great deal of trouble, he went back as poor as he was before.

He was thirty miles from his own house, and thinking of the pleasure of seeing his children again, when he lost his way in a great forest. It was snowing terribly, and the wind was so strong that he was twice thrown off his horse. With night coming on, he began to worry about starving, or freezing to death, or being devoured by the wolves that were howling all around him.

Suddenly, looking down a long avenue of trees, he saw a distant light. Then, going a little further, he realized the light came from a palace that was illuminated from top to bottom. Thanking God, the merchant hurried there but was surprised to find no one in the courtyard. His horse followed him and seeing a large stable open, the hungry creature went in and began to devour the hay and oats. The merchant tied him up and entered the house.

He saw no one in the large hall, but he found a good fire and a table with a dinner on it. Since the rain and snow had soaked him to the bone, he came near the fire to dry himself. "I hope," he said, "that the master of the house or his servants will excuse the liberties I'm taking. I suppose it won't be long before some of them appear."

He waited a considerable time, but when the clock struck eleven and still no one had come, he was so hungry that he could resist no longer. Trembling, he took some roasted chicken. After this, he drank a few glasses of wine. Growing more bold, he went out of the hall and crossed through several grand rooms with magnificent furniture. Finally, he came to a room with a good bed in it and, since he was very tired and it was past midnight, he decided it was best to shut the door and go to sleep.

It was ten the next morning when the merchant woke up, and he was astonished to see a new set of clothes had been laid out for him in place of the soiled ones he had arrived in yesterday. "Certainly," he said, "this palace must belong to some kind fairy who has seen my distress and pitied me." Then he looked through a window but instead of seeing winter's snow, he saw arbors filled with the most beautiful of flowers.

When the merchant returned to the great hall where he had eaten supper the night before, he found a cup of chocolate ready for him on a little table. "Thank you, good Madam Fairy," he said aloud, "for providing me with a breakfast. I am very grateful to you for all your kindness." Then the good man drank his chocolate and went to look for his horse.

Passing through an arbor, he remembered Beauty's request and gathered a branch of roses on which there were several blossoms. At that same moment, he heard a great noise and saw such a frightful beast coming towards him that he nearly fainted. "You are very ungrateful," said the Beast in a terrible voice. "I have saved your life by receiving you into my castle and, in return, you steal my roses, which I value more than anything else in the world. You shall die for it. I will give you a quarter of an hour to prepare yourself and say your prayers."

The merchant fell on his knees and lifted up both his hands. "My Lord," he said, "forgive me. I did not mean to offend you when I gathered a rose. It was for one of my daughters who asked me to bring her one."

"My name is not *My Lord*," replied the monster, "but *Beast*. And I don't like flattery. I like people who say what they think. So, don't imagine I can be persuaded by any sweet talk or flattering lies. But you say you have daughters. I will forgive you on one condition: that one of your daughters comes here, of her own free will, to take your place. Do not argue or try to bargain with me. Leave, but swear that if your daughter refuses to come in your place, you will return within three months."

The merchant had no intention of sacrificing one of his daughters, but he thought that by appearing to consider the Beast's proposal he would at least have the chance of seeing his children once more and saying farewell. So, he gave his promise that he would return, and the Beast told him he might leave whenever he wished. "But," the Beast added, "you shall not depart empty-handed. Go back to the room where you fell asleep. There you will see a great empty chest. Fill it with whatever you like, and I will send it to your home." Then the Beast withdrew.

"Well," said the good man to himself, "if I must die, I shall at least have the comfort of leaving something to my poor children." He returned to the bedroom and finding an abundance of gold pieces, he filled the great chest the Beast had mentioned.

Then the merchant took his horse out of the stable and left the palace with a sadness as great as the joy with which he had first entered it. The horse, of his own accord, took one of the roads of the forest, and in a few hours the good man was home.

When he arrived, his children gathered round him. But instead of receiving their embraces with pleasure, he looked on them, held up the branch of roses in his hands and burst into tears. "Here, Beauty," her father said, "take these roses. Little do you realize how

31

much they are likely to cost your unfortunate father." Then he told them about his experiences in the forest.

Right away, the two oldest sisters started weeping and saying unkind things about Beauty, who was not crying at all. "Look at that little wretch," they said. "She would not ask for fine clothes, as we did. No, she wanted to be different and now she will be the death of our poor father. Even now, she does not shed a tear."

"Why should I?" answered Beauty. "Father will not suffer on my account. Since the monster will accept of one of his daughters, I will deliver myself up to his fury. I am happy to think that my death will save my father's life."

"No, sister," said her three brothers, "that will not be necessary. We will go find the monster and either kill him or perish in the attempt."

"Do not imagine any such thing, my sons," said the merchant. "The Beast's power is so great that you can have no hope of overcoming him. I am pleased by Beauty's kind and generous offer, but I cannot accept it. I am old and don't have long to live, so I don't have so much to lose — except for a few years with you, my children."

"Listen, father," said Beauty, "you will not go to the Beast's palace without me. You can't stop me from following you." In fact, no matter what the others said, Beauty still insisted on going to the palace. On their part, her sisters were delighted by the idea of Beauty's departure because her virtues and friendly nature made them spiteful and jealous.

Now the merchant was so troubled by the thought of losing his daughter that he had forgotten all about the chest full of gold. But at night when he retired to rest, no sooner had he shut the door to his room than, to his great astonishment, he found the chest beside his bed. The merchant was determined, however, not to tell his children that he had become rich because they would have wanted to return to town and he was resolved not to leave the country. But he shared the secret about the gold with Beauty who told him that, in his absence, two gentlemen had come and courted her sisters. She begged her father to give them fortunes and let them marry. Beauty loved her sisters no matter how they treated her.

Then the time came for Beauty to depart. Her brothers were really concerned about her, but her sisters were not. They rubbed their eyes with an onion to force out some tears to make it seem as if they were heartbroken. Only Beauty did not shed tears at this parting, because she did not want to increase anyone's sorrow.

The horse took the direct road to the palace and towards evening Beauty and her father saw the place, illuminated from top to bottom. The horse went off by himself into the stable, and the merchant and his daughter came into the great hall where they found a magnificent meal laid out for them. The merchant had no heart to eat, but Beauty, trying to appear cheerful, sat down at the table and encouraged him to do the same. Afterwards, she thought to herself, "The Beast must plan to fatten me up before he eats me, since he provides such a lavish meal."

After they had eaten, they heard a great noise. The merchant, all in tears, said goodbye to his poor child because he thought the Beast was coming to separate them. Beauty was frightened by the Beast's horrid form, but she summoned up as much courage as she could and when the monster asked her if she had come willingly, she trembled and said that she had. "Good," the Beast answered. "I am much obliged. And as for you, my good man, please leave tomorrow morning and never think of coming here again. Goodnight, Beauty."

"Goodnight, Beast," she replied as he went away.

"Oh, daughter," said the merchant, embracing Beauty, "I am frightened to death. Believe me, you had better go back and let me stay here."

"No, father," said Beauty with determination. "You shall set out tomorrow morning and leave me to the care and protection of God."

They went to bed and thought they would not close their eyes all night, but just as soon as they laid down, they fell fast asleep. Then Beauty dreamed that a fine lady came and said to her, "I am pleased, Beauty, by your goodness. This act of giving up your life to save your father's shall not go unrewarded." Beauty awoke and told her father about the dream. But though it comforted him a little, he still couldn't help but cry bitterly when he had to leave his dear child.

As soon as he was gone, Beauty sat down in the great hall and started to cry as well. Still, she was a courageous person, so she prayed to God and decided to make the most of the little time she thought she had left to live. She believed that the Beast would eat her up that night.

To pass the time, Beauty decided to walk around and investigate the castle. It was a delightful and impressive place. But she was greatly surprised when she came upon a door over which was written the words "BEAUTY'S APARTMENT." She opened the door and was dazzled by the magnificence of everything within. She was especially impressed by a large library, a harpsichord, and several music books. "Well," she said to herself, "I see he will not let me grow bored in the little time I have left." Then she reflected, "If I was only going to live for a day, all these preparations wouldn't have been necessary."

Inspired with fresh courage, she went to the bookshelf, took down a book, and read these words written in gold letters:

> *Welcome Beauty, banish your fear,*
> *You are the queen and mistress here:*
> *Speak your wishes, speak your will,*
> *Swift obedience meets them still.*

"Alas," she sighed, "there is nothing I wish for more than to see my poor father and know how he is doing." As soon as she said this, something amazing occurred. Looking into a great mirror, she saw her own home and her father arriving there with a very sad face. Her sisters went to meet him and made every effort to appear sorrowful, but they could scarcely conceal their happiness at having got rid of their sister. A moment later, everything disappeared, and Beauty realized this magical vision had been a kindness from the Beast.

At noon, she found her dinner ready and throughout the meal she was entertained by excellent music, though she couldn't see any musicians. When night came and she sat down to supper, she heard the noise the Beast made and could not help but be terrified. "Beauty," said the monster, "will you let me sit with you while you dine?"

"You can do as you please," Beauty answered with a tremble.

"No," replied the Beast, "you alone are mistress here. You need only bid me to be gone, if my presence is troublesome, and I will immediately withdraw. But tell me, do you not think me very ugly?"

"That is true," said Beauty, "for I cannot tell a lie. But I believe you are a good person."

"So I am," said the monster. "But then, besides my ugliness, I lack intelligence. I know very well that I am just a poor, stupid creature."

"A stupid person would never say that," replied Beauty. "Fools never realize what they lack but always overestimate their own intelligence."

"Eat then, Beauty," said the monster, "and try to amuse yourself in your palace, for everything here is yours. I would be very uneasy if you were not happy."

"You are very generous," answered Beauty. "I am pleased by your kindness and when I consider that, I hardly notice your ugliness."

"Yes, yes," said the Beast, "my heart is good, but still I am a hideous monster."

"Among mankind," answered Beauty, "there are many who deserve that name far more than you. I prefer you, just as you are, to those who, under a human form, hide a false and corrupt heart."

"If I was smart enough," replied the Beast, "I would make a fine compliment to thank you. But, as I am not so clever, I can only say that I am greatly obliged to you."

Beauty ate a hearty supper and grew less afraid of the Beast. But she nearly fainted in fear when at last he spoke and asked her, "Beauty, will you marry me?"

Some time passed before she could make an answer, because she was afraid of making him angry if she refused. At last, however, she trembled and said, "No, Beast."

As soon as she said this, the poor monster gave out a sigh which changed into a frightful hissing that echoed throughout the palace. But Beauty recovered from her fright when the Beast continued in a mournful voice. "Then farewell, Beauty," he said, as he left the room, turning back, now and then, to look at her.

When Beauty was alone, she felt a great deal of compassion for the Beast. "It's a great shame," she said, "that anyone so good should be so ugly."

For the next three months, Beauty was content to live in the palace. Every evening the Beast paid her a visit and talked with her during supper. His conversation showed that he had common sense, but he wasn't especially witty or clever. Still, each day Beauty discovered something new and admirable in him. Moreover, seeing the monster so often, she grew accustomed to his ugliness and far from dreading his visits, she actually looked forward to nine o'clock when the Beast joined her. There was only one thing that gave Beauty concern: every night before she went to bed, the monster always asked her if she would be his wife.

One day she finally said to him, "Beast, you make me very uneasy. I wish I could say I will marry you, but I am too honest to say that will ever happen. Still, I shall always value you as a friend. You have to be satisfied with that."

"I must," the Beast sighed, "because I know how I look to others. Still, I love you. But what good is that? I ought to be happy that you stay here. Promise me that you will never leave."

Beauty blushed at these words. She had seen in her magic mirror how her father was worried sick by his loss of her, and she longed to see him again. "I could promise you that," Beauty replied, "on one condition. I have a great a desire to see my father. Please let me. My heart will break if you refuse me this request."

"I would rather die myself than cause you any pain," answered the monster. "I will send you to your father, but you will remain with him and I will die of grief."

"No," said Beauty, "I wouldn't do that. I give you my promise to return in a week. The mirror has shown me that my sisters are married and that my brothers have left and joined the army. My father is alone. Let me stay with him for just one week."

"You shall be there tomorrow morning," said the Beast. "But remember your promise. Then, when you want to return, just lay your ring on a table before you go to bed. When you awake, you will be here. Good night and farewell, Beauty."

Beauty went to bed, but she was saddened by seeing the Beast so sorrowful. When she awoke the next morning, by magic, she found herself in her father's house. She summoned the maid by giving the bell by her bedside a little shake; but when the good woman saw Beauty, she was so startled that she gave out a loud shriek. This sent her father running upstairs, and then he nearly died with joy to see his dear daughter again. He held her fast in his arms for nearly a quarter of an hour.

After these greetings, Beauty began to think about getting up, only she was worried she had no clothes to put on. But the maid said that in the next room she had just found a large trunk full of gowns that were covered with gold and diamonds. Speaking out loud, Beauty thanked the Beast for his kindness and chose one of the plainest dresses to wear, saying she intended to make a present of the others to her sisters. As soon as she said this, the trunk disappeared. Her father suggested that, maybe, the Beast wanted her to keep them for herself. As if in agreement, both the trunk and the gowns reappeared.

Beauty dressed herself and, in the meantime, word was sent to her sisters who hurried home with their new husbands. Both were very unhappy. The eldest had married an extremely handsome gentleman, but he was so conceited he never thought of anyone but himself and he never paid any attention to his wife. The second had married a very clever man, but he used his wit to insult and torment everybody, his wife most of all.

Beauty's sisters were sick with envy when they saw her dressed like a princess and more beautiful than ever. Despite her kindness to them, they could hardly stifle their jealousy when she told them how happy she was. When her sisters could stand it no longer, they went down into the garden and one said to the other, "Is she so much better than us that she deserves such happiness?"

"Sister," said the oldest, "a thought just occurred to me. Let's find a way to keep her here for more than a week. Maybe, then, the monster will be so enraged at her for breaking her promise that he will devour her."

"Yes," answered the other, "let's show her as much kindness as possible." After they had agreed to this, they went up and behaved so affectionately to their sister that poor Beauty wept for joy. When the week was up, they cried and tore their hair. In fact, they seemed so sorry to part with her that Beauty promised to stay a week longer.

In the meantime, Beauty grew anxious about the pain she might be causing the poor Beast, whom she sincerely loved and really longed to see again. On her tenth night in her father's house, she dreamt she was in the palace garden and she saw the Beast lying on

37

the lawn and near death. In a dying voice, he reproached her for her ingratitude.

Beauty awoke in the middle of the dream and burst into tears. "Am I not very wicked," she said, "to be unkind to him who has been so kind to me? It's not his fault that he is ugly and not especially clever. He is kind and good, and that should be enough. Why did I refuse to marry him? I could be happier with the Beast than my sisters are with their husbands. Good looks or cleverness in a husband is not what makes a woman happy; instead, it is virtue and kindness — and the Beast has those qualities. It is true that I don't feel infatuated with him, but I do feel gratitude, respect, and friendship. I will not make him miserable. If I were ever to be so ungrateful, I wouldn't be able to forgive myself."

Having said this, Beauty got up, put her ring on the table, and then lay down again. As soon as she was in bed, she fell asleep. And when she awoke the next morning, she was overjoyed to find herself back in the Beast's palace. She put on one of her finest dresses to please him and impatiently waited for evening. But when the clock struck nine, no Beast appeared.

Beauty then feared she had been the cause of his death, and she ran all about the palace, crying and wringing her hands. After having looked for him everywhere, she remembered her dream and ran to the canal near the garden where she had seen him. There she found the poor Beast, stretched out, unconscious, and near death. Beauty threw herself upon him and finding his heart still beating, she fetched some water from the canal and poured it on his head.

The Beast opened his eyes and said to Beauty, "You forgot your promise, and I was so saddened by the loss of you that I resolved to starve myself. But since I have had the happiness of seeing you once more, I can die satisfied."

"No, dear Beast," said Beauty, "you must not die. Instead, live to be my husband. From this moment on, I give you my hand and swear to be none but yours. I thought I only wanted to be your friend, but the grief I now feel convinces me that I cannot live without you."

As soon as Beauty said these words, it was as if some great event had occurred; the palace began to sparkle with light, and fireworks could be seen and music heard. But she noticed none of this because when she turned to her dear Beast, how great was her surprise! The Beast had disappeared, and in his place she beheld a handsome prince more beautiful than the God of Love, thanking her for breaking the spell that had made him look like a monster. As dazzled as she was by his good looks, Beauty still couldn't help but ask, "But where is the Beast?"

"You see him in front of you," said the prince. "A wicked fairy condemned me to remain in that form and to hide my intelligence, until a beautiful maiden should agree to marry me. In all the world, only you were won over by the goodness of my character. Now, in offering you my crown, I can hardly repay my obligation to you."

Beauty was surprised and pleased. She gave the charming prince her hand and together they went into the castle. In the great hall, Beauty was overjoyed to find there her father and all her family, who had been transported there by the beautiful lady who had appeared in her dream. "Beauty," said this lady, "come and receive the reward of your good choice. You have preferred virtue over good looks and cleverness, and you now deserve to find a person in whom both these qualities are united. You are going to be a great queen, and I hope that honor will not lessen your virtues or make you forget yourself."

"As for you, dear ladies," said the fairy to Beauty's two sisters, "I know your hearts and all the malice they contain. Become two statues but keep your power of thought after this transformation. You shall stand before your sister's palace gate, and it will be your punishment to constantly behold her happiness. You will not be able to return to your former state until you have recognized your faults, but I think it likely that you will always remain statues. Pride, anger, gluttony, and idleness are sometimes conquered, but the conversion of a malicious and envious heart is a very difficult miracle."

At that moment, the fairy waved her wand and, in the blink of an eye, everyone in the hall was transported to the prince's kingdom. His subjects received him with joy, and he married Beauty and lived with her for many years because their perfect happiness was founded on virtue.

THE TALE: CLOSE READING

The list of the characters who appear in Beaumont's tale reads like a *Dramatis Personae* composed of stock characters:

> The Merchant
> Beauty
> Sisters
> Brothers
> Beast
> Fairy
> Sisters' Husbands

Still, despite their generic names, the major characters have specific traits that make them distinct personalities.

THE MERCHANT, as his name suggests, has a life that revolves around money. While the virtues and vices of other characters are subjects of much discussion in this story, the topics most often associated with him are wealth and poverty. He is able to be lavish when it comes to his children's education or their extravagant life in town; he is bankrupted and needs to retire to the country and work like a peasant; then the Beast provides him with a chest of gold, and he has some largesse to distribute. Like the stock market on a tumultuous day, his lucre vacillates.

Another characteristic of the Merchant is his hard luck. He seems more harassed than Job. The whims of fate sink his ship, destroy his fortune, and send him in dire poverty to the country. At the first glimmer of hope, when one of the ships comes in, his fiduciary dreams are dashed when his creditors get to the harbor before him. This Jonah can't even travel through a forest without being beset by a snowstorm, wolves, and hunger. And even when he does such an innocent thing as pluck a rose, he ends up pleading for his life and sacrificing his beloved daughter.

As a father, the Merchant has a special relationship with Beauty. She cares for him and he prefers her over his other daughters. In the absence of a spouse, he also depends on her for counsel; for example, when the Beast provides the chest of gold, then the father consults only Beauty, and together they decide whether it would be best if others in the family were advised about their return to prosperity. The Merchant's special relationship with Beauty is also suggested by his health which seems to vary in direct proportion to his proximity to his daughter: he grows ill when Beauty is absent and improves when she returns.

With regards to his other daughters, the Merchant is clearsighted. Beauty may be deceived by her duplicitous sisters, but her father is no dupe and has their measure. When Beauty's sisters criticize her, for example, calling her a peasant for her cheerfulness in the midst of their rural squalor, "The good merchant did not agree with them. He knew Beauty was better than her sisters in virtue as well as looks. She was humble and hardworking, but her father especially admired her patience because her sisters not only left her all the work, but insulted her every chance they got."

This suggests something else about the Merchant—his weakness or powerlessness. If he knows Beauty's shiftless sisters are persecuting her and shirking their work, why does he do nothing to stop them? No strong *paterfamilias*, he also does not rein in his older daughters when they live in town, nor does he have any say at the end of the tale when the fairy punishes them. And when he insists that Beauty will not go to the Beast's castle in his place, all Beauty need do is insist more emphatically that she *will* go in order to win the argument. His powerlessness is also apparent in scenes with the Beast when he is pictured on his knees and pleading for his life, or when the Beast tells him to depart and leave his daughter behind; then the Merchant can only weep and lament his sad fate. This father's lack of assertiveness may also be said to be something he passes along to his beloved daughter.

BEAUTY may be especially attractive, but after the opening paragraphs her looks are not mentioned. Instead, her virtues are stressed. She is described as kindly, generous, humble, hardworking, patient, cheerful, etc. In fact, the catalog of her excellences is so long that some readers may find Beauty an unrealistic character and something of a goody-goody. But if Beauty seems too good to be true, the fault lies in her lopsided selflessness.

Perhaps Beauty's most representative scene is the one where she is about to depart for the Beast's castle and apparently leave her family behind forever. On that occasion, "Beauty did not shed tears at this parting, because she did not want to increase anyone's sorrow." This concern with others' feelings over her own, this repression and deference, is typical of Beauty.

Beauty always seems attentive to others before herself. She defers to her sisters. She is solicitous to the Beast. And, of course, she is devoted to her father: twice she turns down suitors in order to remain with and comfort him; and with no thoughts about herself, she offers to sacrifice her own life so that her father may live.

That same self-sacrificial nature is evident when the family is stripped of their luxuries and they move to the country. Rising at four in the morning, cleaning and doing housework, preparing the meals—Beauty helps the family and plays the uncomplaining servant while her sisters sleep in and evade work. Without feelings of righteousness or indignation, Beauty also endures her sisters' constant insults. And putting others' interests before her own and asking nothing for herself, Beauty requests only a rose from her father and she makes that request only so that her sisters' long shopping list will not seem so immoderate.

Beauty's self-effacement is so complete we might wonder, when it comes to her personality, whether there is any "there" there. Does she have desires of her own? Can she possibly be offended? Is there someone there to be offended? Can this long-suffering character ever stand up for herself and her own interests? If answers to these questions come at all, they come in the second half of Beaumont's tale.

When Beauty travels to the Beast's castle, her circumstances are reversed. No longer the servant, she is the mistress of all she surveys and treated like a queen. Instead of work necessitated by poverty, she can spend her days at leisure in a luxurious apartment furnished with books and a harpsichord. And instead of her sisters' constant insults, her host showers her with kindness and attention. At the Beast's castle, Beauty's customary life of self-sacrifice is replaced with opportunities for self-indulgence.

But even in these favorable circumstances, Beauty still cannot imagine situations where she puts her own interests first. When she can have whatever she wishes, her concerns concern another and she asks the magic mirror to show her how her father is getting along and she begs permission to visit the old man because she has seen how lonely he is. Unaccustomed to consulting her own feelings, instead of anger or despair at her confinement, "when Beauty was alone, she felt a great deal of compassion for the Beast." And when the Beast gives her permission to return home, this woman-accustomed-to-serving-others feels no joy of her own but, instead, "was saddened by seeing the Beast so sorrowful."

Beauty is, in fact, so other-directed, so sacrificial, that we may wonder whether she has desires of her own, whether it is possible for her to be assertive. That is why choice becomes so important in the tale. Beauty has free will and, in considering the Beast's marriage proposal, she is finally obliged to exercise it and declare *her own* desires. The whole story, as it were, holds its breath waiting for her to decide.

The critical moment is the occasion when she tells the Beast, "From this moment on, I give you my hand." When she explains her motives, something important is revealed: "I thought I only wanted to be your friend, but the grief I now feel convinces me I cannot live without you." In other words, she first considered him and his needs; but then she looked elsewhere, inside herself, and consulted her *own* feelings and discovered her *own* needs and desires. This marks the reorientation of this otherwise sacrificial and other-directed woman, a salutary moment in her self-development and maturation.

BEAUTY'S SISTERS exist in contrast to her. They are older; she is younger. They are pretty; she is prettier. The language between them is always comparative, and Beauty is "better." While Beauty is humble, her sisters are proud and "put on airs." While Beauty "speaks kindly to poor people," her vain sisters are social climbers who refuse to associate with other merchants' daughters and spend time only with people of the upper classes. When the family loses its wealth and is forced to retire to the country, society gossips feel sorry for Beauty's misfortune but they welcome the way this will humble the uppity sisters: "Let them go and put on airs while milking the cows," the gossips say.

In one of her many comparative sentences, Beaumont describes Beauty's sisters as gadabouts ("Every day they went out to parties, balls, plays, and concerts") while Beauty is described as a stay-at-home maiden who "spent her time home reading good books." The older sisters are also materialistic; for example, when their father departs for town in hopes of recovering some of his wealth, they ask for gowns, ribbons, head-dresses, and all kinds of finery. Beauty asks only for a rose and does so only to be obliging.

Beauty is also unconcerned about marriage and on two occasions turns down suitors. In contrast, her sisters seem to stake their self-importance on making the best match possible. At first, they will only marry a duke or an earl. Then, when they lose their wealth, they are surprised that their suitors disappear as well. Finally, in the country, they take what's available and settle on rural husbands.

When the family is forced to move to the country, Beauty faces penury with cheery resolution, rising at four each day to begin her chores and finishing the day with reading, singing, or playing the harpsichord. Her sisters, *au contraire*, "did not know how to spend their time." Indolent, they rise at ten and spend their days lamenting their misfortune and never lending a hand.

Beauty's sisters are also hypercritical: they laugh at their younger sister for reading books, they mock the way she takes to country life as if she were a peasant, they accuse her of showing off when her request for a rose puts their father's life in jeopardy—in short, they "insulted her every chance they got." Beauty, on the other hand, is always friendly, sweet-tempered, and kind to her sisters. As Beaumont's narrator observes, "Beauty loved her sisters no matter how they treated her."

Finally, the sisters differ in what they value in a partner. Beauty grows unconcerned about the Beast's looks and lack of wit; so, in the changed prince, the fairy rewards Beauty for her discrimination: "You have preferred virtue over good looks and cleverness, and you now deserve to find a person in whom both these qualities are united." The sisters, on the other hand, suffer for their marital choices: "The eldest had married an extremely handsome gentleman, but he was so conceited he never thought of anyone but himself and he never paid any attention to his wife. The second had married a very clever man, but he used his wit to insult and torment everybody, and his wife most of all."

The sisters' vices are many, but—as the fairy says when she changes them into living statues—the greatest of these is "a malicious and envious heart." In fact, envy, it should be noted, is the sisters' most fundamental reaction to Beauty's very nature:

"Her virtues and friendly nature made them spiteful and jealous."

As for their malice, it is of a particular kind. The sisters are hypocrites. They rub their eyes with onions in order to appear sad at Beauty's departure. According to the Beast's magic mirror, they make every effort also to appear sorrowful when their father returns home without Beauty, but "they could scarcely conceal their happiness at having got rid of their sister." And when their younger sister returns home for a visit, they conspire to delay her return (hoping this might put her in jeopardy) by appearing to be terribly aggrieved at the idea of her departure. These siblings are duplicitous.

Interestingly enough, this theme of appearance and reality intimately connects the sisters with the Beast. The sisters' duplicity corresponds with the Beast's doubleness since his animal ugliness covers his virtuous nature. Beauty may, in fact, have this in mind when she says to the Beast, "I prefer you, just as you are, to those who, under a human form, hide a false and corrupt heart."

THE BEAST in Beaumont's tale is only thinly sketched. We know a good deal more about the Beasts who appear, for example, in the films by Jean Cocteau and Disney Studios. But the Monsieur Monster who appears in Beaumont's story is something of a mystery man. We don't know until the end of the tale, for example, that this prince was changed into a hideous creature by a wicked fairy (for reasons unknown) and obliged to hide his true identity until a beautiful maiden should agree to marry him.

Essentially, Beaumont's Beast is paradoxical. On the one hand, he is horrific and frightens the Merchant and Beauty, and they cower at his appearance. On the other hand, this scary creature is also pitiable and in need of petting: he sighs in sorrow when Beauty rejects his marriage offers, and he whines in grief at her departure, saying he will die if she is absent too long.

The Beast is also paradoxical in being immensely powerful. He is able to compel the Merchant and Beauty to do his bidding; as the Merchant tells his sons, "The Beast's power is so great that you can have no hope of overpowering him." On the other hand, he is a courtly pussycat who surrenders the reins of power to the woman he puts on a pedestal. He tells Beauty, "You alone are the mistress here. You need only bid me to be gone, if my presence is troublesome, and I will immediately withdraw." And when she worries that her request to return home will be rejected, he tells her he cannot refuse her, "I would rather die than cause you any pain."

The Beast is also paradoxical in being extraordinarily generous. He provides hospitality for the storm-battered Merchant and a farewell gift of a chest of gold. With Beauty, too, he is magnanimous, providing her with a magic mirror, an apartment, a library and harpsichord, even a trunk of fine dresses when she goes traveling. On the other hand, he seems bizarrely begrudging when he gets enraged over the loss of some roses.

Frightening but pitiable, powerful but deferential, generous but mean — these are some of the contradictions within Beaumont's paradoxical Beast. Still, there is a logic to these pairs since they consist of recognizable opposites. Less logical, however, is the central paradox of the Beast, an oxymoron of Beauty's making: she says the Beast is ugly *but* he is good and kind.

THE FAIRY is the Judge in Beaumont's fairy tale, her *conte de fée*. When she first appears in Beauty's dream, the Fine Lady has a judicial tone: "I am pleased, Beauty, by your goodness. This act of giving up your life to save your father's shall not go unrewarded." At the end of the story, she serves as a substitute for the Almighty on Judgment Day, saying to Beauty, "Come and receive the reward of your good choice," while telling her sisters, "As for you, dear ladies, I know your hearts and all the malice they contain," fitting them to their punishments.

To a certain extent, the censorious Fairy finds her counterparts in the society gossips who, in the manner of a chorus, comment upon Beauty's sisters and her family's fall from wealth ("They don't deserve to be pitied," "We feel sorry, however, for Beauty," etc.). And this fairy magistrate also seems reincarnated in the story's judgmental narrator. After all, this storyteller not only provides facts about characters and events, but numerous asides and commentary that are critical in nature (e.g., "Beauty was also better than her sisters," "The older two were proud," etc.).

Ultimately, behind this fairy judge (as well as the censorious gossips and the righteous narrator), we may detect the presence of Madame Beaumont, governess. In the lessons about virtue and vice, in the parceling out of rewards and punishments, in the scoldings and the good examples, we may sense the presence of a tutor in the nursery surrounded by her juvenile charges. This suggests a way that we might turn from a close reading of the text alone to a biographical understanding of the story

THE AUTHOR: AN ARRANGED MARRIAGE

Jeanne-Marie Le Prince de Beaumont was born in Rouen, France, in 1711. She received an excellent education during her childhood. In fact, we may have a portrait of that in the opening of the tale when she describes Beauty's father: "He was a sensible man and spared no expense for his children's education, and he hired all kinds of tutors."

In 1743, while in her early twenties, she entered into an arranged marriage with a Monsieur de Beaumont. Her husband was a minor aristocrat but also, according to reports, a "dissolute libertine."[1] The marriage was not a happy one and was annulled two years later.

A lone woman, Beaumont departed France in 1746 and traveled to England. There she worked for fourteen years as a governess. During this time, she made a name for herself by writing books for children and adolescents. At the age of fifty-one, she returned to France and married two years later. By the time of her death in 1780, she had published more than seventy books.

In terms of understanding "Beauty and the Beast," two features of Beaumont's life are salient: her arranged marriage and her career as a governess. With regards to the first, it should be noted that Beaumont lived in times when old ideas about arranged marriages were being challenged by new notions of romantic love. In the *ancien regime*, scant attention was given to the possibility of love-in-marriage, and marriage was often an alliance based on such practical concerns as class and wealth; indeed, in Beaumont's tale, Beauty's sisters think along these lines. On the other hand, against these conventional marital notions, some progressive thinkers (among them, fairy-tale writer Charles Perrault) spoke of the possibility of conjugal friendship and romantic marriages, advocating

---

1   Zipes, *Beauty and the Beast and Other Classic French Fairy Tales* 131.

the idea that one should wed for no other consideration but love.[1] We might wonder what side Beaumont's "Beauty and the Beast" takes in this controversy.

At first the story seems to present something like an arranged marriage. When Beauty comes to the Beast's castle, her situation resembles that of a maiden whose hand is being given to the *seigneur* by her father. Indeed, the fact that marriage is the primary issue here is dramatically suggested when the Beast does not devour Beauty (as she fears and presumes will happen) but, instead, asks for her hand in marriage—a question he repeats each night.

The Beast's repeated question, on the other hand, might be adduced as evidence that Beaumont's story concerns a romantic marriage. Beauty's assent is sought. Differing from what is customary in arranged nuptials, Beaumont stresses that Beauty has free will. And the voluntary nature of Beauty's decision—on which, in fact, the whole tale turns—might suggest that this is a story about romantic love and love-in-marriage.

In fact, this is how many people mistakenly remember the story's conclusion. Trained to expect the familiar romantic denouement, most contemporary readers, it seems, blithely pass over Beaumont's own conclusion and amend the tale in their own minds so that it becomes a conventional love story. Ask people to retell "Beauty and the Beast," as I have, and they will typically summarize the story in this fashion: "Beauty has a troubled relationship with the Beast, but eventually she realizes that she loves him and declares her love, and then the Beast changes into a handsome prince." That is how most people recall the conclusion of "Beauty and the Beast," but that is not what happens in Beaumont's tale.

In truth, when Beaumont's Beauty first considers the possibility of marriage, she is motivated more by practicality and gratitude than by *amour*:

> "Am I not very wicked," she said, "to be unkind to him who has been so kind to me? ... Why did I refuse to marry him? I could be happier with the Beast than my sisters are with their husbands.... It is true that I don't feel infatuated with him,

---

1 Cf. Marina Warner, *From the Beast to the Blonde: On Fairy Tales and their Tellers* (New York: Farrar, Straus, & Giroux, 1995) 277-79.

but I do feel gratitude, respect, and friendship. I will not make him miserable. If I were ever to be so ungrateful, I wouldn't be able to forgive myself."

Here we don't see a woman swept away by passion and love, but someone calmly calculating her prospects and obligations. Even at the moment when the Beast is near death and Beauty comes to him and agrees to wed, we don't see romantic rapture and love. Instead, Beauty offers a thoughtful statement about deep attachment and friendship:

"No, dear Beast," said Beauty, "you must not die. Instead, live to be my husband. From this moment on, I give you my hand and swear to be none but yours. I thought I only wanted to be your friend, but the grief I now feel convinces me that I cannot live without you."

Beaumont seems to take a middle position, then, in her era's cultural debate between arranged marriages and romantic marriages. Her story does not simply present an arranged marriage where a father gives his daughter's hand to the *grande seigneur*, since Beauty's free will and assent play such a large part in the story's resolution. On the other hand, and despite how readers misremember the tale, Beaumont does not really present a romantic marriage; Beauty is not swept off her feet by love but enters into something like a companionable relationship. In the end, Beauty is persuaded to marry not by her passions but by her sentiments of gratitude and attachment.

BIOGRAPHICAL APPROACHES: THE STORY OF A GOVERNESS

After her own arranged marriage was annulled, Beaumont traveled to England and worked as a governess from 1746 until 1760. During that time, Sarah Fielding published her very popular work *The Governess, or little female academy* (1749), a book that presents a teacher and her nine pupils who tell moral tales to each other. Beaumont followed Fielding's example and created a similar work in French in her *Magasin des enfans* (1756), and then translated the book into English as *The Young Misses Magazine* (1759). Beaumont's

"Beauty and the Beast" is a story told within this book, and we can understand more about the tale from the context in which it was introduced.

The Young Misses Magazine is organized as a series of imaginary conversations between a governess, Mrs. Affable, and her six pupils. The book's title page indicates that the work presents a collection of stories, anecdotes, and lessons meant to both teach and entertain:

> *The Young Misses Magazine,*
> *Containing Dialogues Between*
> *A Governess and Several Young Ladies of Quality her Scholars:*
> *In Which*
> *Each Lady is made to speak according to her particular*
> *Genius, Temper, and Inclination;*
> *Their several Faults are pointed out, and the easy Way to mend*
> *them, as well as to think, and speak, and act properly; no less*
> *care being taken to form their Hearts to Goodness, than to*
> *enlighten their Understandings with useful Knowledge.*
> *A short and clear Abridgement is also given of the Sacred and Profane*
> *History, and some Lessons in Geography.*
> *The Useful is blended throughout with the Agreeable, the Whole*
> *being interspersed with proper Reflections and Moral Tales.*[1]

The first thing to notice is the audience to whom Beaumont is apparently writing. She calls her work *The Young Misses Magazine* and imagines conversations taking place between her governess and six pupils who are identified as "Lady Sensible, twelve [years old]; Lady Witty, twelve; Lady Mary, five; Lady Charlotte, ten; Lady Trifle, ten; [and] Lady Tempest, thirteen."[2] In other words, Beaumont's book and her "Beauty and the Beast" seem addressed to young females, and not ordinary girls but "Young Ladies of Quality"—aristocrats between the ages of five and thirteen.

The other thing to notice is Beaumont's didactic intent. The title page promises that Beaumont's book will teach lessons to the young ("Faults are pointed out, and the easy Way to mend them, as well as [ways] to think, and speak, and act properly"), but that this

1 *Visions and Revisions* 190–91.
2 *Visions and Revisions* 190–91.

will not be a dry catalog of moral injunctions and lessons in manners since the book aims to both teach *and* delight ("the Useful is blended throughout with the Agreeable"), and the way these two goals can be met is by means of edifying stories ("the Whole being interspersed with proper Reflections and Moral Tales"). Signaling even more the book's didactic intent, Beaumont creates an imagined educational milieu in her frame story in which the governess, Mrs. Affable, tells these stories to her pupils.

When "Beauty and the Beast" is positioned within these contexts — within a book that announces its didactic intentions and as a story told by a governess to her students — it can be more clearly recognized as a Moral Tale meant to teach lessons. But what lessons? There are many, both explicit and implicit, but among them we might list:

- that it is admirable to be dutiful and concerned with one's parents;
- that reading good books should be preferred over such pastimes as attending parties and balls;
- that when it comes to matters of class, it is best to be humble instead of "putting on airs";
- that hard work in rural settings makes one healthy and cheerful and is to be preferred to idleness and metropolitan life;
- that honesty (like Beauty's) is more admirable than duplicity (like that of her sisters); and
- that in choosing spouses, virtue and kindness are more important than good looks and a ready wit.

But more than any of these, I suggest, the great lesson of "Beauty and the Beast" concerns that personality trait referred to in the name Beaumont has chosen for her narrator and governess: "Mrs. Affable." A not so common word these days, "affable" suggests "mild-mannered" and "friendly," "amiable," or "equable." And this is precisely Beauty's virtue: what the people in town mean when they say Beauty is "sweet-tempered" and has an "agreeable nature," that cheerful equanimity she possesses when the family loses their wealth and she is obliged to labor in the country, her "friendly nature" which so irks her sisters and charms the Beast. But "affable" not only provides the best description of Beaumont's

Beauty, it also describes the Beast and what is commendable in him (his kindness, gentleness, and friendliness). The lesson the tale teaches, then, is that amiability or "affability" is commendable in a woman and desirable in a potential husband.

In choosing Mrs. Affable as the narrator of her story, in a very straightforward way, Beaumont makes her "Beauty and the Beast" the Story of a Governess. Since Beaumont was employed at the time as a governess, we might say that "Beauty and the Beast" is doubly her story. But there is still a third way in which Beaumont's tale might be seen as the Story of a Governess.

One of the most curious facets of Beaumont's tale concerns the issue of power: on the one hand, Beauty is subordinate and the Beast is dominant, compelling the Merchant to do his bidding and making Beauty his prisoner; on the other hand, Beauty is in charge, and the Beast tells her that her desires take precedence and that she can bid him to come or go as she wishes.

This power dynamic can be seen as an echo of the frame story and the working conditions of a governess. Mrs. Affable, after all, is an inferior, a servant and an employee from a lower social station than that of her aristocratic pupils; on the other hand, she is the governess and in this way the children's superior, an adult and disciplinarian. This dynamic, in other words, may provide a model for the vacillations of power in the relationship between Beauty and the Beast, and this is a third way Beaumont's tale might be seen as the Story of a Governess.

But there is still a fourth way in which the story might be seen in this fashion, when we consider tradition. From Charlotte Bronte's title character in *Jane Eyre* to Julie Andrews's role in "The Sound of Music," the Story of a Governess has familiar features: there is a pronounced social gap between the classes of the two principal characters, but eventually the Marm marries the Master and the downstairs maid becomes the upstairs doyenne. In other words, Beaumont's tale was not only written by a governess (Beaumont herself) and told by a governess (Mrs. Affable), it also echoes the familiar Story of a Governess in its contrast between the merchant's daughter and her aristocratic host, in their eventual nuptials, and in her elevation from country servant to lady of the manor. In this way, Beauty finds in the Beast her own Mr. Rochester and Baron Von Trapp.

THREE

AMONG THE CRITICS

Only after Beauty decides to leave her father's house to be reunited with the Beast—that is, after she has resolved her oedipal ties with her father—does sex, which before was repugnant, become beautiful.

—BRUNO BETTELHEIM, *The Uses of Enchantment* (1976)

The theme of this aristocratic tale involves "putting the bourgeoisie in their place."

—JACK ZIPES, *Breaking the Magic Spell* (1979)

Beauty stands in need of the Beast, rather than vice versa.... He holds up a mirror to the force of nature within her, which she is invited to accept and allow to grow, [namely] ... her female erotic pleasures in matching and mastering a man who is dark and hairy, rough and wild.

—MARINA WARNER, *From the Beast to the Blonde* (1994)

"BEAUTY AND THE BEAST" PROVIDES A convenient way to examine how meaning is discovered in, or imposed on, fairy tales. Professionals, scholars, and various kinds of specialists have explained the tale in dozens of ways.

Among these, we can detect three main trends. Psychological critics have focused attention on Beauty and suggested she has a "problem" (with sex). Socio-historical critics have seen the tale as a reactionary condemnation of social-climbing by the bourgeoisie or merchant class. Finally, feminist critics—while at first faulting the tale for advocating womanly sacrifice and submissiveness—have come to endorse "Beauty and the Beast" for presenting a desirable exploration of feminine erotics.

PSYCHOLOGICAL READINGS

Among the earliest interpreters of "Beauty and the Beast" were Jungian critics Maria Von Franz and Joseph Henderson.[1] Typically, the followers of Carl Jung see the various characters in a tale as representations of different facets of a single individual's personality. Problems arise, they suggest, when individuals reject a part or parts of their personality. The aim of Jungian therapy is for an individual to acknowledge and integrate all the parts of their personality into a harmonious whole, and this resolution is often symbolized in a tale by a marriage.

A concept important to Jungians is the "*anima*" and the "*animus*." Jungians noticed that in men's dreams what is forbidden, dangerous, and erotic often comes in the form of a woman (an *anima*); in the case of women's dreams, the forbidden, dangerous, and erotic often comes in the form of a male (an *animus*). In their interpretation of "Beauty and the Beast," then, Jungian critics see the Beast as Beauty's *animus* — as a part of her personality that she has denied and excluded, a part that is animal-like and sexual. Jungians argue that Beauty's task in the tale is to face reality rather than turn away from it, to acknowledge and integrate that part of her personality she regards as beastly and has rejected.[2]

Two things make this task difficult, they suggest. First, Beauty is something of a Goody Two Shoes. Events early in the story suggest that she has embraced an unreal and exaggerated life of virtue, and Beaumont certainly goes to great lengths to tell us of Beauty's supernal goodness and her self-sacrificing ways. If she is to be saved, Beauty must venture forth from her antiseptic existence and make contact with the Beast. Moreover, this too good girl must fall: the all-too-virtuous Beauty must sin and betray the Beast and recognize that she has done so. Only in this way can she escape her Shirley-Temple-like life of saccharine goodness and dutiful self-denial.

---

1   Joseph Henderson, "Beauty and the Beast," and Marie-Louise Von Franz, "The Process of Individuation," *Man and his Symbols*, ed. Carl G. Jung (Garden City, NJ: Doubleday, 1964) 137-40 and 193-95, respectively.
2   Von Franz 194.

A more significant impediment to Beauty's coming to acknowledge and accept her *animus* is the incest taboo. Growing up with her father, Beauty has driven all thought of sexuality out of her mind. By means of the Beast, however, she comes into contact with the erotic and awakens to the possibility of love. In her prolonged contact with the Beast, her childhood sexual repression (originally maintained because of the incest taboo) must give way and be replaced by trust and love.

If these remarks fairly represent the Jungians' view of the story, the Freudians are best represented by the ideas of Bruno Bettelheim in his *The Uses of Enchantment* (1977).[1] With regard to "Beauty and the Beast," Bettelheim generally follows the lead of the Jungians but differs slightly in identifying Beauty's problem as an oedipal one.

A Freudian concept, the oedipal complex refers to a period in most children's lives when they feel a rivalry with the same-sex parent and a special bond of affection with the opposite-sex parent. Interestingly enough, many of Bettelheim's analyses of other fairy tales focus on the rivalry between the child and same-sex parent; numerous stories, he points out, feature antagonistic relationships between young women and mother figures like the witch or stepmother. But "Beauty and the Beast" focuses on the other side of the oedipal relationship, on the special bond of affection that exists between Beauty and her father. Indeed, we can only wonder how this tale might have been different had Beauty's mother (or her surrogate) been present.

Freudians, we should add, see nothing necessarily sick or aberrant about the oedipal complex; most children go through a period when they are a "momma's boy" or a "daddy's girl." The oedipal complex only becomes a problem when someone gets frozen at this developmental stage and does not outgrow it. In fact, as Bettelheim suggests, when the oedipal period is successfully negotiated, love for a parent can be a prelude to the transfer of affection to someone outside the family:

1   Jacques Barchilon was probably the first to employ Freudian thinking in understanding the tale, and Bettelheim appears to have borrowed from him. Barchilon, "Beauty and the Beast: From Myth To Fairy Tale," *Psychoanalysis and the Psychoanalytic Review* 46,4 (Winter 1959): 19-29.

No other well-known fairy tale makes it as obvious as "Beauty and the Beast" that a child's oedipal attachment to a parent is natural, desirable, and has the most positive consequences of all, if during the process of maturation it is transferred and transformed as it becomes detached from the parent and concentrated on the lover. Our oedipal attachments, far from being a source of our greatest emotional difficulties (which they can be when they do not undergo proper development during our growing up), are the soil out of which permanent happiness grows if we experience the right evolution and resolution of these feelings.[1]

To support his diagnosis of Beauty's oedipal difficulties, Bettelheim points to the young woman's special connections with her father. First, while her sisters go out to parties and are concerned with courtship, Beauty shuns this kind of romantic life and prefers to remain at home with her father. And second, while her sisters are eager to marry, Beauty twice turns down suitors, saying she wishes to stay longer with her father.

But in marshaling evidence to suggest that Beauty has a special bond of affection with her father, Bettelheim overlooks additional proofs that might be used to support his view. For instance, when Beauty resides at the Beast's castle, we learn that every second thought of hers concerns her father and his well-being, so much so that she regularly looks in the Beast's magic mirror to get news of him; and when given permission by the Beast to leave his castle, she flies to her father's side. Indeed, following Bettelheim's ideas, we might view Beaumont's story as a series of Beauty's trial separations from her father until, finally, she can leave the nest and remain with her admirer.

Understanding Bettelheim's view of the story as essentially recounting Beauty's transference of her love from her father to the prince, we can begin to understand Bettelheim's notion of how beastliness enters the story. According to this psychologist, as long as Beauty has a special bond of affection with her father, she sees sex as animal-like and loathsome because of the incest taboo. Or, to

---

1 Bruno Bettelheim, *The Uses of Enchantment* (New York: Vintage Books, 1977) 307.

say this differently, as long as Beauty has a special bond of affection with her father, she sees other men as beastly. Once she works through her relationship with her father and separates from him, Beauty can then see the handsome prince as he is.

Though this is not exactly said by Bettelheim, the logical implication of his view is that the Prince has *always* looked like the Prince. Beauty — because of the incest taboo and her oedipal attachment to her father — has not seen the prince correctly and has imagined him a beast. Once she works through her relationship with her father and separates from him, she can see the Prince as he is — *and as he has always been.*

And it is here where we might begin a critique of psychological interpretations of the tale, by noticing how both the Jungians and Freudians have narrowed the story to a discussion of Beauty and *her* problems. Such a view is not wrong, but it is incomplete. After all, the title of "Beauty and the Beast" suggests dual billing; and while Beauty may certainly have a problem with her relationships, the Prince (trapped in the form of a beast) has manifest problems of his own that should not be overlooked.

Moreover, in directing attention away from the Beast's physical transformation and towards Beauty's emotional transformation, both Jungians and Freudians have come to see the tale as an account of *feminine* maturation. Beauty passes through various developmental stages. She learns and matures. But if this is, equally, the Beast's story, then we may need to consider his development. What is it that *he* learns? In what ways, does *he* need to mature?

We might even hazard some answers here. Perhaps the prince was changed into a beast, as is the case in some folk tales, because of unwelcome sexual misconduct and animal-like aggressiveness with women. If that is so, then "Beauty and the Beast" might talk about *a male's* needing to learn not to force himself on women and his demonstration that he can be a gentleman. In other words, the tale presents a test of his ability (in amorous engagements) to wait patiently until the woman says "Yes."

Again, in overlooking the Beast's story and in remaking Beaumont's tale into the story of "Beauty and Her Problems," psychological critics have not erred but they have limited our understanding of the story. Other kinds of myopia can be noticed when we pay attention to the ideology behind these psychological

approaches. Consider the Jungians, for example. In their formula-
tions of the *anima* (the female dream figure of men) and the *animus*
(the male dream figure of women), Jungians, we should note,
display a distinct predisposition to heterosexuality. This same
predisposition plays itself out in the way Jungians focus on
male/female relationships in "Beauty and the Beast." While these
relations are important and are foregrounded in this romantic story,
attention to them should not come at the expense of ignoring
female/female and male/male relations in the story — all of which,
we might note, are conflicted.

A similar kind of shortsightedness limits Freudian understand-
ings of the story. Bettelheim emphasizes that it is *Beauty's* oedipal
affection which makes difficult her detaching from her father and
her aligning herself with the Beast. But we might ask: Is she the
only one who has problems with separating? Is attachment only *her*
problem? Beauty's father, we might note, collapses in illness and
very nearly dies when he is separated from his daughter, and he
bounces back to health upon her return. Oedipal attachment, we
might observe, is not a one-way street.[1]

And Beauty's father is not the only one to suffer from deathlike
swoons — or, perhaps, the self-indulgent tantrums we associate with
spoiled children — when Beauty absents herself. The Beast, too,
collapses and is near death when Beauty leaves his side. If
Bettelheim's argument is that such dependency is a kind of imma-
turity, then we might argue that poor Beauty is surrounded by
masculine whiners desperate for her nurturance, and this unfairly
compels Beaumont's Florence Nightingale to shuttle between
needy males, at her father's home and the Beast's castle. Indeed,
Beauty is only permitted happiness at the end, when her family

---

1 This notion that other characters have problems in the tale — and that psychological critics are shortsighted in viewing the story only as an account of
Beauty and *her* problems — is also suggested in another way. Bettelheim's ideas
lead to the interesting suggestion that the prince has always looked like the
prince but Beauty (because of her oedipal attachment to her father) mistakenly
views him as a beast. But here is the catch: Beauty's father *also* sees the Beast. If
we wish to be consistent, then, we need to say that the father's equally mistak-
en vision of the Prince reveals the father's own oedipal attachment to his
daughter: his unwillingness to give up his daughter and his notion that her
suitors are unsuitable beasts.

comes to the Beast's castle and she is no longer asked to choose between father and husband.

Again, in offering these reservations to the Jungian and Freudian interpretations of the tale, I am not suggesting that these psychological readings of "Beauty and the Beast" are wrong. Instead, my aim is to add more complexity and depth to them. In raising questions about the consistency and thoroughness of their arguments, however, I am still playing within their ballpark and working within the mind-set of psychological criticism. Other critics might raise more comprehensive questions and ask whether this is the right ballpark, at all, in which to take up the meanings of Beaumont's story.

SOCIO-HISTORICAL READINGS

Jack Zipes is a well-known and prolific commentator on fairy tales whose methodology is socio-historical or Marxist. Zipes vehemently objects to Bettelheim's psychological approach to the fairy tales, arguing that Bettelheim sees these stories as ahistorical documents that address timeless human problems. Instead, Zipes insists, these tales must be seen precisely within their historical and cultural contexts. And when this is done, we notice how they have been reshaped in different times and locales not to address universal human issues, but to push specific social agendas.[1]

In "Beauty and the Beast," Zipes suggests, we see class struggle: the story presents the quarrel between the nobility and the rising merchant class or bourgeoisie. The aim of Beaumont's aristocratic tale, Zipes explains, is to "[put] the bourgeoisie in their place."[2]

With regard to the role of class in the story, Zipes is entirely convincing. Unlike the classic folk tale, at the outset of Beaumont's tale, we are not introduced to, say, a king and queen. Instead, front and center is an entirely new set of characters—a merchant and his family. They are *nouveau riche*. Moreover, Beauty's sisters are vulgar social climbers who insist they will only marry a duke or an earl. And, of course, these *arrivistes* get their comeuppance when their father loses his fortune.

---

1 Cf. Jack David Zipes, *Breaking the Magic Spell: Radical Theories of Folk and Fairy Tales* (Austin, TX: University of Texas Press, 1979; London: Methuen, 1984) 160–82.

2 Zipes, *Breaking the Magic Spell* 9.

Opposite the merchant and his family stands the Beast. Zipes suggests he is a figure for the aristocracy, "old money," a nobleman living in a castle. According to Zipes, the message of the story, then, is that the merchant class (in the face of their aristocratic betters) ought to be humble like Beauty and not put on airs like her sisters.

Zipes's approach to Beaumont's tale suggests how meaning can be found by positioning "Beauty and the Beast" within its historical context, particularly in terms of the rise of the bourgeoisie. In that regard, we might follow his example but go a bit further in order to gather an even more comprehensive understanding of the story.

One of the principal architects of the rise of the bourgeoisie was Jean Baptiste Colbert (1619-83), the minister of Louis XIV. Faced with massive government debts and looking for advice, the king turned not to the members of his court or to the nobility, but to this professional civil servant, the son of a prosperous merchant family. Colbert thought the way to put France on a sound financial footing was to run the government as a business and put the merchant at center stage. Moreover, he was impressed by how the English and the Dutch had increased their wealth by becoming commercial nations with ships that sailed the world and engaged in trading enterprises. Colbert saw to it that France followed their examples. He encouraged the building of ships, the formation of private trading companies among groups of investors, and the extension of commerce to the East and West Indies as well as northern Europe and the eastern Mediterranean.

At home, Colbert hated idlers and slackers—landlords, bureaucrats, nobles, clergymen, and others who wiled away their days with luxurious pastimes, who lived in the cities and depended upon the labors of others who worked on their distant estates. Convinced that every citizen should work and produce, Colbert developed a number of economic measures meant to frustrate the privileged and undermine their lives of ease. Under his mercantile system, productive merchants and manufacturers were rewarded, and wealth began to gradually shift to this merchant class and away from the privileged whose families for years had derived their income from others.

In the decades following Colbert and his policies, the gradual erosion of the *ancien régime* left the nobility in a sorry state. While

they might claim the grandeur of their titles and possibly the ownership of vast estates, aristocrats were often at the brink of financial
ruin and unable to pay taxes—especially because they were now
required to do so in a new way, by using money and paying in the
new currency. Moreover, they could not easily find a solution to
their financial woes by engaging in activities like trade or manufac-
turing since such commercial pursuits were often viewed as common and beneath members of the nobility.

So, on the one hand, those who laid claim to titles like "Duke"
or "Earl" seemed to be headed towards extinction. On the other
hand, the bourgeoisie, the merchant class, was on the rise. To be
sure, wealth fluctuated. Great fortunes were both made and lost as a
result of investments in tobacco, mining, foundries, cotton mills,
banks, maritime trade, and other activities. But boom or bust, the
merchant class (as a whole) was gaining the upper hand.

Of course, the nobility (on their way down) and the merchant
class (on their way up) did occasionally find a meeting ground.
Cash-poor, the nobility at least had the grandeur of their titles.
Class-less, the bourgeoisie had money—even though it might have
been acquired in the sordid and common world of commerce, and
even though aristocrats might look down their noses at them as
nouveau riche. Typically enough, a happy compromise was reached
when, say, the wealthy owner of cotton mills arranged for his
daughter to be married to a destitute nobleman. In this way, the
aristocrat could pay his taxes and keep the family estate, while the
merchant and his family gained a title and an entrance into high
society.

It may be immediately obvious how the historical circumstances
described here reappear in the situation found in Beaumont's
"Beauty and the Beast." Beaumont sets her story in a world of
merchants and nobility, of trading ships and fluctuating fortunes, of
merchants' daughters with aspirations to upward mobility, and so
forth. But what is perhaps more interesting is how Beaumont's tale
differs from, or reacts to, its times. Most obvious is the fact that the
union between Beauty and the Beast is not presented as a marriage
of convenience between a wealthy merchant's daughter and an
impoverished nobleman. Instead, we have the opposite.

In Beaumont's tale, the nobleman is not hurting for cash; it is the
merchant's family that is down on its luck. Moreover, the merchant

and his family are considerably helped by the magnanimous Beast and his chests of gold, his largesse and sense of *noblesse oblige*. In fact, as a figure for the aristocrat, the Beast presents an appealing picture—landed and kind, generous and refined, and in every way noble. In other words, in the midst of changing times, Beaumont seems to offer a kind of backwards-looking endorsement of the nobility, a flattering and conservative portrait of the *ancien régime*.

But, besides honoring the aristocrat, we should also notice how Beaumont responds to changing times by offering a reactionary criticism of the new and rising merchant class. Beauty's sisters and their vulgar class aspirations are particularly singled out for disapproval. Moreover, in her vision of the merchant's slide from urban prosperity to rural poverty, Beaumont seems to go out of her way to emphasize that status is a precarious thing among the bourgeoisie because (unlike the landed gentry) social station is tied to money and wealth, and fortunes could and did fluctuate. Ultimately, Beaumont seems to suggest that the merchant class would be better if they were more like Beauty—that is to say, if they went back to the farm and became once again hardworking and uncomplaining peasants; in the evenings, she suggests, they can turn to improving books and music.

When Beaumont's tale is seen in its historical context, then, we can detect the author's aristocratic airs, patronizing attitudes, and conservative views. Seen in this way, her tale is not so much a reflection of her era as it is a reaction to it: a kind of aristocratic backlash to changing times.

FEMINIST READINGS

The fortunes of the fairy tales among feminist critics may be divided into two phases. A first generation of feminist critics condemned the tales as reflections of a patriarchal culture and found abundant evidence in them of the victimization of women.[1]

---

1 Cf. Marcia K. Lieberman's "Some Day My Prince Will Come: Female Acculturation Through the Fairy Tale" and Karen E. Rowe's "Feminism and Fairy Tales" in *Don't Bet on the Prince: Contemporary Feminist Fairy Tales in North America and England*, ed. Jack Zipes (New York: Methuen, 1986) 185-200 and 209-26, respectively. See also Ruth B. Bottigheimer, *Grimm's Bad Girls and Bold*

However, a second generation of feminists—a loose collection of writers, Jungian essayists, and critics—came to endorse them as female stories and saw in these "old wives' tales" visions of feminine empowerment.[1] What has been the history of fairy tales in general has also been the history of "Beauty and the Beast" in particular.

Those feminists who object to "Beauty and the Beast" see it as an admiring portrait of a self-sacrificial maiden and argue that Beaumont's story conveys the objectionable lesson that women should be submissive. Beauty puts others' interests before her own, especially her father's interests, when she rejects suitors, resettles in the country in order to comfort the old man, and finally takes his place at the Beast's castle. When the family moves to the country, Beauty (like some uncomplaining Cinderella) represses her own feelings and remains upbeat, rising at four in the morning and doing the chores. In Beauty's going to the Beast's castle and in her agreeing to marry him, these feminists also see the situation of women pledged to arranged marriages by their fathers; in that case, the message to young aristocratic girls in Beaumont's story seems to be that they should acquiesce to arrangements that have been made for them. Moreover, the tale suggests that if her selected spouse should strike her as a beast, a young woman should know that a clever and well-meaning woman can change a brute into a companionable husband.[2] In summary, as one critic suggests, when we consider the admirable heroine who gives her name to this tale, we are obliged to conclude that "the mark of beauty for a female is to be found in her submission, obedience, humility, industry, and patience."[3]

When the story is seen in this way, first-generation feminists seem entirely correct and Beaumont emerges from their assessments as a matronly co-conspirator coaching young women to bow to traditional and patriarchal values. Other evidence, however,

   Boys: The Moral and Social Vision of the Tales (New Haven, CT: Yale University Press, 1987).

1 Cf. Warner; Pinkola Estés; Angela Carter, *The Bloody Chamber* (New York: Penguin Books, 1993); Maria Kolbenschlag, *Kiss Sleeping Beauty Good-Bye* (New York: Bantam Books, 1981).

2 Cf. Warner 293.

3 Jack Zipes, *Fairy Tales and the Art of Subversion: The Classical Genre for Children and the Process of Civilization* (New York: Wildman Press, 1983) 38, 40-41.

suggests that this is too simple an understanding. Indeed, it might be possible to construct a counter-argument and argue that Beaumont was an early feminist.

"Beauty and the Beast" appeared in Beaumont's book for young women, *The Young Misses Magazine,* and in the introduction to that work Beaumont presented strikingly radical and forward-looking views for her times. Against the commonly held opinion that only boys should be schooled, Beaumont declared her conviction that young women should be educated and encouraged to be intelligent, not just viewed as fodder for marriage:

> Some will think, that the instructions to be given here are too serious for ladies from fifteen to eighteen years of age. But to satisfy this objection, [I need only say] that I have merely [written] down the conversations that have passed between me and my [students]; and experience has taught me that those instructions are not above their reach.... We don't have a true [understanding] of the capacity of [young women]; nothing is out of their reach.... Now-a-days ladies read all sorts of books, history, politicks, philosophy and even such as concern religion. They should therefore be in a condition to judge solidly of what they read and able to discern truth from falsehood.[1]

If we admit the possibility that Beaumont might be considered a proto-feminist, then we may question the opinions of first-generation feminists who condemned her and her tale. For example, note that Beaumont's Beauty is not always submissive. When she first sees the Beast, she recoils in horror and does not repress her feelings; and when he asks her if she finds him ugly, her answer is direct and candid and in the affirmative. When Beauty returns to visit her father, she is not catering to the Beast's wishes but indulging her own desires. In fact, self-indulgence, more than self-sacrifice, seems to characterize her time at the Beast's castle, where she has a room of her own and every kind of luxury. At these moments, it might be argued, the tale does not speak of compliance but of feminine independence and autonomy.

1 Quoted in *Visions and Revisions* 17.

Moreover, it can be argued further, first-generation feminists do not offer a complete view of Beauty when they regard her as a self-sacrificial and powerless victim. In several ways, Beaumont offers a tale in which Beauty is in charge. Although the Beast is a huge and formidable creature, it is Beauty who calls the shots: she is the mistress of the house, the Beast insists, and everything and everyone (including the Beast himself) is at her command. Moreover, the tale dramatically emphasizes Beauty's power of choice: she must come to the Beast's castle of her own free will; she is not to be coerced but must freely choose to marry; she alone holds the power to transform the Beast; and, indeed, through much of the tale he waits upon her decision. In fact, Beauty seems to inhabit a world where males (her father, the Beast) are weak and where women have power.

These facts suggest something important: that "Beauty and the Beast" is not a story of feminine submissiveness but of feminine empowerment. Here may be found the reason for something noted earlier in this book—namely, the story's unusual popularity among women.

This is the point at which second-generation feminists, such as Marina Warner, have taken up the story and endorsed it. Inspired by the "pagan" and "earthy" feminism of writer Angela Carter, Warner sees "Beauty and the Beast" as not only dealing with power transactions but with "the complicated character of the female erotic impulse."[1]

In a fashion, Warner sees Beaumont's "Beauty and the Beast" as the familiar kind of story seen in popular women's romance novels: the charged encounter between the nice girl and the dark or dangerous male. In Warner's eyes, Beauty is going for "a walk on the wild side." And in this way, "Beauty and the Beast" addresses the attraction women feel towards males who are appealing not so much because of their looks but because of their dark and sexy nature, their animal magnetism.

In advancing her views, Warner subsumes and answers other interpretations of the tale. Jungian and Freudian critics, for example, have suggested that the Beast represents Beauty's own sexual or animal nature which she is resisting because of her special bond of

1 Warner 313.

affection with her father and the incest taboo. Warner is willing to accept the view that the Beast represents Beauty's sexual nature, but she steadfastly refuses to find a "problem" in that. Instead, she suggests, for example, that Bettelheim's views reveal his prudery and discomfort with feminine sexuality since he feels obliged to stigmatize Beauty's encounter with sexuality as showing oedipal difficulties and arrested development. On her part, Warner finds the encounter powerful and positive: Bettelheim's interpretation of the tale, Warner complains, "takes the exuberance and the energy from female erotic voices."[1]

At the same time, Warner also goes beyond the notion implicit in the interpretations of Marxists and first-generation feminists: namely, that Beauty is a victim. Beauty is not subjugated, Warner notes; once she gets to the Beast's castle, she is the mistress of all she surveys, and the huge and formidable Beast waits on her approval. If anything, the equation of power is tipped in her favor. She might, in fact, be seen as a dominatrix in several senses of the word, not excluding the sexual one. For Warner, "Beauty and the Beast" is a story of "female erotic pleasures in matching and mastering a man who is dark and hairy, rough and wild."[2]

Oedipal difficulties and sexual anxiety, the *noblesse oblige* and uppity bourgeoisie, womanly deference and feminine erotics — the spectrum of meanings this fairy tale produces is one measure of the story's potency and prism-like perfection.

1   Warner 313.
2   Warner 318.

FOUR

SOURCES

It is impossible to trace the origins of "Beauty and the Beast" back to some alpha, some original source from which all other versions flowed. That is as it should be. The story of a woman with an animal husband is as old as the hills. In response to common existential problems, numberless individuals have imagined (at different times and all over the globe) tales about beastly spouses and their transformations.

Stories of animal grooms were, no doubt, told by storytellers for centuries before they were ever written down. In their most common form, frequently found in Africa and Asia, these tales tell of "The Woman Who Married a Snake." One of the earliest records of this story appeared when it was written down in Sanskrit in the *Panchatantra*, a classical Indian text that probably dates to the time of Christ. A century later, Apuleius recorded a similar story in Latin as the myth of "Cupid and Psyche," and in printed form it would come to be widely distributed in Europe.[1]

In the years and centuries that followed, Beauty-and-the-Beast-like tales were shaped from Apuleius's myth and from oral folktales, but the next notable appearance of animal groom stories in print occurred in Italy in the sixteenth and seventeenth centuries. Several tales in Giambattista Basile's *The Pentameron* (*Pentamerone*, 1634-36) tell Cupid-and-Psyche-like stories of a snake husband or of wives who mistakenly believe their spouses to be monsters and who need to go in search of them once they are lost.[2] On the other hand, stories of "animal husbandry" that appeared in Giovanni Francesco Straparola's *The Pleasant Nights* (*Le piacevoli notti*, 1550) seem to have been drawn from indigenous folklore. For

---

1 Cf. Ruth B. Bottigheimer, "Beauty and the Beast," *The Oxford Companion to the Fairy Tales*, ed. Jack Zipes (New York: Oxford University Press, 2000) 45.

2 Bottigheimer 47. Basile's "Pinto Smalto" appears in Hearne's *Beauties and Beasts* 145-50.

instance, one of the most amusing of Straparola's tales is "Pig King" ("Re Porco"), the story of a swinish prince who enjoys wallowing in a filthy and muddy bed. His first two wives object to being defiled in this way and, in the manner of Bluebeard, he kills them. His third wife, however, is not so fickle about the fecal and her lack of squeamishness eventually effects her husband's transformation from pig to prince.[1]

From Italy, the history of making fairy-tales crosses over into France and the salon. Gatherings of aristocrats and intellectuals for entertainment and conversation, salons became a fashion in France near the end of the seventeenth century.[2] Besides musical performances and drawing-room theatricals, it was customary for individuals to provide entertainment by telling "fairy stories." Ostensibly repeating old stories heard from their servants or nursemaids, these aristocratic storytellers, in fact, often made use of oral folktales or written works and then embellished them in their own manner. Some of these stories, intended for an adult and upper-class audience, eventually found their way into print.

The several volumes of Madame d'Aulnoy's *Fairy Stories* (*Les contes des fées*, 1697-98) provide examples of these literary productions of the salon, and a number of her tales tell animal groom stories in which the prince appears as a frog or serpent. Her story that most resembles "Beauty and the Beast" is "The Ram" ("Le Mouton") where the prince appears in that titular form, but it ends differently: the ram pines away when his beloved is absent and, upon her return, dies in her arms.[3] As an aside, we should not be sheepish but note that biographical facts may explain Aulnoy's enthusiasm for stories about beastly husbands and their demise: like Beaumont, she was unhappily wed in an arranged marriage; but while Beaumont sought a divorce, Aulnoy went a bit further and unsuccessfully plotted to have her husband executed by making false charges to the authorities about him.[4]

---

1 Straparola's "Pig King" is printed in Maria Tatar's *The Classic Fairy Tales* (New York: W.W. Norton and Company, 1999) 42-47.

2 Cf. Zipes, *Beauty and the Beast And Other Classic French Fairy Tales*, xiv-xix.

3 Zipes has translated "The Ram" in *Beauty and the Beast And Other Classic French Fairy Tales* 250-67.

4 Zipes, *Beauty and the Beast And Other Classic French Fairy Tales* 194.

Other examples of the salon fairy tale appeared about the same time when Charles Perrault published a collection of tales titled *Histories or Stories from Times Past* (*Histoires ou contes du temps passé*, 1697). Of these, the most interesting as a source for "Beauty and the Beast" is his "Riquet of the Tuft" ("Riquet à la Houppe"), the story of a beautiful (but unintelligent) girl who is persuaded by an ugly (but witty) prince to marry him. He promises that if she will remain married to him for a year, she will be granted intelligence; that condition is met and when she does receive her gift, her husband appears to her as "the most handsome man in the world." The value Perrault places on *both* beauty and wit (intelligence) recalls how these two qualities are equally prized in Beaumont's "Beauty and the Beast." But also of interest is the ambiguous conclusion to "Riquet of the Tuft" since Perrault leaves unclear whether the prince goes through an actual physical transformation or whether his different appearance is due to a perceptual change once his wife acquires intelligence. This ambiguity may be echoed in Beaumont's tale and in Beauty's similar perceptual change.

The first appearance of a story with the name of "Beauty and the Beast" occurred when Madame Gabrielle de Villeneuve, an *habitué* of the salons, published a novel-length version of the tale in 1740. As Betsy Hearne explains, it is an unusually complicated work with an army of characters, but it is essentially concerned with matchmaking, the suitability of marriage partners, and the approval of parents — resolved in this case when it is revealed in the conclusion that the peasant Beauty is actually of noble blood.[1]

Intended for an adult and aristocratic audience, Villeneuve's version is, in retrospect, striking in the way the story is centered around sex. The prince was changed into a beast for rejecting the amorous advances of a fairy. Instead of Beaumont's Beast nightly asking Beauty whether she will marry him, Villeneuve's Beast repeatedly asks, "Will you go to bed with me?" And instead of the Beast transforming into a prince once Beauty speaks of her affection and agrees to marry, Villeneuve's Beast only transforms after their wedding night together: more than music, sex seems to soothe the savage beast.

1   *Visions and Revisions* 21-25.

Beaumont's version of "Beauty and the Beast" appeared a little more than a dozen years later, in French in 1756 and in English in 1759. In coining her own version, Beaumont seems to have been aware of the myth of "Cupid and Psyche" since she makes a bow in that direction after the Beast has been transformed: she describes the handsome prince "as more beautiful than the God of Love." She may have made use of other sources as well, for example, Aulnoy's "The Ram" and Perrault's "Riquet of the Tuft." But she clearly made use of Villeneuve's work, bringing to it a wanted economy in her abridgment of her predecessor's long-windedness and in deleting all the other's talk about sex. After all, Beaumont was transporting the tale from adults-in-the-salon to children-in-the-nursery, and she was creating a new thing—literature for children.

To understand Beaumont's invention, we need to turn aside for a moment and notice cultural developments in her milieu — specifically, the rise of the concept of childhood and Children's Literature. As Philippe Ariès has argued in his *Centuries of Childhood*,[1] the notion of "childhood" did not exist prior to the sixteenth century; while his ideas have since been questioned, he does at least make a convincing case that this was the situation in France. The invention of "children" is, of course, an idea difficult for contemporary readers to comprehend; for us, the notion of childhood is so widespread and institutionalized that it seems to have the force of nature. But Ariès suggests we can understand the absence of "childhood" prior to the sixteenth century by recalling that in earlier times, in agricultural societies, the young were not sheltered and cozened in a special period of their development; instead, once they had passed through their first few tender years, they joined with adults in meeting the labor-intensive demands of their lives. As paintings from these times also suggest, "children" were not separated from "adults" in dress, activities, or entertainments. Indeed, these differentiated concepts did not exist.

Change came in the sixteenth and seventeenth centuries. While these developments can only be sketched here, it was during this time that the notion arose of the "child" as a special creature with

---

1 Philippe Ariès, *Centuries of Childhood*, trans. Robert Baldrick (New York: Random House, 1962).

unique needs and a distinct nature. As paintings suggest, children and adults were now separated in clothing styles that were considered appropriate to each; as home designs from the period indicate, it now became more customary to create a children's room or nursery, from which the young would venture to the parlor to sometimes entertain the adults. What was arising, in other words, was a notion of "childhood" as a protected period of time through which the aristocratic young would transit, a period when they might be immune from work and their time given over to education and play.

For this new creature, the "Child," new books came to be written which addressed their special nature. Certain topics (e.g., manners and deportment) were judged appropriate, and other subjects (e.g., sex) were deemed unsuitable until the child had grown older. In other words, once the notion of the Child and Childhood began to receive wider cultural acceptance, literature for children came to be developed.

John Newbery, the English bookseller, is generally regarded as the creator of the genre of "Children's Literature" when, in the 1740s, he established a trade of producing and distributing books meant for the young and that, for example, retold Aesop's fables or recounted the mishaps of Goody Two-Shoes. Arriving in England in 1746, Beaumont was Newbery's contemporary and aware of these developments. In fact, Beaumont's "Beauty and the Beast" might be regarded as the very first great work in this new genre of Children's Literature.

When we look back from this milestone story, we can see how Beaumont forever altered the history of the tale by aiming her version at this new market, addressing her story to young and marriageable girls. But before it reached the nursery, this tale had had a long evolution: arising as the story of an animal groom in oral and possibly Asian sources, appearing in Apuleius's "Cupid and Psyche," passing into and out of folklore and literary works in the sixteenth and seventeenth centuries, and emerging as an adult "fairy tale" in the salons at the end of the seventeenth century and into the eighteenth century. Just as we know something about a child from its parents, we get a better understanding of Beaumont's "Beauty and the Beast" when we consider it in terms of its antecedents.

APULEIUS'S "THE MARRIAGE OF CUPID AND PSYCHE"

Scholars have pointed to the myth of "Cupid and Psyche" as one of the earliest versions of "Beauty and the Beast." While the myth no doubt existed in an earlier oral form, one of the first written records of the tale appeared in a chapter of Apuleius's The Golden Ass. *Apuleius was born in 123 A.D. in the area now known as Algeria. His Latin text appeared in the middle of the second century.*

Apuleius's story was well known by the time Beaumont penned her "Beauty and the Beast." By 1469, the Latin text had been printed and widely distributed throughout Europe. In France, the text was published at least four times in the first half of the seventeenth century; in the second half of that century, French translations appeared, for example, in La Fontaine's "Amours de Psyché et de Cupidon" and in Molière and Corneille's "Psyché, a tragedie-ballet."[1] The story was equally accessible in English. My own version here, for example, is a modernization of the 1566 translation by William Adlington.

Once upon a time, in ancient Greece, there lived a King and Queen who had three daughters. The two oldest were uncommonly beautiful. But Psyche, the youngest, was so extraordinarily beautiful she seemed almost divine.

Hearing of her beauty, people came from far and near to have a look at her and admire her. They paid her so much attention that it seemed as if the goddess Venus, herself, had come to earth. In fact, a rumor was started that a second Venus had appeared.

Stories of Psyche's beauty spread all over Greece and to distant parts, and people came to do her honor and present her with flowers and garlands. Calling this girl "the new Venus," people neglected to honor the actual goddess, temples dedicated to Venus fell into disrepair, and the ceremonies to her were ignored.

Venus, herself, was angered by this loss of honor: "Who is it that uses my name? No earthly woman shall lay claim to my honors. This girl shall soon repent her ways."

So, Venus called her son Cupid, the winged god who is a mischief-maker, the one who shoots his arrows of love this way and that, causing trouble and upsetting marriages. Showing him Psyche,

---

1 Bottingheimer 45; *Visions and Revisions* 13.

Venus begged her son, "If you love me, do me this favor. Shoot one of your fiery arrows at my rival, that human impostor. Make her wretched. Make her fall in love with the poorest, ugliest, and vilest creature alive." After saying that, Venus kissed her son and departed.

In the meantime, Psyche was taking no pleasure in her astonishing beauty. She might be praised and adored, but no one asked for her hand in marriage. Her sisters weren't treated as extraordinary, and each had married a king. But Psyche remained single, and all she could do was lament her solitary life. Maybe the world was pleased by Psyche's beauty, but she wasn't pleased by it herself.

Psyche's father was also unhappy that his daughter had not married and, fearing that the gods bore some grudge against her, went and consulted the Oracle of Apollo. The father said the required prayers and made the required sacrifice, then he asked where a husband might be found for his daughter. The answer he received from the Oracle was unexpected:

> Dress Psyche for a funeral
> And leave her on the mountain top.
> Her husband will no human be
> But a winged snake, a monster so fierce
> That even the gods are afraid of him.

The king returned home, sad and sorrowful, and told his wife everything the Oracle had said. For many days, they wept and lamented their lot, but there was nothing they could do to avoid what had been prophesied. When the day came for Psyche's wedding, a ghastly bridal ceremony took place. The customary joyful songs were replaced by mournful dirges. The people of the city joined with her family in weeping and lamenting. Even Psyche wept, drying her eyes with her bridal veil.

Acting as if she were going to her funeral instead of her wedding, Psyche urged her parents, "Do not suffer anymore. This is my hard fate, not yours. Do not beat your breasts and pull your hair. Now you see the reward for my unusual beauty. Now you see the damage caused by envy. When people honored my beauty and called me the new Venus, you should have cried. Now I see that people have dishonored Venus and that the goddess is behind my suffering. Bring me to the mountain top. I am eager to meet my monster husband. Why would I want to delay my destruction?"

So they left her at the appointed place, and everyone departed in tears and darkness. At home, her miserable parents were consumed with sorrow. Meanwhile, alone and abandoned, Psyche was weeping and trembling when a gentle wind lifted her from the mountain and carried her down into a deep valley of fragrant flowers. There she fell into a deep sleep.

When she awoke, Psyche found herself in a grove of trees alongside a river. Nearby was a palace so princely that it must have been intended for a god. Ivory and precious metals had been used in its construction, and the wooden walls were carved with pictures of beasts that seemed to jump out at her. The floor and different corners of the building were so decorated with precious stones that when the sun shone, reflected light was everywhere. It looked like a place fit even for Jupiter himself.

Feeling confident, Psyche entered the palace. She was amazed by the abundance of riches she found there, none under lock and key. Then an invisible voice spoke to her: "Why do you marvel at these riches? These are all yours. You are the Lady of this house. When you wish, retire to your room to rest and bathe. We, these voices that you hear, are your servants. We will summon you when it is time for dinner."

After she had rested and bathed, she saw a table set for her. When she sat down, wonderful dishes and wines were brought by these invisible servants. Psyche could hear their voices but saw no one. Then musicians played and sang for her, but again she could see no one.

Finally, at the end of these festivities and with night approaching, she retired to her bed. Then her husband came to her and, making love to her, consummated the marriage. In the early hours before morning, he departed. While she was at first surprised, these nocturnal visits continued and she grew accustomed to them and found them pleasurable.

Then one night, Psyche's husband spoke to her, "My dear wife, you are in great danger. Your sisters think you are dead and will retrace your steps to the mountain top. If you hear them weeping and lamenting, do not call to them or even look towards them. If you do, you will bring great sorrow to me and misfortune to yourself." Psyche said she was happy to obey.

But after her husband departed, Psyche began to feel sorry for herself. Here she was all day, alone, as if in a prison, deprived of human conversation, and her husband had commanded her not to communicate with her sisters or even see them. She spent the day weeping and went to bed without having eaten.

When her husband came and embraced her that night, he complained, "Is this the kind of a wife you are? Is this how you are going to keep your promise to me? Weeping night and day? Even sobbing while we embrace? Alright, do as you wish. But remember you are bringing on your own destruction, and you will regret it when it is too late."

Then she begged him for his approval, asking if she might see her sisters, saying she should die unless she saw them. At length, he gave in and even provided her with gold and jewels to give them. But he warned her once again, "Your sisters will try to persuade you to discover what I look like. Do not give into that curiosity or you will lose me and all that is ours."

"Dear husband," Psyche replied, "though I have never seen your face, I don't care. I would rather die than be separated from you. I love you. But let me ask just one more favor. Command the winds to carry my sisters here, as they once carried me." Then she kissed him, called him "sweetheart" and other endearing names, and in this way she persuaded him. And just before the morning light came, he departed as usual.

Then Psyche's sisters came to the mountain top and called out her name in lamentations. But when she heard them, Psyche came from the house and said, "Here am I, the one you are weeping for. Torment yourselves no longer." And with that, the gentle winds raised the sisters from the mountain and gently brought them to the valley. Then they were reunited, and there was such kissing and hugging and crying that I cannot tell it all.

Psyche then invited her sisters into the palace and showed them all her treasures and had her invisible servants bring them every kind of delicacy. Then a great envy arose in their hearts, and they began to question their younger sister. "Who is this husband of yours," they asked curiously, "who has such wealth?" But Psyche, remembering her promise to her husband, made up a story that he was a handsome young man who loved to spend his days hunting in the nearby hills and valleys. And to distract them further, Psyche filled their laps with gold and silver and jewels, before commanding the winds to carry them back.

After they were brought back to the mountain and were making their way home, the two sisters talked enviously about Psyche's good fortune: "Here we are, born of the same parents, but we were married to foreign husbands and have to live far from our friends and own country. But Psyche! She seems to have a god for a husband, and as for riches! Did you see the piles of jewels, the glittering robes, and the floor of gold that we walked on? If she has such a husband as she says, then there is no luckier woman in the world. And if her husband is a god, it may be that one day he will make her immortal as well. She already acts like a goddess, commanding invisible voices to serve her and telling the winds what to do."

Then the oldest sister complained, "Look how bad I've got it. My husband is older than my father, and bald and feeble to boot. He keeps me locked up in the house all day."

The other sister answered her, "You think you have it bad. My husband is doubled over with rheumatism, and I have to rub him with lotions and oils that stain my lovely white hands. I'm treated more like a servant than a wife."

"But maybe you think as I do," she continued, "and cannot stand our young sister's happiness. Did you notice how she treated us in a patronizing manner, casting gold into our laps and then having us taken away by the winds when she grew tired of our company? As I live and breathe, I will deprive her of all her happiness. And if you feel the way I do, let's figure out a way to bring her down. But we must do so in secret. In the meantime, we must tell no one, especially our parents, of her good fortune. In this way, we will find a way to show her that we are not her inferiors but worthier than she is. For the time being, let's go home to our contemptible husbands and our poor houses. There will be time enough to plan a way to humble her." Having conspired in this fashion, they hid the wealth that Psyche had given them and returned to their homes, plotting their own sister's destruction.

That night, Psyche's husband warned her again, "Don't you see the great danger you are in and why you must be careful? Your conniving sisters are laying a trap for you. They will try to persuade you to find a way to see my face; but if you do, as I have warned you, you will never see me again. If these wicked creatures come again, and I know they will, let them speak but say nothing yourself. Or if you cannot do that, then say nothing about your husband. If you can do that, then our child, who now grows in your belly, will become an immortal god. If you fail, the child will only be a mortal creature." In this way, Psyche discovered that she was to be a mother and that a child was on the way. Soon she marveled at how big her belly became.

In the days that followed, the wicked sisters made plans to return in order to carry out their evil plot. Once more, Psyche's husband warned her, "Our day of danger draws close. Your sisters will soon be here to bring you down. Please, Psyche—for my sake and yours and for the sake of our unborn child—do not listen to these accursed women. They will come to the mountain and weep and lament, hoping that out of pity you will give in to them."

When Psyche heard these words, she sighed, "For a long time now, you have had the proof of my love. Doubt me not. I will remain faithful. Nonetheless, grant me a boon: command the winds to transport my sisters here. You will not let me see your face. At the very least, let me be comforted by seeing my sisters' faces. I swear to you that I will do nothing to compromise you or to endanger our relationship or the child that now lives in my belly." Softened by her words, and overcome by her tears and embraces, her husband gave into her. And when morning came, he departed as usual.

When her sisters came back, they did not even stop first to visit with their parents but went directly to the mountain top. Once more the winds carried them to the valley. Then they entered the palace and embraced their victim. "Little Psyche," they said with amazement, "you are with child! What a joy that will be in a house already filled with so many treasures." In this way, little by little, they sought to win Psyche's confidence. They spent time with her, relaxing, dining, and listening to music together.

Eventually, they began to work their plot against Psyche, asking her about her husband and his history. But Psyche had forgotten the story she had invented on the previous occasion, and so this time she invented an entirely new story and described her husband as a merchant and middle-aged. Having already said too much, she filled her sisters' laps with gold and silver and had the winds take them away.

77

On their way back, the two sisters spoke with each other: "What do you think of Psyche's lie? First, her husband is a young hunter. Now, he is a middle-aged merchant. How could he grow old so quickly? I'll tell you what I think. I think she has never seen her husband's face, and he must be some god. That means the baby she will give birth to will also be a god, and our sister — how irritating this is! — will be known as 'the mother of a god.' Let's figure a way to put our upstart sister in her place."

Once more they returned to the mountain top. Once more the gentle winds carried them into the valley and to the palace door. Forcing tears from their eyes, they accosted their sister: "Psyche, you are so naive. You think yourself happy and safe. But we are your sisters and we worry about you. We have been told that the person you lie with every night is a great poisonous serpent with a huge gaping mouth. Remember what the oracle of Apollo said, that you would marry a deadly serpent? People in this area saw such a creature swimming in the river last night, and they say it will not be long before he shows his true nature and devours you and your child. Come away with us to safety, Psyche. Do not linger here where, in the end, you will be swallowed up. We did not want to spoil your happiness, but we had to tell you about this."

Then poor Psyche grew afraid and entirely forgot her husband's warnings. "My dear sisters," she said in a trembling voice, "I thank you for your concern, and I worry that what people have told you about my husband may be true. I have never seen his face and know nothing about his background. He comes to me at night, and I have never seen him in the daylight. For all I know, he may be a beast, as you suggest. If there was only some way I could sneak a look at him, but he has threatened me with all kinds of harm and pain if I do. What can I do?"

That was just the opening they were looking for, and the conniving sisters offered her a plan: "Here is the best thing. Put a razor under your pillow and hide an oil lamp in your bedroom. After he comes to you and has fallen asleep, take the lamp out and use the razor to cut off the serpent's head. In this way, you will be saved. We will find another, handsome man for you to marry." Then, having caused all the harm they could and worried about their own safety, the sisters traveled by the winds back to the mountain top and hastened away to their distant homes.

78

Now Psyche tossed this way and that. Sometimes she was resolved to follow her sisters' suggestions. Other times, she was uncertain. But when night came, she prepared for the awful event.

After her husband came to bed and made love with her, he fell asleep. Then Psyche brought out the lamp and took the razor in her hand. But when she came to the bedside, the lamp shone on the man she had been sleeping with — on the sweetest beast of all beasts, on the most beautiful of all the gods, on Cupid himself! Psyche was amazed when she beheld his divine beauty, his golden hair, his milk-white neck, his rosy cheeks, his shining wings with their trembling feathers. She counted herself lucky that this was the father of her child.

At the foot of the bed, lay his bow and arrows — those same arrows that Cupid shoots at others to make them fall in love. And curiously taking up one of those arrows, she accidentally pricked herself. Then love was added to the love she already felt, and she fell upon Cupid, kissing and kissing him. And so eager was she for the touch of his body that she tipped the lamp and a drop of burning oil fell on his right shoulder. Alas, that was the end of things. Being burned, Cupid awoke and perceived that his wife had broken her promise, and he departed.

But Psyche grabbed his leg as he flew up and held on, until her strength gave out and she fell down to the ground. Then he swept down and confronted her, "Oh, Psyche. Do you have any idea what I have done because of my love for you? My mother commanded me to do you harm and arrange your marriage to some horrible and ugly human. Instead, I disobeyed her, came down from heaven, fell in love, and took you as my wife. Did I seem such a beast to you that you would plan to cut my head off with a razor? Did I not warn you that your sisters would trick you in this way? I will punish them severely, but you I will punish only with my departure."

And with those words, he took flight into the air. With her eyes, Psyche followed her husband as long as she could. But when she could see him no longer, she threw herself on the ground in despair.

There was a shepherd nearby, a god in disguise, who saw her distress and approached her, saying, "Please excuse me for speaking. I am just a poor herdsman, but old age has made me wise. From your pale complexion, your sobs and tears, I'd say you are in love.

Let me give you some advice. Quit grieving. Cupid has a heart that can easily be won if you are devoted." When Psyche heard these words, she thanked the shepherd and went in search of her lost husband.

When she had traveled some ways, she chanced to come to the city where one of her sisters lived. So, they met, and her sister asked Psyche what brought her to these parts. Psyche replied, "Remember the advice you gave me that I should kill the beast I slept with every night? Well, when I brought forth the lamp, I discovered that it was the son of Venus, Cupid himself, who was sharing my bed. And I was so stricken with pleasure and the desire to embrace him, that I could not contain myself and accidentally spilled some oil from the lamp on him. He woke up and seeing me armed with a razor, knew I was up to no good. So, he told me to depart and to take my things with me. Then, sister, he said he would take you as a wife in my place. And he commanded the winds to take me away."

Psyche had scarcely finished her tale when her wicked sister ran home, made some excuse to her husband, and departed. When she arrived at the mountain top, she cried out, "Cupid, take me, your more worthy wife!" and jumped from the edge. But the winds did not come and bear her up. Instead, she fell from that great height and on to the rocks below where her body was broken into many parts on which birds of prey and wild beasts feasted.

And justice wasn't long delayed for the other sister. Psyche came to the city where she lived and told her the same story. This sister likewise hurried to the mountain top and suffered the same grisly end. Then Psyche traveled from one country to the next, looking for her husband. But he had retreated to the heavens where, in his mother's chambers, he nursed the horrible wound he had got from the oil of the burning lamp.

Then a seagull flew to Venus and told her that Cupid was burned and in danger of dying. Moreover, the bird added, there were rumors that her son had been spending his time with a harlot in the mountains. "So, my son has got a sweetheart," Venus replied. "Tell me, little bird, who she is and what kind of goddess or divinity she is."

"I know not what she is," the bird answered, "but her name is Psyche."

Venus was indignant: "I'll tell you what she is! She is that human impostor who claimed my name. And as for my son, what does he think I am—some kind of madam who procures companions for men, since he came to know her through me?"

Venus departed immediately for her chamber where she found her wounded son and chastised him, "Is this how you honor your mother? Instead of obeying my command and bringing trouble to my enemy, you embrace her and make her my daughter-in-law? Do you think that you alone can have children and that I am too old to have another son who would be even worthier than you? Think again! I will go even farther. I will adopt one of my slaves and give him the wings and bow and arrows that I gave to you. You were brought up badly and have often offended your elders, especially me, your mother. Moreover, you pass your time with wenches and harlots. Well, you shall soon repent and will pay dearly for this affair.

"Now, what should I do to tame my delinquent son? Should I call on the goddess Sobriety—even though she is my sworn enemy? Well, there is no other I can turn to. Sobriety will reform you, my son. She will correct and scold you. She will unbend your bow and take away your arrows. She will quench your fire and diminish your bodily urges. Because of all the trouble you have caused me, I won't feel content until you have been brought into line, until I have cut your golden locks and given you a decent haircut, until I've trimmed your wings and your wild ways." And with that, Venus departed from her chambers in a great rage.

In the meantime, Psyche traveled here and there, seeking her divine husband. She did not think he could be won over by sweet words, but she hoped that if she was religious and offered up constant prayers, he might eventually show mercy.

Meanwhile, Venus had grown tired of searching for Psyche on sea and land. In her great chariot, she flew to heaven and persuaded Jupiter to let her make use of his messenger Mercury. Then she gave this command to Mercury: "You know how long I have sought this girl and have not been able to find her. Now there is nothing to do but for you to make an announcement far and wide. Say that I will give a reward to whoever finds her, and that I will punish anyone who might hide her." That said, she departed to her chambers.

81

Mercury did not delay but proclaimed his announcement throughout the world. If anyone knew the whereabouts of Psyche, they were to tell Mercury and in reward they would receive seven sweet kisses from Venus. Hearing this, every man was inflamed with desire and went to search for Psyche.

This proclamation made clear to Psyche how hopeless her case was, so she approached the house of Venus. There one of the goddess's servants spied her and, seizing her by the hair, dragged Psyche into Venus's presence—all the while promising the girl that pain and punishment would teach her a lesson in humility and respect.

When Venus saw Psyche, she laughed in the way angry people sometimes do. "Oh goddess, sweet goddess," Venus said sarcastically, "have you come to visit your husband whom you have wounded so grievously? Let me welcome you like a daughter-in-law. Where are my handmaidens, Sorrow and Sadness? Ah, here they are." And Venus handed Psyche over to the two, who cruelly tormented her according to the instructions of their mistress.

And after they had scourged her with whips and rods, they brought her back to Venus who laughed again, saying, "Look how she thinks I will pity her because of her great belly, which she has got by playing the whore. Does she think I am happy, a woman as young as I am, to be called a grandmother? Oh, won't it be wonderful to have the son of a harlot known as my grandchild! Wait a minute! I am a fool to call her son my grandson. It was a marriage between unequals. There were no witnesses. Moreover, the parents did not give their consent. Therefore, this is not a legitimate marriage and the child will be born a bastard—if the mother lives long enough to deliver it." After she had spoken these words to Psyche, Venus seized the girl and pulled her hair and tore her clothes.

Then Venus took a great quantity of different grains (wheat, barley, poppy seeds, lentils, chick peas, and beans) and mixed them together in a great heap on the ground. Then turning to Psyche, she said, "I don't see how you can ever expect to get a husband if you can't act like a servant. Let's see what kind of servant you are. Separate these various grains according to their kind, and do so by nightfall." Having given Psyche her task, Venus departed to a banquet.

Psyche collapsed, stunned by the task Venus had given her. But an ant came by and, cursing the cruelty of Venus, took pity on the girl and called to all the other ants, "Come quickly and help this girl, the wife of Cupid, or she will be in great danger." So they came, one after another, and separated the various grains into different piles. Then they ran away.

When night came, Venus returned home, drunk and crowned with garlands of flowers. When she saw how the grains had been sorted, she said to Psyche, "This is not the work of your hands but of the god that loves you." And she gave Psyche only a morsel of bread and then went to bed. In the meantime, Cupid had been locked in his chambers to prevent his misbehavior and to keep him from talking to his love. In this way, the two lovers were separated.

When morning came, Venus called Psyche to her, "See that far-off forest with a river running through it? Massive wild sheep live there, and their fleece is golden. Go and bring me some of their wool."

Faced with such a hopeless task, Psyche was resolved to end her sorrows by drowning herself in the river. But when she went down by the riverbank, growing there was an enchanted reed that spoke to her: "Psyche, do not pollute my waters with your death. Listen. Be careful of the great sheep who live here. As long as the sun is up, they are dreadful and furious with sharp horns that can kill you. But as soon as the sun goes down, they are no longer violent. Then you can go among the bushes and you will find little snatches of their golden wool caught on the briars."

Psyche took the reed's advice, gathered up bits of wool in her apron, and took them to Venus. The goddess was no more happy with Psyche's having completed this task than she was with her having completed the first one. "I know who is responsible for this work and it is not you," she said. "But let me test you further. See the top of that distant hill, the one with a stream running down it, with water all black and deadly that feeds the rivers of Hell? Go and draw me a jar of that water." And she gave Psyche a crystal vessel and threatened her if she should fail.

Psyche hurried away to the mountain top but soon perceived the task was impossible. The water came bursting out of an unreachable crag, and where it fell to the ground there were dragons who never slept keeping watch. Even the water seemed to be saying, "Run away. Run away. Or you will be slain." The situation was so impossible that Psyche stood stock still, staring into space. Things were so bad, she could not even weep.

But an eagle, remembering a favor done him by Cupid, came from the skies to help the wife of Cupid. "Poor woman," he said, "do not think you can take even a drop of this water. The gods themselves are afraid of it. Let me return the favor I owe your husband." With that, the eagle took the flask, flew past the dragons and into the chasm, filled the jar, and returned it to her.

Psyche was happy to be able to bring the water to Venus, but Venus was not happy or appeased to receive it. "You must be a witch to pull these things off," Venus insisted. "But enough of that. Take this box to Hell and meet with the goddess Proserpina. Tell her to send me a little of her beauty, as much as I need for a day, because I have used up what I had while caring for my injured son. But return quickly because I must prepare myself for a banquet tonight with the gods."

Then Psyche knew her luck had come to an end because no mortal had ever gone to Hell and returned. Thinking to end her misery, she went to a tall tower to throw herself off and commit suicide. But the tower, magically, spoke to her: "Don't give up so easily. This is the last test. If you commit suicide, you will go to Hell but you will never return. Listen to me. There is another way. Go to the tall hill in Sparta. There you will find a passageway that leads to Hell, to the underworld and palace of Pluto. But do not go there empty-handed. In each hand carry a barley cake soaked in honey and in your mouth carry two coins.

"Remember, too, that in the land of the dead there is no pity. When you have gone a fair ways, you will meet a lame donkey carrying wood and a lame man who will ask you to pick up the sticks that have fallen; pass them by without a word. Then you will come to Charon who ferries the dead across the water and who requires everyone to pay a fare; have him take one of the coins out of your mouth. As you are traveling, an old man will swim by and ask in a pitiful way to be taken into the boat; do not listen to him. On the shore you will also see old women sitting by their spinning wheels and they will ask you for help, but do not help them because they are only temptations created by Venus so that you will put down your barley cakes—and if you do that, you will never return to this world.

84

"Finally, you will see a ferocious three-headed dog who guards the entrance to Proserpina's palace. To preserve yourself from harm, you must give him one of the cakes and he will allow you to enter. Proserpina will then invite you to a fine dinner, but you must decline and sit on the ground and say you wish only for brown bread. When you have eaten, tell her what you seek, then take the box and return. To the three-headed dog, give the other cake. To Charon, the ferryman, give your last coin. In this way, you will find your way back to the world. But be careful: do not look into the box or be curious about divine beauty."

Then it all happened as predicted. But once Psyche had returned to the world, she could not help but be curious about the little box of divine beauty she carried. "Surely, there will be no harm if I just use a little of it on my face and make myself more beautiful for my husband." But when she opened the box, she could find nothing inside; instead, something seemed to come out of the box that made her feel sleepy, and soon she fell into a deep slumber.

By now, Cupid had recovered from his injury and was missing Psyche terribly; so he found a way to get out the window of the locked room where he was being held, and he flew to his wife. Finding her in a deep slumber, he wiped the sleep from her eyes and put it back in the box. Then he poked her with one of his arrows and scolded her, "Curiosity has got you into trouble again. Well, go now to my mother with your gift. In the meantime, I will go to the other gods and see if there is a way to resolve this dispute."

Cupid flew directly to Jupiter, told him of his problems and asked for the great god's help. Jupiter laughed, "You rascal! You've never shown me the least bit of respect, and you've plagued me with problems all your life. You've filled me with lust and led me into all kinds of affairs. You've tempted me into various adulteries. Because of your doings, I've had to transform myself into all kinds of foul beasts in order to carry on my liaisons in secret. But because I remember bouncing you on my knee when you were a child, I'll see that this all turns out as you want it. I will help you on one condition: if you encounter another earthly girl of uncommon beauty, you must return the favor by introducing her to me."

That said, Jupiter summoned all the gods and goddesses to a great council. There he said, "You all know Cupid, this wild and irresponsible young man. He has found a maiden and made her pregnant. Let him settle down now and get married." Then Jupiter turned to Venus: "Don't look so forlorn, my dear. You will not be dishonored by having a mortal in your family. I will make Psyche into an immortal like us and arrange for the couple to have a legitimate wedding."

So, Jupiter had his servant bring Psyche to his palace and he gave her a cup of ambrosia, the drink of the gods, saying, "Swallow this, my dear, and it will make you immortal." Then a great wedding feast was prepared, and Cupid and Psyche were officially married. Not long after, a daughter was born to them and they named her Pleasure.

Exogamy

Like two different individuals, Apuleius's "Cupid and Psyche" and Beaumont's "Beauty and the Beast" have different looks but if we were to x-ray both stories, we would notice that they share similar skeletal structures. Three sisters are featured in both, and the youngest is the most beautiful but does not marry. This heroine is led to expect death from a beast but is instead pampered at a magical and luxurious castle. Into her life, on a nightly basis, comes a mysterious male whose identity is concealed from her but who is kind and generous. In time, her two unhappily married sisters grow jealous and plot against their youngest sister. As a result of that plot and against her better judgment, the heroine breaks a promise and hurts the hero. After a long separation, the heroine seeks the hero, is reunited with him, and marries.

There are also differences, of course. Beaumont's Beast, for example, is not a god. Still, both tales tell of an inequality between marriage partners: in "Cupid and Psyche" between gods and mortals, in Beaumont's tale between a merchant family and an aristocrat. On the other hand, Cupid is not really a beast but only rumored to be one by the oracle and by Psyche's sisters. Here, scholars suggest, Apuleius deviated from tradition; in most versions of the story he would have drawn on, the mysterious male is, in fact, a snake.[1] Moreover, as other Greek myths indicate, gods often

1 *Visions and Revisions* 15; Gwyneth Hood, "Husbands and Gods as Shadowbrutes: 'Beauty and the Beast' from Apuleius to C.S. Lewis," *Mythlore* 15 (Winter 1988): 35.

took on animal shapes to carry on their love affairs with mortals and sometimes became trapped, for a time, in their bestial metamorphoses.

But perhaps the greatest difference between Cupid and the Beast is the amount of time they are on stage. While Beaumont's Beast waits in the wings for Beauty's decision, Cupid has a larger and more active role in his own story. Indeed, if Beaumont's "Beauty and the Beast" tells a story of feminine maturation, Apuleius's "Cupid and Psyche" adds a parallel story of masculine maturation as we watch how the rascally and irresponsible God of Love becomes a sober and settled husband and father.

Psyche also differs from Beauty. Apuleius's myth is frankly about sex, and Psyche enjoys the nightly visits of her paramour and (subsequently) falls in love with him. Beaumont's story, on the other hand, is about courtship; Beauty's relationship with the Beast is essentially platonic. In one, sexual union precedes familiarity. In the other, the sequence is reversed, and familiarity precedes any eventual union.

Psyche also has heroic tasks to perform. While in Beaumont's tale the hero is trying to win a bride, in Apuleius's myth the heroine goes searching for her missing husband. Psyche is flawed and makes mistakes, so in the second half of the myth she undergoes a series of trials that test her. Beauty, however, from the beginning of her story, seems without fault and virtuous; if she is tested at all, it is her perception that is tested and her ability to find values behind appearances.

In that regard, Beaumont's "Beauty and the Beast" seems more "psychological" and Apuleius's myth more "external." As E.R. Dodds has shown, the Greeks had difficulty reckoning with invisible and inner issues like desires and feelings, and so they converted them into externalized forms or personages; thus, love becomes the freestanding and separately existing God of Love, chastity the goddess Diana, and so forth.[1] In the same way, Apuleius's myth is more "externalized" than Beaumont's fairy tale: while the Beast suffers hurt feelings, Cupid suffers from an actual wound; while Beauty has all kinds of emotional difficulties, Psyche has concrete problems to face in the world at large.

1   E.R. Dodds, *The Greeks and the Irrational* (Berkeley, CA: University of California Press, 1951).

Psyche also differs from Beaumont's Beauty in the way she must change. In the beginning of her story, Beauty is humble, self-sacrificial, and compliant — a kind of Cinderella who goes about her domestic chores. In the second phase of her life at the Beast's castle, what is constantly emphasized is her power of choice: if she is to come to the Beast's demesne, it must be voluntarily; everything in the castle awaits her commands since she is the Mistress there; and her decision to marry the Beast is entirely a matter of free will. In a fashion, Beaumont's "Beauty and the Beast" can be seen as a story of a deferential heroine who must finally learn to be self-assertive.

Psyche's problems, on the other hand, are the tragic results of her self-assertion: her giving in to her curiosity and disobeying her husband despite his warnings. In the latter half of her tale, she has to demonstrate the humbleness and compliance that Beauty already possesses; in this phase of the story, in her domestic chores, Psyche has to become the kind of Cinderella that Beauty is from the start. In other words, Psyche learns to surrender her free will and submit to Fate: Cupid knows full well what will happen when Psyche's sisters visit, but he permits her to make her mistake and learn from the tragedies that follow. As events proceed and Venus casts her net around her, Psyche realizes the hopelessness of her situation; in surrendering to Venus, she surrenders to forces larger than herself. If Beaumont's "Beauty and the Beast," then, speaks of the need for self-assertion, Apuleius's "Cupid and Psyche" heads in the opposite direction and speaks of the need for submissiveness.

Even so, Psyche's self-assertiveness is treated in the myth not as a form of arrogance but as a "tragic flaw." Moreover, in the manner of a "fortunate fall," her mistakes do, ultimately, produce good results; while she should be more compliant, her disobedience does eventually effect a more satisfactory transformation of her relationship with Cupid. In fact, when she makes a mistake a second time — giving into curiosity again and opening Prosperpina's box of beauty when she has been warned not to do so — Psyche's husband views this as the result of an endearing and understandable fault of women (i.e., vanity), forgives her, and wipes sleep from her eyes.

But we should understand Cupid's indulgent attitude toward his wife's mistakes as something more than patronizing. Giving into her curiosity and disobeying her husband may reveal Psyche's "tragic flaw," but her actions are also motivated by a deserving reason: a wish to know more about her mysterious husband, her nightly visitor. At the beginning of her relationship, Psyche's life is strictly divided between night and day, between her nocturnal and amorous escapades and her lonely, everyday existence. She wants something more. Not content with being a sex object, she seems to say, "Sure, the sex is good, but who are you?" Not content with her honeymoon existence in the luxurious palace, with the life of a kept woman, she seeks a deeper familiarity with her husband and a more complete marriage. Seen in that way, the indulgent attitude towards her mistakes seems more understandable; and given the beneficent results, her "tragic flaw" hardly seems a flaw at all.

But Psyche is not the only one with a problem in the myth. In Beaumont's story, Beauty suffers oedipal problems in the difficulty she has in separating from her father; indeed, during her tenure with the Beast, she is constantly thinking of him and she retreats to her father when given the chance, before she sorts things out. Psyche's parents, on the other hand, play only a small role in the myth, but Venus looms large. It is Cupid who seems to suffer oedipal problems in Apuleius's myth. In making his alliance with Psyche, Cupid is at odds with his mother; he disobeys her and keeps his romance secret from her. And when he is disappointed by Psyche, Cupid (in a manner similar to Beauty) retreats to his mother's house until things are sorted out.

Both the fairy tale and the myth also suggest that oedipal difficulties are not confined to the child alone. Beauty's father has a special bond of affection with her and shares secrets with her that he does not share with his other daughters. As a result of this special relationship, his own oedipal tie, this father grows ill when separated from his daughter and revives when Beauty returns. In fact, the Beast can be seen as his rival; and Beauty's father is not only reluctant to let go of her, but also seems unwilling to let Beauty grow up and out of their father-daughter bond.

Change genders and we see the very same situation in the myth. Cupid's mother also has a rivalrous connection with Psyche and is unwilling to let go of her son and let Cupid grow up. Among other reasons, Venus wishes to freeze her son in adolescence because admitting he is mature enough to be a husband and father would mean admitting that she has grown older, old enough to be a grandmother.

In a rivalrous oedipal situation, we would expect a character to have problems in bonding with a partner because of a problematic relationship with their opposite-sex parent. Such is the case with Beauty (and her father) and with Cupid (and his mother). But we also note in Beaumont and in Apuleius that the motherless Beauty and fatherless Cupid have a more favorable relationship with a same-sex parent figure. In "Beauty and the Beast," the maternal fairy appears in Beauty's dream to encourage her; and in "Cupid and Psyche," Jupiter, the Olympian *paterfamilias*, takes Cupid's side.

But as much as this psychological understanding may explain these tales, such an understanding does not quite offer a complete view of these stories. Cupid's problems with his mother may be present in the background, but the myth seems to foreground Psyche's mother-in-law problems; by implication, of course, Beaumont's story might also be read as an account of the Beast's father-in-law problems. When we focus, then, on Psyche's mother-in-law problems, we can see a new way of reading "Cupid and Psyche" as a tale about exogamy and this reading yields new ways of looking at "Beauty and the Beast."

Exogamy (or "marrying out") describes the difficulties an individual faces when leaving family and clan behind and entering into the spouse's family or clan as an outsider. As Erich Neumann suggests, the early parts of "Cupid and Psyche" present a vision of marriage as a threat to the family.[1] The oracle's foretelling of a monstrous wedding, the ghastly procession of Psyche in her bridal gown while women are lamenting and beating their breasts, the funereal atmosphere as if a virgin were to be thrown into a volcano or as if she were about to be sacrificed to King Kong—all this suggests the deep pain of separation from the family which is a part of exogamy.

Even though Psyche separates from her family and clan, when she is transported to Cupid's luxurious palace, she does not gain entrance into new forms of affiliation. Her husband only visits her at night, not quite accepting her or granting her full admission into

---

1 Erich Neumann, *Amor and Psyche: The Psychic Development of the Feminine*, trans. Ralph Manheim (Princeton, NJ: Princeton University Press, 1956) 62.

his life. Moreover, she does not gain entrance into her spouse's family and clan: no other living person inhabits the palace. Even as she falls in love with Cupid, the cost of amour is loneliness and isolation. As Gwyneth Hood observes about Psyche, "She has lost her virginity without gaining real intimacy with her husband, and given up a family without gaining entrance into a new one."[1]

The sisters' visits amount to a test of her allegiance in this exogamous situation, and Psyche is ambivalent. On the one hand, her growing love for her husband, as well as the pleasure of their erotic union, puts her at odds with her siblings and challenges her loyalty to her family; so, for example, she lies to her sisters about her husband's identity and takes his side. Her sisters, on the other hand, after their own unhappy marriages, have reverted to family loyalty and depend upon this in arguing that Psyche should go behind her husband's back and against his wishes. Psyche is torn between her husband and her sisters, but decides against her husband and loses.

In this exogamous competition between loyalties, events could have turned out differently. In the fairy tale "Bluebeard," for example, the husband is a murderous monster and the heroine is saved by her sisters and brothers, by a reversion to family loyalty. But in the myth, after Psyche has made her tragic choice and injured her husband, Cupid accuses her by saying that *he* broke with his mother in entering into this union and implies that *she* has failed to transfer her allegiance from her family when they became a couple. Later, when Psyche goes in pursuit of Cupid and arranges the deaths of her sisters, we understand symbolically that she has finally transferred her allegiance to him, just as we see, in terms of exogamy, how old ties can be poisonous (once a new relationship is entered into) when Psyche's sisters plot against her.

To win her husband, Psyche has to win the acceptance of her mother-in-law. Venus will not admit this outsider, her son's wife, this mortal. But Psyche throws herself at her mother-in-law's feet and begs for admission to Venus's household.

The tests that Venus then devises for Psyche address issues that might face any new bride when seeking admission to her spouse's family and clan. An anthropologist might say that her mother-in-law wants to know whether Psyche—after she has led a petted

1 Hood 38.

existence as the most beautiful woman in the world, after she has enjoyed a pampered life during her honeymoon at Cupid's palace — can do the washing and help with the chores. The trials that Venus devises for Psyche are meant to test her willingness to be humble and subservient in a new household. They are also meant to test her feminine skills.

Psyche is asked to complete four tasks, and the first three are clearly tests of feminine competence: she is to sort grains, gather wool, and fetch water. The fourth task (to gather the box of beauty in a trip to Hell) is more complex but essentially tests her ability to remain "on task," not to become distracted, and to follow advice. Except for a last-minute lapse, Psyche succeeds.

In comparison, we should note that while Psyche needs to demonstrate to her mother-in-law her willingness to be subservient and her feminine competencies, Beaumont's Beauty already possesses that nature and those skills. From the start of her story, Beaumont's character is already humble and playing the servant. Moreover, besides doing the housework, Beauty, we are told, is accomplished in other "feminine" ways: she spins, reads, and plays the harpsichord.

It is Jupiter who finally arranges for the outsider's full admission into her new circle. Jupiter restores Psyche's husband to her and makes peace between her and her mother-in-law. But besides admission to her husband's family, Psyche also wins admission to the clan when Jupiter sanctions their marriage and offers her the cup of ambrosia which will change her from a mortal into an immortal, so that she may join with the other Olympian gods.

Issues of exogamy are thus resolved, but in different ways in Apuleius's myth and Beaumont's fairy tale. In the myth, Psyche painfully leaves her family behind and painfully wins admission to her mother-in-law's household and her new clan, at the expense of her relationship with her own family. Beauty also undergoes a painful separation from her family, also faces a painful choice between her family and her partner, and also chooses her beloved over her family. But in the end, at her wedding to the Beast, Beauty not only gains a princely husband and admission to his kingdom as his wife, but her family is restored to her (albeit, with her sisters as statues). In Beaumont, what had seemed a choice "between" suddenly dissolves as Beauty gets her cake and eats it too.

Madame de Villeneuve's "Beauty and the Beast"

Though inspired by similar tales, Madame Gabrielle de Villeneuve's "Beauty and the Beast" marks the first appearance in print of a story by this name. Published in 1740 in her La jeune amériquaine, et les contes marins, *this work provided a basis for Beaumont's later version in 1756. Instead of a short story, however, Villeneuve's work more closely resembles a romantic novel; it is some two hundred pages in length and full of miscellaneous characters and complications.*

If we now know Villeneuve's version of the story at all these days, it is because of a redaction of the tale in Andrew Lang's The Blue Fairy Book *(1889) in which Villeneuve's lengthy novel was reduced to twenty pages. This version, which appears below, was the most well-known version of "Beauty and the Beast" at the turn of the nineteenth century.*

Once upon a time, in a very far-off country, there lived a merchant who had been so fortunate in all his undertakings that he was enormously rich. As he had, however, six sons and six daughters, he found that his money was not too much to let them all have everything they fancied, as they were accustomed to do.

But one day a most unexpected misfortune befell them. Their house caught fire and was speedily burnt to the ground, with all the splendid furniture, the books, pictures, gold, silver, and precious goods it contained; and this was only the beginning of their troubles. Their father, who had until this moment prospered in all ways, suddenly lost every ship he had upon the sea, either by dint of pirates, shipwreck, or fire. Then he heard that his clerks in distant countries, whom he trusted entirely, had proved unfaithful; and at last from great wealth he fell into the direst poverty.

All that he had left was a little house in a desolate place at least a hundred leagues from the town in which he had lived, and to this he was forced to retreat with his children, who were in despair at the idea of leading such a different life. Indeed, the daughters at first hoped that their friends, who had been so numerous while they were rich, would insist on their staying in their houses now they no longer possessed one. But they soon found that they were left alone, and that their former friends even attributed their misfortunes to their own extravagance and showed no intention of offering them any help. So nothing was left for them but to take their departure to the cottage, which stood in the midst of a dark forest and seemed to be the most dismal place upon the face of the earth. As they were too poor to have any servants, the girls had to work hard, like peasants, and the sons, for their part, cultivated the fields to earn their living. Roughly clothed, and living in the simplest way, the girls regretted unceasingly the luxuries and amusements of their former life; only the youngest tried to be brave and cheerful. She had been as sad as anyone when misfortune overtook her father, but, soon recovering her natural gaiety, she set to work to make the best of things, to amuse her father and brothers as well as she could, and to try to persuade her sisters to join her in dancing and singing. But they would do nothing of the sort, and, because she was not as doleful as themselves, they declared that this miserable life was all she was fit for. But she was really far prettier and cleverer than they were; indeed, she was so lovely that she was always called Beauty. After two years, when they were all beginning to get used to their new life, something happened to disturb their tranquillity. Their father received the news that one of his ships, which he had believed to be lost, had come safely into port with a rich cargo. All the sons and daughters at once thought that their poverty was at an end, and wanted to set out directly for the town, but their father, who was more prudent, begged them to wait a little, and, though it was harvest time, and he could ill be spared, determined to go himself first, to make inquiries. Only the youngest daughter had any doubt but that they would soon again be as rich as they were before, or at least rich enough to live comfortably in some town where they would find amusement and gay companions once more. So they all loaded their father with commissions for jewels and dresses which it would have taken a fortune to buy; only Beauty, feeling sure that it was of no use, did not ask for anything. Her father, noticing her silence, said, "And what shall I bring for you, Beauty?"

"The only thing I wish for is to see you come home safely," she answered.

But this only vexed her sisters, who fancied she was blaming them for having asked for such costly things. Her father, however, was pleased, but as he thought that at her age she certainly ought to like pretty presents, he told her to choose something.

"Well, dear father," she said, "as you insist upon it, I beg that you will bring me a rose. I have not seen one since we came here, and I love them so much."

So the merchant set out and reached the town as quickly as possible, only to find that his former companions, believing him to be dead, had divided between them the goods which the ship had brought; and after six months of trouble and expense he found himself as poor as when he started, having been able to recover only just enough to pay the cost of his journey. To make matters worse, he was obliged to leave the town in the most terrible weather, so that by the time he was within a few leagues of his home he was almost exhausted with cold and fatigue. Though he knew it would take some hours to get through the forest, he was so anxious to be at his journey's end that he resolved to go on; but night overtook him, and the deep snow and bitter frost made it impossible for his horse to carry him any further. Not a house was to be seen; the only shelter he could get was the hollow trunk of a great tree, and there he crouched all the night which seemed to him the longest he had ever known. In spite of his weariness the howling of the wolves kept him awake, and even when at last the day broke he was not much better off, for the falling snow had covered up every path, and he did not know which way to turn.

At length he made out some sort of track, and though at the beginning it was so rough and slippery that he fell down more than once, it presently became easier and led him into an avenue of trees which ended in a splendid castle. It seemed to the merchant very strange that no snow had fallen in the avenue, which was entirely composed of orange trees, covered with flowers and fruit. When he reached the first court of the castle he saw before him a flight of agate steps, and went up them, and passed through several splendidly furnished rooms. The pleasant warmth of the air revived him, and he felt very hungry, but there seemed to be nobody in all this vast and splendid palace whom he could ask to give him something to eat. Deep silence reigned everywhere, and at last, tired of roaming through empty rooms and galleries, he stopped in a room smaller than the rest, where a clear fire was burning and a couch was drawn up closely to it. Thinking that this must be prepared for someone who was expected, he sat down to wait till he should come and very soon fell into a sweet sleep.

When his extreme hunger wakened him after several hours, he

was still alone; but a little table, upon which was a good dinner, had been drawn up close to him, and, as he had eaten nothing for twenty-four hours, he lost no time in beginning his meal, hoping that he might soon have an opportunity of thanking his considerate entertainer, whoever it might be. But no one appeared, and even after another long sleep, from which he awoke completely refreshed, there was no sign of anybody, though a fresh meal of dainty cakes and fruit was prepared upon the little table at his elbow. Being naturally timid, the silence began to terrify him, and he resolved to search once more through all the rooms, but it was of no use. Not even a servant was to be seen; there was no sign of life in the palace! He began to wonder what he should do, and to amuse himself by pretending that all the treasures he saw were his own, and considering how he would divide them among his children. Then he went down into the garden, and though it was winter everywhere else, here the sun shone, and the birds sang, and the flowers bloomed, and the air was soft and sweet. The merchant, in ecstasies with all he saw and heard, said to himself, "All this must be meant for me. I will go this minute and bring my children to share all these delights."

In spite of being so cold and weary when he reached the castle, he had taken his horse to the stable and fed it. Now he thought he would saddle it for his homeward journey, and he turned down the path which led to the stable. This path had a hedge of roses on each side of it, and the merchant thought he had never seen or smelt such exquisite flowers. They reminded him of his promise to Beauty, and he stopped and had just gathered one to take to her when he was startled by a strange noise behind him. Turning round, he saw a frightful Beast, which seemed to be very angry and who said, in a terrible voice, "Who told you that you might gather my roses? Was it not enough that I allowed you to be in my palace and was kind to you? This is the way you show your gratitude, by stealing my flowers! But your insolence shall not go unpunished." The merchant, terrified by these furious words, dropped the fatal rose, and, throwing himself on his knees, cried, "Pardon me, noble sir. I am truly grateful to you for your hospitality, which was so magnificent that I could not imagine that you would be offended by my taking such a little thing as a rose." But the Beast's anger was not lessened by this speech.

"You are very ready with excuses and flattery," he cried, "but that will not save you from the death you deserve."

"Alas!" thought the merchant, "if my daughter could only know what danger her rose has brought me into!"

And in despair he began to tell the Beast all his misfortunes, and the reason of his journey, not forgetting to mention Beauty's request.

"A king's ransom would hardly have procured all that my other daughters asked," he said, "but I thought that I might at least take Beauty her rose. I beg you to forgive me, for you see I meant no harm."

The Beast considered for a moment, and then he said, in a less furious tone, "I will forgive you on one condition—that is, that you will give me one of your daughters."

"Ah!" cried the merchant, "if I were cruel enough to buy my own life at the expense of one of my children's, what excuse could I invent to bring her here?"

"No excuse would be necessary," answered the Beast. "If she comes at all she must come willingly. On no other condition will I have her. See if any one of them is courageous enough, and loves you well enough to come and save your life. You seem to be an honest man, so I will trust you to go home. I give you a month to see if any of your daughters will come back with you and stay here, to let you go free. If none of them is willing, you must come alone, after bidding them good-bye for ever, for then you will belong to me. And do not imagine that you can hide from me, for if you fail to keep your word, I will come and fetch you!"

The merchant accepted this proposal, though he did not really think any of his daughters could be persuaded to come. He promised to return at the time appointed, and then, anxious to escape from the presence of the Beast, he asked permission to set off at once. But the Beast answered that he could not go until next day.

"Then you will find a horse ready for you," he said. "Now go and eat your supper, and await my orders."

The poor merchant, more dead than alive, went back to his room, where the most delicious supper was already served on the little table which was drawn up before a blazing fire. But he was too terrified to eat, and only tasted a few of the dishes, for fear the

Beast should be angry if he did not obey his orders. When he had finished he heard a great noise in the next room, which he knew meant that the Beast was coming. As he could do nothing to escape his visit, the only thing that remained was to seem as little afraid as possible; so when the Beast appeared and asked roughly if he had supped well, the merchant answered humbly that he had, thanks to his host's kindness. Then the Beast warned him to remember their agreement, and to prepare his daughter exactly for what she had to expect.

"Do not get up to-morrow," he added, "until you see the sun and hear a golden bell ring. Then you will find your breakfast waiting for you here, and the horse you are to ride will be ready in the courtyard. He will also bring you back again when you come with your daughter a month hence. Farewell. Take a rose to Beauty, and remember your promise!"

The merchant was only too glad when the Beast went away, and though he could not sleep for sadness, he lay down until the sun rose. Then, after a hasty breakfast, he went to gather Beauty's rose, and mounted his horse, which carried him off so swiftly that in an instant he had lost sight of the palace, and he was still wrapped in gloomy thoughts when it stopped before the door of the cottage.

His sons and daughters, who had been very uneasy at his long absence, rushed to meet him, eager to know the result of his journey, which, seeing him mounted upon a splendid horse and wrapped in a rich mantle, they supposed to be favorable. He hid the truth from them at first, only saying sadly to Beauty as he gave her the rose:

"Here is what you asked me to bring you; you little know what it has cost."

But this excited their curiosity so greatly that presently he told them his adventures from beginning to end, and then they were all very unhappy. The girls lamented loudly over their lost hopes, and the sons declared that their father should not return to this terrible castle and began to make plans for killing the Beast if it should come to fetch him. But he reminded them that he had promised to go back. Then the girls were very angry with Beauty and said it was all her fault because if she had asked for something sensible this would never have happened; they complained bitterly that they should have to suffer for her folly.

Poor Beauty, much distressed, said to them, "I have, indeed, caused this misfortune, but I assure you I did it innocently. Who could have guessed that to ask for a rose in the middle of summer would cause so much misery? But as I did the mischief it is only just that I should suffer for it. I will therefore go back with my father to keep his promise."

At first nobody would hear of this arrangement, and her father and brothers, who loved her dearly, declared that nothing should make them let her go; but Beauty was firm. As the time drew near she divided all her little possessions between her sisters, and said good-bye to everything she loved, and when the fatal day came she encouraged and cheered her father as they mounted together the horse which had brought him back. It seemed to fly rather than gallop, but so smoothly that Beauty was not frightened; indeed, she would have enjoyed the journey if she had not feared what might happen to her at the end of it. Her father still tried to persuade her to go back, but in vain. While they were talking the night fell, and then, to their great surprise, wonderful colored lights began to shine in all directions, and splendid fireworks blazed out before them. All the forest was illuminated by them, and even felt pleas-antly warm, though it had been bitterly cold before. This lasted until they reached the avenue of orange trees, where [there] were statues holding flaming torches, and when they got nearer to the palace they saw that it was illuminated from the roof to the ground, and music sounded softly from the courtyard. "The Beast must be very hungry," said Beauty, trying to laugh, "if he makes all this rejoicing over the arrival of his prey."

But, in spite of her anxiety, she could not help admiring all the wonderful things she saw.

The horse stopped at the foot of the flight of steps leading to the terrace, and when they had dismounted, her father led her to the little room he had been in before, where they found a splendid fire burning, and the table daintily spread with a delicious supper.

The merchant knew that this was meant for them, and Beauty, who was rather less frightened now that she had passed through so many rooms and seen nothing of the Beast, was quite willing to begin, for her long ride had made her very hungry. But they had hardly finished their meal when the noise of the Beast's footsteps was heard approaching, and Beauty clung to her father in terror, which became all the greater when she saw how frightened he was. But when the Beast really appeared, though she trembled at the sight of him, she made a great effort to hide her terror and saluted him respectfully.

This evidently pleased the Beast. After looking at her he said, in a tone that might have struck terror into the boldest heart, though he did not seem to be angry, "Good-evening, old man. Good-evening, Beauty."

The merchant was too terrified to reply, but Beauty answered sweetly, "Good-evening, Beast."

"Have you come willingly?" asked the Beast. "Will you be content to stay here when your father goes away?"

Beauty answered bravely that she was quite prepared to stay.

"I am pleased with you," said the Beast. "As you have come of your own accord, you may stay. As for you, old man," he added, turning to the merchant, "at sunrise tomorrow you will take your departure. When the bell rings get up quickly and eat your breakfast, and you will find the same horse waiting to take you home; but remember that you must never expect to see my palace again."

Then turning to Beauty, he said, "Take your father into the next room, and help him to choose everything you think your brothers and sisters would like to have. You will find two traveling-trunks there; fill them as full as you can. It is only just that you should send them something very precious as a remembrance of yourself."

Then he went away, after saying, "Good-bye, Beauty; good-bye, old man"; and though Beauty was beginning to think with great dismay of her father's departure, she was afraid to disobey the Beast's orders. The two of them went into the next room, which had shelves and cupboards all round it. They were greatly surprised at the riches it contained. There were splendid dresses fit for a queen, with all the ornaments that were to be worn with them; and when Beauty opened the cupboards she was quite dazzled by the gorgeous jewels that lay in heaps upon every shelf. After choosing a vast quantity, which she divided between her sisters—for she had made a heap of the wonderful dresses for each of them—she opened the last chest, which was full of gold.

"I think, father," she said, "that, as the gold will be more useful to you, we had better take out the other things again, and fill the trunks with it." So they did this; but the more they put in the more room there seemed to be, and at last they put back all the jewels and dresses they had taken out, and Beauty even added as many more of the jewels as she could carry at once; and then the trunks were not too full, but they were so heavy that an elephant could not have carried them!

"The Beast was mocking us," cried the merchant; "he must have pretended to give us all these things, knowing that I could not carry them away."

"Let us wait and see," answered Beauty. "I cannot believe that he meant to deceive us. All we can do is to fasten them up and leave them ready."

So they did this and returned to the little room, where, to their astonishment, they found breakfast ready. The merchant ate his with a good appetite, as the Beast's generosity made him believe that he might perhaps venture to come back soon and see Beauty. But she felt sure that her father was leaving her for ever, so she was very sad when the bell rang sharply for the second time and warned them that the time had come for them to part. They went down into the courtyard, where two horses were waiting, one loaded with the two trunks, the other for him to ride. They were pawing the ground in their impatience to start, and the merchant was forced to bid Beauty a hasty farewell; and as soon as he was mounted he went off at such a pace that she lost sight of him in an instant. Then Beauty began to cry and wandered sadly back to her own room. But she soon found that she was very sleepy and, as she had nothing better to do, she lay down and instantly fell asleep. And then she dreamed that she was walking by a brook bordered with trees and lamenting her sad fate, when a young prince, handsomer than anyone she had ever seen, and with a voice that went straight to her heart, came and said to her, "Ah, Beauty! you are not so unfortunate as you suppose. Here you will be rewarded for all you have suffered elsewhere. Your every wish shall be gratified. Only try to find me out, no matter how I may be disguised, as I love you dearly, and in making me happy you will find your own happiness. Be as true-hearted as you are beautiful, and we shall have nothing left to wish for."

"What can I do, Prince, to make you happy?" said Beauty.

"Only be grateful," he answered, "and do not trust too much to your eyes. And, above all, do not desert me until you have saved me from my cruel misery."

After this she thought she found herself in a room with a stately and beautiful lady, who said to her, "Dear Beauty, try not to regret all you have left behind you, for you are destined to a better fate. Only do not let yourself be deceived by appearances."

Beauty found her dreams so interesting that she was in no hurry to awake, but presently the clock roused her by calling her name softly twelve times, and then she got up and found her dressing-table set out with everything she could possibly want; and when her toilet was finished she found dinner was waiting in the room next to hers. But dinner does not take very long when you are all by yourself, and very soon she sat down cosily in the corner of a sofa, and began to think about the charming Prince she had seen in her dream.

"He said I could make him happy," said Beauty to herself. "It seems, then, that this horrible Beast keeps him a prisoner. How can I set him free? I wonder why they both told me not to trust to appearances? I don't understand it. But, after all, it was only a dream, so why should I trouble myself about it? I had better go and find something to do to amuse myself."

So she got up and began to explore some of the many rooms of the palace.

The first she entered was lined with mirrors, and Beauty saw herself reflected on every side and thought she had never seen such a charming room. Then a bracelet which was hanging from a chandelier caught her eye, and on taking it down she was greatly surprised to find that it held a portrait of her unknown admirer, just as she had seen him in her dream. With great delight she slipped the bracelet on her arm and went on into a gallery of pictures, where she soon found a portrait of the same handsome Prince, as large as life, and so well painted that as she studied it he seemed to smile kindly at her. Tearing herself away from the portrait at last, she passed through into a room which contained every musical instrument under the sun, and here she amused herself for a long while in trying some of them and singing until she was tired. The next room was a library, and she saw everything she had ever wanted to read, as well as everything she had read, and it seemed to her that a whole lifetime would not be enough to even read the names of the books, there were so many. By this time it was growing dusk, and wax candles in diamond and ruby candlesticks were beginning to light themselves in every room.

Beauty found her supper served just at the time she preferred to have it, but she did not see anyone or hear a sound, and, though her father had warned her that she would be alone, she began to find it rather dull.

But presently she heard the Beast coming, and wondered tremblingly if he meant to eat her up now.

However, as he did not seem at all ferocious, and only said gruffly, "Good-evening, Beauty," she answered cheerfully and managed to conceal her terror. Then the Beast asked her how she had been amusing herself, and she told him all the rooms she had seen.

Then he asked if she thought she could be happy in his palace, and Beauty answered that everything was so beautiful that she would be very hard to please if she could not be happy. And after about an hour's talk Beauty began to think that the Beast was not nearly so terrible as she had supposed at first. Then he got up to leave her, and said in his gruff voice, "Do you love me, Beauty? Will you marry me?"

"Oh! what shall I say?" cried Beauty, for she was afraid to make the Beast angry by refusing.

"Say 'yes' or 'no' without fear," he replied.

"Oh! no, Beast," said Beauty hastily.

"Since you will not, good-night, Beauty," he said.

And she answered, "Good-night, Beast," very glad to find that her refusal had not provoked him. And after he was gone she was very soon in bed and asleep and dreaming of her unknown Prince. She thought he came and said to her:

"Ah, Beauty! why are you so unkind to me? I fear I am fated to be unhappy for many a long day still."

And then her dreams changed, but the charming Prince figured in them all; and when morning came her first thought was to look at the portrait and see if it was really like him, and she found that it certainly was.

This morning she decided to amuse herself in the garden, for the sun shone, and all the fountains were playing; but she was astonished to find that every place was familiar to her, and presently she came to the brook where the myrtle trees were growing where she had first met the Prince in her dream, and that made her think more than ever that he must be kept a prisoner by the Beast. When she was tired she went back to the palace, and found a new room full of materials for every kind of work—ribbons to make into bows and silks to work into flowers. Then there was an aviary full of rare birds, which were so tame that they flew to Beauty as soon as they saw her, and perched upon her shoulders and her head.

"Pretty little creatures," she said, "how I wish that your cage was nearer to my room, that I might often hear you sing!

So saying she opened a door and found, to her delight, that it led into her own room, though she had thought it was quite the other side of the palace.

There were more birds in a room farther on, parrots and cockatoos that could talk, and they greeted Beauty by name; indeed, she found them so entertaining that she took one or two back to her room, and they talked to her while she was at supper; after which the Beast paid her his usual visit, and asked her the same questions as before, and then with a gruff "good-night" he took his departure, and Beauty went to bed to dream of her mysterious Prince. The days passed swiftly in different amusements, and after a while Beauty found out another strange thing in the palace, which often pleased her when she was tired of being alone. There was one room which she had not noticed particularly; it was empty, except that under each of the windows stood a very comfortable chair; the first time she had looked out of the window it had seemed to her that a black curtain prevented her from seeing anything outside. But the second time she went into the room, happening to be tired, she sat down in one of the chairs, when instantly the curtain was rolled aside, and a most amusing pantomime was acted before her; there were dances, and colored lights, and music, and pretty dresses, and it was all so gay that Beauty was in ecstasies. After that she tried the other seven windows in turn, and there was some new and surprising entertainment to be seen from each of them, so that Beauty never could feel lonely any more. Every evening after supper the Beast came to see her, and always before saying good-night asked her in his terrible voice, "Beauty, will you marry me?"

And it seemed to Beauty, now she understood him better, that when she said, "No, Beast," he went away quite sad. But her happy dreams of the handsome young Prince soon made her forget the poor Beast, and the only thing that at all disturbed her was to be constantly told to distrust appearances, to let her heart guide her, and not her eyes, and many other equally perplexing things, which, consider as she would, she could not understand.

So everything went on for a long time, until at last, happy as she was, Beauty began to long for the sight of her father and her brothers and sisters; one night, seeing her look very sad, the Beast asked her what was the matter. Beauty had quite ceased to be afraid of him. Now she knew that he was really gentle in spite of his ferocious looks and his dreadful voice. So she answered that she was longing to see her home once more. Upon hearing this the Beast seemed sadly distressed, and cried miserably.

"Ah! Beauty, have you the heart to desert an unhappy Beast like this? What more do you want to make you happy? Is it because you hate me that you want to escape?"

"No, dear Beast," answered Beauty softly, "I do not hate you, and I should be very sorry never to see you any more, but I long to see my father again. Only let me go for two months, and I promise to come back to you and stay for the rest of my life."

The Beast, who had been sighing dolefully while she spoke, now replied, "I cannot refuse you anything you ask, even though it should cost me my life. Take the four boxes you will find in the room next to your own, and fill them with everything you wish to take with you. But remember your promise and come back when the two months are over, or you may have cause to repent it, for if you do not come in good time you will find your faithful Beast dead. You will not need any chariot to bring you back. Only say good-bye to all your brothers and sisters the night before you come away, and when you have gone to bed turn this ring round upon your finger and say firmly: 'I wish to go back to my palace and see my Beast again.' Good-night, Beauty. Fear nothing, sleep peacefully, and before long you shall see your father once more."

As soon as Beauty was alone she hastened to fill the boxes with all the rare and precious things she saw about her, and only when she was tired of heaping things into them did they seem to be full.

Then she went to bed, but could hardly sleep for joy. And when at last she did begin to dream of her beloved Prince she was grieved to see him stretched upon a grassy bank, sad and weary, and hardly like himself.

"What is the matter?" she cried.

He looked at her reproachfully, and said, "How can you ask me, cruel one? Are you not leaving me to my death perhaps?"

"Ah! don't be so sorrowful," cried Beauty; "I am only going to assure my father that I am safe and happy. I have promised the Beast faithfully that I will come back, and he would die of grief if I did not keep my word!"

"What would that matter to you?" said the Prince "Surely you would not care?"

"Indeed, I should be ungrateful if I did not care for such a kind Beast," cried Beauty indignantly. "I would die to save him from pain. I assure you it is not his fault that he is so ugly."

Just then a strange sound woke her—someone was speaking not very far away; opening her eyes she found herself in a room she had never seen before, which was certainly not nearly so splendid as those she was used to in the Beast's palace. Where could she be? She got up and dressed hastily, and then saw that the boxes she had packed the night before were all in the room. While she was wondering by what magic the Beast had transported them and herself to this strange place she suddenly heard her father's voice, and rushed out and greeted him joyfully. Her brothers and sisters were all astonished at her appearance, as they had never expected to see her again, and there was no end to the questions they asked her. She had also much to hear about what had happened to them while she was away, and of her father's journey home. But when they heard that she had only come to be with them for a short time, and then must go back to the Beast's palace for ever, they lamented loudly. Then Beauty asked her father what he thought could be the meaning of her strange dreams, and why the Prince constantly begged her not to trust to appearances. After much consideration, he answered, "You tell me yourself that the Beast, frightful as he is, loves you dearly, and deserves your love and gratitude for his gentleness and kindness; I think the Prince must mean you to understand that you ought to reward him by doing as he wishes you to, in spite of his ugliness."

Beauty could not help seeing that this seemed very probable; still, when she thought of her dear Prince who was so handsome, she did not feel at all inclined to marry the Beast. At any rate, for two months she need not decide, but could enjoy herself with her sisters. But though they were rich now, and lived in town again, and had plenty of acquaintances, Beauty found that nothing amused her very much; and she often thought of the palace, where she was so happy, especially as at home she never once dreamed of her dear Prince, and she felt quite sad without him.

Then her sisters seemed to have got quite used to being without her, and even found her rather in the way, so she would not have been sorry when the two months were over but for her father and brothers, who begged her to stay and seemed so grieved at the thought of her departure that she had not the courage to say good-bye to them. Every day when she got up she meant to say it at night, and when night came she put it off again, until at last she had a dismal dream which helped her to make up her mind. She thought she was wandering in a lonely path in the palace gardens, when she heard groans which seemed to come from some bushes hiding the entrance of a cave and, running quickly to see what could be the matter, she found the Beast stretched out upon his side, apparently dying. He reproached her faintly with being the cause of his distress, and at the same moment a stately lady appeared, and said very gravely:

"Ah! Beauty, you are only just in time to save his life. See what happens when people do not keep their promises! If you had delayed one day more, you would have found him dead."

Beauty was so terrified by this dream that the next morning she announced her intention of going back at once, and that very night she said good-by to her father and all her brothers and sisters, and as soon as she was in bed she turned her ring round upon her finger, and said firmly, "I wish to go back to my palace and see my Beast again," as she had been told to do.

Then she fell asleep instantly and only woke up to hear the clock saying, "Beauty, Beauty" twelve times in its musical voice, which told her at once that she was really in the palace once more. Everything was just as before, and her birds were so glad to see her! But Beauty thought she had never known such a long day, for she was so anxious to see the Beast again that she felt as if suppertime would never come.

But when it did come and no Beast appeared she was really

frightened; so, after listening and waiting for a long time, she ran down into the garden to search for him. Up and down the paths and avenues ran poor Beauty, calling him in vain, for no one answered, and not a trace of him could she find; until at last, quite tired, she stopped for a minute's rest, and saw that she was standing opposite the shady path she had seen in her dream. She rushed down it, and, sure enough, there was the cave, and in it lay the Beast—asleep, as Beauty thought. Quite glad to have found him, she ran up and stroked his head, but, to her horror, he did not move or open his eyes.

"Oh! he is dead; and it is all my fault," said Beauty, crying bitterly.

But then, looking at him again, she fancied he still breathed, and, hastily fetching some water from the nearest fountain, she sprinkled it over his face, and, to her great delight, he began to revive.

"Oh! Beast, how you frightened me!" she cried. "I never knew how much I loved you until just now, when I feared I was too late to save your life."

"Can you really love such an ugly creature as I am?" said the Beast faintly. "Ah! Beauty, you only came just in time. I was dying because I thought you had forgotten your promise. But go back now and rest, I shall see you again by and by."

Beauty, who had half expected that he would be angry with her, was reassured by his gentle voice, and went back to the palace, where supper was awaiting her; afterward the Beast came in as usual, and talked about the time she had spent with her father, asking if she had enjoyed herself, and if they had all been very glad to see her.

Beauty answered politely, and quite enjoyed telling him all that had happened to her. And when at last the time came for him to go, and he asked, as he had so often asked before, "Beauty, will you marry me?"

She answered softly, "Yes, dear Beast."

As she spoke a blaze of light sprang up before the windows of the palace; fireworks crackled and guns banged; and across the avenue of orange trees, in letters all made of fire-flies, was written: "Long live the Prince and his Bride."

Turning to ask the Beast what it could all mean, Beauty found that he had disappeared, and in his place stood her long-loved Prince! At the same moment the wheels of a chariot were heard upon the terrace, and two ladies entered the room. One of them Beauty recognized as the stately lady she had seen in her dreams; the other was also so grand and queenly that Beauty hardly knew which to greet first.

But the one she already knew said to her companion:

"Well, Queen, this is Beauty, who has had the courage to rescue your son from the terrible enchantment. They love one another, and only your consent to their marriage is wanting to make them perfectly happy."

"I consent with all my heart," cried the Queen. "How can I ever thank you enough, charming girl, for having restored my dear son to his natural form?"

And then she tenderly embraced Beauty and the Prince, who had meanwhile been greeting the Fairy and receiving her congratulations.

"Now," said the Fairy to Beauty, "I suppose you would like me to send for all your brothers and sisters to dance at your wedding?"

And so she did, and the marriage was celebrated the very next day with the utmost splendor, and Beauty and the Prince lived happily ever after.

Déjà Vu

In Villeneuve's "Beauty and the Beast" (as we have it in Andrew Lang's famous redaction), Beauty falls into a "tender trap." While Villeneuve's version is quite similar to Beaumont's, there are subtle differences that shape her story into a vision of an arranged marriage. All the events in Beauty's waking life and in her dream life — the entertainments provided her and the riches she is given to distribute, her interactions with the Beast and her father, her dream visions of the Prince and the Grand Lady — are arranged to "bring her around" and finally win her assent.

In Beaumont's tale, Beauty seems a long-suffering and hard-pressed Cinderella, a nearly solitary figure in a friendless world. This situation is aggravated by Beaumont's sisters who plot against her. The sisters in Villeneuve, however, are in no way as malicious; moreover, all the siblings share in the work necessitated by the family's fall from fortune, and Villeneuve's Beauty only differs from her sisters in not complaining. Absent, in other words, are Beaumont's conniving kin and with them the contrast between Beauty's virtues and her sisters' venality, her sincerity and their hypocrisy, her peasant-like humility and their nouveau-riche uppityness, her hardworking nature and their petted indolence.

In her largely friendless world, Beaumont's Beauty has only one ally in her father. The same can't be said in Villeneuve's tale, where Beauty's father is seen in a less flattering light. In Beaumont, when the merchant arrives at the castle of his unknown host and finds himself at a table set with food, he waits "a considerable time" before giving into his hunger and trembles through his meal in fear that he may be committing some *faux pas*. The father in Villeneuve is nowhere near as circumspect: famished and finding himself in front of a table set with food, "he lost no time in beginning his meal." The next morning and after another hospitably provided meal, the father in Beaumont imagines all this generosity the work of a kind fairy and thanks her. In Villeneuve, that gratitude is absent; marveling at all the treasures in the castle, the father opines, "All this must be meant for me."

The avarice of this last statement suggests something about the father in Villeneuve, as does the bargain he strikes with the Beast after he is caught taking the rose. When the Beast proposes to let the merchant go if one of his daughters volunteers to come in his place, Beaumont's father only appears to entertain this idea, saying he will ask them, but he says this only in order that he may go home and bid them adieu; he has no intention of allowing this substitution. In Villeneuve, the father says something quite curious to the Beast's proposal: "If I were cruel enough to buy my own life at the expense of one of my children's, what excuse could I invent to bring her here?" Perhaps smitten by all the riches he has seen in the castle, Villeneuve's indigent father seems more than ready to sacrifice his daughter and is only slowed by the problem of how she might be persuaded. In fact, as later events might suggest, this father becomes a kind of co-conspirator with the Beast when he interprets his daughter's dreams.

Villeneuve's mysteriously hospitable castle of the Beast also seems to conspire to woo Beauty. Fireworks and music greet her arrival, and during the remainder of her waking days the house caters to her every wish and provides her with recreations lest she grow bored. In dramatic contrast to her penurious work life at home, Villeneuve's potential bride is beguiled with an aviary full of birds to amuse her, a library with every book she might care to read, a music room where she can play instruments and sing, even sewing materials should she care to pass the time in that way. When tired of walks in the lovely arbor or the luxurious home, she can turn to the equivalent of cable television: in one room, Beauty can look out any of eight windows and see a different theatrical or pantomime.

This wooing continues nonstop in Beauty's dream life when she is visited nightly by a handsome Dream Prince (whom she falls in love with) and a Grand Lady (who turns out to be a fairy). In Beaumont, Beauty only has one dream when the Fairy comes and assures her that her sacrifice for her father will not go unrewarded; good to her word, the Fairy Lady appears at the end of Beaumont's tale to reward Beauty and punish her sisters. But in Villeneuve, the Great Lady and the Dream Prince have more steady employment in Beauty's dreams, and their messages are not so much promises of rewards but instructions on the topic of "reality versus appearances."

In a quite heavy-handed and too obvious way, Villeneuve's Beauty is sent to Night School and regularly instructed by her dream visitors:

"Try to find me out, no matter how I may be disguised." (Dream Prince)
"Do not trust so much your eyes." (Dream Prince)
"Do not let yourself be deceived by appearances." (Great Lady)

Every night, she has repeating dreams that feature these visitors and she finds them pleasant with one exception: "The only thing that at all disturbed her was to be constantly told to distrust appearances, to let her heart guide her, and not her eyes, and many equally perplexing things, which, consider as she would, she could not understand."

Since she goes to school every night and since the lessons are so constant, Villeneuve's perplexed Beauty seems a slow student. So, even more clues are given to her that the handsome prince who visits her in dreams (and whom she has fallen in love with) is the

Beast. As she wanders about the castle, Beauty finds a bracelet hanging in a chandelier and the picture it contains is of the very same prince who visits her in her dreams. In a scene Disney Studios would later employ in their film, Beauty wanders into a gallery and notices a portrait of the same prince who visits her in her dreams; and then, to confirm her *déjà vu* experience, after she has once more dreamt of the prince, she returns to the gallery and confirms that the portrait is a picture of him. When she turns down the Beast's offer of marriage, that night (in an unmistakable moment of ventriloquism) her Dream Prince asks how she can be so unkind. And when she persuades the Beast to permit her to return to her father despite his being heartbroken at her departure, his double, the Dream Prince asks again how she can be so unkind to him.

Despite this abundance of clues, Villeneuve's Beauty still can't figure things out. We might wonder how she can be so dim. To be sure, Beauty comes to believe, without any foundation whatsoever, that the prince is being held captive in the castle by the Beast. But the truth is that Beauty has fallen in love with the handsome Dream Prince and resists identifying him with the Beast, his unsightly double.

When Beauty returns home and confides her dreams to her father, he plays the therapist. With perhaps a measure of self-interest, he interprets her dreams in the following fashion: "You tell me yourself that the Beast, frightful as he is, loves you dearly, and deserves your love and gratitude for his kindness and gentleness; I think the Prince must mean you to understand you ought to reward him by doing as he wishes you to, in spite of his ugliness." Beauty realizes her father is correct but still resists this notion because of her love for her Dream Prince. Responding to her father's dream interpretation, "Beauty could not help seeing that this seemed very probable; still, when she thought of her Prince who was so handsome, she did not feel at all inclined to marry the Beast."

Beauty's resistance is notable. Against all force of logic and evidence, Villeneuve's Beauty maintains a strict separation between the Prince and the Beast. Even more than in Apuleius's myth where the separation of daytime from nighttime is a given condition of Psyche's life, Beauty in Villeneuve's story willfully maintains that division in the face of constant intimations that night and day are not that distinct. And despite more than a few experiences of the "uncanny," with *déjà vu* experiences that signal the link between her dreams and her waking life, this Beauty resists making a link between her Dream Prince and the Beast.

Bettelheim might argue that this resistance reveals an immature attitude towards sex as something that is beastly, an attitude she must outgrow.[1] But if we were to seek a psychological explanation, it might be more accurate to say that Beauty's situation resembles that of a neurotic—say, that of a woman who is in love with a movie star or some other ideal male and who, as a result, is unable to form a relationship with an average or less becoming male.

But more than a picture of psychological dilemmas, Villeneuve's "Beauty and the Beast" seems to reflect a conflict between arranged marriages and love marriages. Villeneuve's Beauty finds herself in a situation where matters have been arranged for her by her father and the Beast, where she is also being wooed by the house during the day and by her dreams at night. In this "tender trap," she still possesses veto power and must give her assent. To be sure, she feels gratitude towards the Beast, but she loves the Prince. So, in her, a competition exists between her feelings of duty and obligation on the one hand and her own romantic desires on the other. The question is: how can this duality be resolved?

In a familiar device from sentimental literature, the imminent death of the righteous shames her into a change of heart. As she lingers at her own home, Beauty is visited in a dream by the Beast who is languishing because she has not returned as she promised. Then the Great Lady appears and chides Beauty for breaking her promise. Conscience-stricken, Beauty returns.

This moment also marks the beginning of a collapse of the dualities she has so strictly maintained between night and day, between dream life and waking life, between the Prince and the Beast. In a psychological way, it is significant that this is the first dream in which the Beast has appeared. Moreover, Beauty subsequently trusts her *déjà vu* experiences when she recalls her dream of the dying Beast languishing near a cave and makes use of the dream to locate where the Beast has fallen ill. Finding him, she admits that

1   Cf. Bettelheim 303-10.

she did not realize how much she loved him until he was near death, and she accepts his marriage proposal.

The events that follow are a bit of a surprise for Beauty. Fireworks go off, guns salute, and fireflies light up with the message "Long Live the Prince and his Bride." The Beast disappears, and in his place is Beauty's long loved Prince. And the Great Lady crosses over from the dreamworld in the company of the Prince's mother, who gives her assent to the marriage and embraces Beauty.

But the ending may come as a bit of a surprise to us, too, because it isn't quite clear how Beauty's gratitude toward the Beast changes into love as well. Ultimately, the decisive issue seems to be The Promise. Reminded of her promise to return to the Beast in two month's time, chastened by the shame she would feel if she were to go back on her word, Beauty abides by her contract and love follows.

But in another way, Villeneuve's Beauty seems to have been promised from the start, though matters await her final assent. She has been in a "tender trap" arranged by a father (who wondered aloud how he might persuade a daughter to come to the Beast's castle and who interprets her dreams as arguing for the giving of her hand); plied by the Beast with gifts and with luxuries; beguiled by a home resplendent with fireworks and arranged for her recreation; instructed nightly by her dreams and the visitations of the Dream Prince and the Great Lady. Everyone and everything seems to await her signing the contract. And she does, finally!

Even so, why Villeneuve's Prince would want such a slow learner and dim partner, such a petted and hesitant spouse, may still seem a bit unclear. To answer that shortcoming in the tale, readers would have to await the arrival of Beaumont's version some twelve years later.

FIVE

FOLK TALE VARIATIONS

FOLKLORISTS HAVE DISCOVERED VERSIONS of "Beauty and the Beast" all over the world. Each incarnation, of course, takes on a local costume: for example, in Germany and Scandinavia the Beast may be a bear; in India and Africa, a snake; in Ireland and England, a dog; in Japan and the Philippines, a monkey; in Italy and Russia, a pig; and in other places, a "monster" who is half human and half animal. As varied as these tales may be, folklorists have found behind their manifold differences an essential unanimity that makes them "Beauty and the Beast" stories. The best gathering of these is Betsy Hearne's *Beauties and Beasts* where twenty-seven tales can be found from around the world (from Norway to Jamaica, from the American Southwest to Indonesia).

In *Women Who Run With the Wolves*, Clarissa Pinkola Estés presents a feminist argument that contemporary women need to recover a missing wildness; as part of that project, she assembles a number of "Beauty and the Beast" tales for women to consider. In another collection and in a similar vein, Maria Tatar presents a handful of related stories in *The Classic Fairy Tales*, especially emphasizing those with plucky women and "Swan Maiden" tales or stories of female beasts.

Responding to the enthusiasm for multiculturalism, contemporary American authors have also recovered and published old folk tales that present variants of the "Beauty and the Beast" story. For example, in *Buffalo Woman*, Paul Goble retells a Native American story from the Osage Nation. John Steptoe has published an African version from Zimbabwe in his marvelously illustrated *Mufaro's Beautiful Daughters*. And well-known children's writer Lawrence Yep has done something similar in *The Dragon Prince: A Chinese Beauty and the Beast*.[1]

---

1   Paul Goble, *Buffalo Woman* (New York: Simon and Schuster, 1984); John

The pleasure in reading these various versions is twofold. If enough of them are consulted, similarities are recognized and what emerges is a sense of the shared story or ur-structure that lies behind them. When that is in place, another pleasure arises. Like the jazz afficionado who appreciates how individual performers can take a well-known tune and work their own improvisations upon it, the reader aware of the core story of "Beauty and the Beast" can be attentive to the way individual tales play their own variations, shortening this part here and lengthening that, leaving some issues in the shadows while foregrounding others, and otherwise doing their own thing.

To first grasp the shared story behind the variants, several methodologies exist. For example, in his encyclopedic *Motif-Index of Folk-Literature*, Stith Thompson continues the work of Antii Aarne and proceeds in the manner of a taxonomical biologist, classifying tales from around the world by species, then genus, then phyla. In his masterful *Morphology of the Folktale*, Vladimir Propp takes another tack and proceeds in the manner of a radiologist, identifying a spinal column of continuity in the shared sequence of events and universal structure of folktales.[1] Combining those methodologies, and consulting dozens and dozens of versions of "Beauty and the Beast," we can say the story typically divides into five acts.

In **Act I**, information is given about the principal characters. Typically, no information is given about the cause of the Prince's transformation. Where details are supplied, however, we learn that he has been cursed by a dwarf or enchanted by a demon stepmother. Sometimes, too, his parents made a hasty wish for a child ("even if it should be a little animal") or something untoward happens — for example, a mother-to-be falls asleep on a path used by fairies and is cursed by them for the inconvenience.

Steptoe, *Mufaro's Beautiful Daughters* (New York: Lothrop, Lee and Shepard, 1987); Lawrence Yep. *The Dragon Prince: A Chinese Beauty and the Beast* (New York: HarperCollins, 1997).

1   Stith Thompson, *Motif-Index of Folk-Literature*, 6 vols. (Bloomington, IN: University of Indiana Press, 1956). Vladimir Propp, *Morphology of the Folktale* (Austin, TX: University of Texas Press, 1968). Cf. Jan-Ojvind Swahn, *The Tale of Cupid and Psyche* (Lund: Gleerup, 1955).

When the maiden is introduced, we are given information about her family. Her father is present but often (although not always) her mother is absent. This Beauty character may have three brothers but she is very likely to have two sisters (or stepsisters), though in a few cases she is one of seven sisters. In any event, she is always the youngest and the most beautiful, and her virtues often contrast with the negative qualities of her sisters.

Sometimes the family has fallen from prosperity; but whatever the case, they are customarily poor. Then something occurs which gives them reason to hope that their circumstances will change: a promise of wealth or a change in status.

At this point, travel enters the story; most frequently, the father goes on a journey. Before he departs, the father asks his daughters what he should bring back for them, and typically the elder sisters ask for luxurious items. The youngest, however, asks for something unusual—for example, a rose, a golden ball, or a singing lark.

"The Singing, Springing Lark," collected by the Grimm Brothers (German, 1812).

Before he departs on a journey, a father asks his three daughters what they would like him to bring back; the elders ask for pearls and diamonds, but the youngest asks for a "singing, springing lark." Fetching the bird, the father is accosted by a lion who threatens to devour him, but the father is able to win his freedom by promising to give the lion the first thing he meets on his return. While the father hopes he might encounter the family's cat or a dog, his youngest daughter is the first to greet him. Keeping her father's promise, the youngest daughter travels to the lion's kingdom only to discover that he is a lion by day and a handsome prince at night. They marry and live happily for a time. Traveling to her sister's wedding, however, the maiden is warned by the lion that if the light from a candle should fall upon him, he will be changed into a dove and they will be separated. Despite the precautions she takes, this calamity occurs, and she must go to the ends of the earth and undergo numerous trials before she eventually rescues her husband from an enchanted princess and effects his transformation.

Like all parts of these varied stories, although there may be extravagant differences between them, **Act II** typically presents the arrangements that bring the maiden in contact with the Beast. Sometimes the Animal Groom initiates the contact—for example, a bear knocks at the family door. Sometimes the maiden initiates contact; in the Irish tale "The Three Daughters of King O'Hara," for example, husbands are wished for and Animal Grooms appear. More typically, in the manner of arranged marriages, a parent serves as a go-between; the Beast's mother approaches suitable partners or the maiden's father encounters a seemingly unsuitable bachelor.

Arrangements are often begun as the result of an inadvertent mistake or hasty promise on the part of the father. Beaumont's father unwittingly breaks a taboo when he snaps off and takes some of the Beast's roses, which the creature prizes more than anything else in the world. Sometimes a father hastily promises his daughter in return for assistance; in the Turkish tale "The Princess and the Pig," in return for help getting his carriage out of the mud, a father rashly promises his daughter to a pig. More common is the father who extricates himself from difficulty by promising the Beast the first thing he encounters when he arrives home; the father hopes he will meet the family dog but, to his sorrow, his youngest daughter is the first to greet him.

In the midst of these events, the Beast has appeared and, as has been suggested, he comes in various zoological forms; he may be, for example, a three-headed serpent, a small-toothed dog, or (in a Tibetan version) a Lion King with an exceedingly large frame and "the eighteen marks of ugliness."[1] Typically, in his meeting with the father, the Beast interrogates the man, extracts information, exacts a promise or strikes a bargain, and ultimately makes the father an unwitting accomplice in the loss of his daughter.

The maiden is then approached with the dilemma and consents to help, agreeing to sacrifice herself or substitute for her father. Her journey to the Beast marks the end of Act II.

1 Ralston 1011.

FIVE: FOLK TALE VARIATIONS

"The Small-Tooth Dog," collected by Sidney O'Addy (England, 1895).

While on a journey, a father is attacked by thieves and then nursed back to health by a large dog. In gratitude, the father promises the dog anything he has, even if it is his most precious thing, and the dog asks for the man's daughter. In a week's time, the dog comes to fetch the girl from her grieving father and carries her on his back to his luxurious home; but after a month, the weeping girl wishes to return and visit her father. The dog is agreeable but first asks, "What do you call me?" Her first answer is an insult ("A great, foul, small-tooth dog") and her canine companion withdraws permission for her journey; later, she changes her answer to a compliment ("Your name is Sweet-as-a-honeycomb") and he begins to carry her to her father's house. These event are repeated at the gate and halfway along the road: each time he asks her what she calls him, she responds with her insult and he turns around; the next time she changes her answer to a compliment, and they continue a little further. At her father's door, these events seem about to be repeated again and the girl about to issue her usual insult but—seeing how her comment would grieve the dog and recalling how good he has been to her—in answer to the dog's question about what she calls him, the maiden says straightaway, "Sweet-as-a-honeycomb." At this, the creature pulls off his dog's head, his fur falls away, and before her stands a handsome prince "with the finest and smallest teeth you ever saw."

Act III presents the encounter between the maiden and the Beast. Typically, she travels to a place where she is more or less confined in a home of extraordinary luxury that contrasts with the impoverished circumstances she has left. Her companion there has a dual nature and is frequently an animal by day but sheds his skin at night and becomes a handsome prince. Sometimes the maiden is unaware that these are the same person.

In the nights that follow, the stories often tell that the Prince sleeps in the maiden's bed, and she enjoys the company of this unknown stranger. In a few stories, however, the opposite is the case and familiarity precedes intimacy; in Beaumont's tale, for example, their evening meals allow her the chance to first get to know and appreciate the Beast.

As happy as she may be with her nocturnal visitor, the maiden eventually grows lonely during the day and begins to miss her family. She seeks permission from the Beast to visit them and, after suitable warnings, he agrees to this. Her return home marks the end of Act III.

"The Enchanted Tsarevitch," collected by Aleksandr Afanasyev (Russian, ca. 1860).

A merchant retrieves a requested flower for his youngest daughter and encounters a three-headed snake. Purchasing his freedom with a promise to surrender the first thing he encounters on his return, the father is obliged to forfeit his daughter. During her first night at the palace, the snake asks that she put his bed outside the door to her room. On the second night, he asks that she put his bed next to hers inside the room. On the third night, he sleeps in her bed. Following that, the maiden returns home on a visit, and her jealous sisters conspire to make her break her promise to the snake by persuading her to stay longer than a day. On her return, she finds the reptile languishing and kissing the creature with all her might, she revives and transforms him into a handsome prince and they marry.

Act IV takes place in the maiden's home where typically her mother or her sisters conspire to undermine her relationship with the Beast by breaking some taboo; often this taboo concerns the secret identity of the Beast/Prince. If he has accompanied her, perhaps the mother burns his animal skin or otherwise exposes him. If the maiden is to return to the Beast, she may be persuaded to spy on him while he is sleeping. Or perhaps she foolishly shares his secret name or enters a forbidden room and discovers something about his true identity. Or maybe the broken taboo is a simpler thing like staying longer than she has promised, as is the case in Beaumont's tale.

In any event, the maiden's action constitutes a betrayal that results in her separation from the Beast. When the next act begins, the maiden must search for her lost partner.

"Whitebear Whittington," collected by Richard Chase (American Appalachia, 1948).

While his two eldest daughters ask for silk dresses, the youngest asks for roses when this father goes on a journey. Before he takes the roses, however, he hears a voice warning him that he will have to surrender whatever first greets him on his return. Regrettably, he first meets his youngest daughter, and a white bear comes to fetch her. Mounting the bear's back, the girl weeps so bitterly at her leaving that she gets a nosebleed and three drops of blood fall on the bear's back. At the bear's fine home, her companion is an animal by day and by night a handsome man who shares her bed. When the maiden wishes to see her father again, the bear warns her not to tell his name; but she is persuaded by others to do so and tells them that her companion's name is "Whitebear Whittington." At this, her husband disappears over the mountain as a man dressed in a white shirt stained by three drops of blood. The maiden then spends seven years looking for him, following his trail marked by white feathers with a red speck. Finally, she comes to an old woman's home and in return for help with the weaving, the girl acquires three golden nuts. Passing through a village, she next comes upon a group of women competing for her husband by seeing who can wash the bloodstains from his shirt. Though her husband does not recognize her, she successfully removes the stains, but another woman claims she did so and spirits him away. Pursuing them, the maiden offers the other woman each of the golden nuts in return for passing three nights with her husband. On the first two nights, the man is drugged and comatose, and she cannot communicate with him. On the third night, however, the handsome husband avoids taking the sleeping potion and they are reunited.

Act V is dramatically abbreviated in Beaumont's "Beauty and the Beast": Beauty realizes she has been inconsiderate, returns to the Beast, finds him languishing, agrees to marry, and revives him. More typically, the maiden goes on a long and arduous journey to recover her missing partner.

Sometimes, in order to follow him, the Beast/Prince provides talismans (e.g., a ring, a horse, a mirror) or marks his trail (e.g., with blood and feathers). Whether that is the case or not, before she can find him, the maiden must weep buckets of tears or wear out many pairs of shoes. She must climb glass mountains or go to the ends of the earth. And she is often obliged to collect magical objects en route and to perform extraordinary tasks.

Often the maiden finds her Prince in his mother's house, as is the case in "Cupid and Psyche." There she must undergo more trials. Often, too, she needs to triumph over a sisterly rival who has supplanted her, and she does so often just before the Prince is about to marry this false bride.

Still, whether the maiden wins her husband or simply revives her partner, issues of identity are resolved in the conclusion: his enchantment is at an end and, if need be, he is transformed into that paragon, the Handsome Prince. Other features of the "happy ending" are also often present as the couple assumes their royal station and evildoers are punished.

"The Serpent and the Grape-Grower's Daughter," collected from Madame Ferrié (France, 1893).

When he removes a stone from his vineyard, a man disturbs a great snake who uses the stone as a door to his home. If the man is not able to persuade one of his three daughters to become the snake's bride, the snake will crush him to death. The elder daughters will have nothing to do with this bargain, but the youngest agrees to save her father's life and marries the snake. At the serpent's castle, the maiden finds every kind of luxury; and at night the snake sheds his skin and becomes a handsome prince who sleeps in her bed. When her sisters come to visit, the prince warns her that his skin is not to be touched when he is sleeping. However, out of jealousy at the younger sister's good fortune, the eldest sister touches the skin, and the siblings suddenly find themselves outside on the ground and the prince gone. For the next seven years, the maiden goes in pursuit of him, filling seven bottles with her tears and wearing out seven pairs of iron shoes. She finally encounters her husband on the day he is about to remarry, and they are reunited to live happily the rest of their days.

In ringing their changes upon this basic pattern, various stories differ in large ways and small; however, at bottom, what can be discovered is the essential unity that leads folklorists to group them as Beauty-and-the-Beast stories. With that pattern in place, we begin to notice the three major deviations from that pattern and their relationship to Beaumont's tale. The first of these are "Swan Maiden" tales (stories of female beasts) or, more properly, cross-gender versions where instead of a disguised bridegroom, we are introduced to a disguised bride; a good example of these is the Grimms' "Ashenputtel," their version of the Cinderella story. Another major variant appears in those stories which give lengthy prominence to the maiden's search for her lost partner; here, a good exemplar is "East of the Sun, West of the Moon." The third significant variant occurs in those tales where the maiden wins the prince not by compliance or amiability, but by defiance and disagreeableness; here, the best example is "The Frog King."

"CINDERELLA"

Jacob and Wilhelm Grimm (1785-1863) were famous German folklorists who collected fairy tales that had been told for years. Many of these appeared in print for the first time when they published Kinder und Hausmärchen *(*Children's and Household Tales*) in 1812 and in several subsequent editions until 1856. "Aschenputtel" ("Ash Daughter") is their version of the story of "Cinderella" and somewhat different from the better known rendition of the tale by Charles Perrault which features, among other things, a fairy godmother and a pumpkin that is changed into a coach. My version of the tale below is based on a translation by Lucy Crane published in 1886.*

There was once the wife of a rich man who fell sick and when she felt her death drawing near, she called her only daughter to her bedside and said, "Dear child, be good and pious, and God will always protect you, and I will look down on you from heaven and watch over you." Then the mother closed her eyes and died.

The maiden remained pious and good, and every day she went to her mother's grave and wept. When winter came, the snow spread a white sheet over the grave. And by the time the spring sun had melted it, her father had taken another wife.

The new wife brought her own two daughters into the household. They were fair of face but vile and black of heart. Now began hard times for the poor stepchild. "Is this stupid creature to sit in the parlor with us?" they asked. "Those who want to eat bread must earn it." And they insisted she work as their kitchen-maid.

The mother and daughters also took away all the stepchild's pretty dresses and made her put on an old grey gown and wooden shoes. "Just look at the pretty princess, now," they laughed as they led her into the kitchen. There she worked hard from morning until night, getting up before dawn, carrying water, lighting the fire, cooking, and washing. Besides this, the sisters did everything they could to torment her—mocking her and emptying her peas and lentils into the ashes so that she was forced to sit and pick them out again.

In the evening, when she was worn out from work, she had no bed to go to. Instead, she had to curl up near the fire and sleep on the hearth that was littered with ashes and cinders. As a result, she always looked dusty and dirty, so they called her "Cinderella."

One day her father was going to a fair, and he asked his two stepdaughters what he should bring back for them. "Beautiful dresses," said one.

"Pearls and jewels," said the other.

"And you, Cinderella," he added, "what will you have?"

"Father," she answered, "break off for me the first tree branch which knocks against your hat on your way home."

So, he bought beautiful dresses and pearls and jewels for his two stepdaughters. And on his way home, as he was riding through a forest, a hazel twig brushed against him and knocked his hat off. So, he broke off the branch and took it with him. When he arrived home, he gave his stepdaughters the things they had asked for, and he gave Cinderella the branch from the hazel tree.

Cinderella took the branch to her mother's grave and planted it there. She wept so much that her tears watered the twig, and it grew into a fine tree. Three times a day, Cinderella would go and sit under that tree where she would weep and pray. Then a little white bird would come, and if Cinderella expressed a wish, the bird would bring her what she wished for.

Now it came to pass that the king gave orders for a festival which would last three days, and all the beautiful young girls in the country were invited so that his son might choose himself a bride. When the two stepsisters heard this, they were delighted. They called Cinderella and said, "Comb our hair, polish our shoes, and fasten our buttons for we are going to a party at the king's palace."

When she heard this news, Cinderella could not help but weep because she wished to attend the ball as well, and she begged her stepmother for permission to go. "You, Cinderella?" the woman replied, "Covered in dirt and ashes as you are, you want to go to the festival? You have no clothes and you have no shoes, but still you want to go to the dance!"

When Cinderella kept on asking, the stepmother finally said, "Alright. I have emptied a bowl of lentils into the ashes of the fire. If you can pick them out again in two hours, you may go with us to the ball."

Then the maiden went out the backdoor and into the garden where she called, "All you tame pigeons, all you turtledoves, all you birds of air, come and help me pick the lentils from the ashes:

> The good go in the dish.
> The others you may keep, if you wish."

Then two white pigeons came, then turtledoves, and finally all the birds under the sky. Chirping and fluttering, landing in the ashes, they began to pick, pick, pick, pick—gathering all the good lentils into the dish. An hour had hardly passed before they were done and flew away.

Then the girl was happy and took the dish to her stepmother, thinking that now she would be allowed to go to the ball. But the stepmother said, "No, Cinderella, you have no clothes and don't know how to dance. If you came with us, people would only laugh and point." But when Cinderella continued to weep in disappointment, the stepmother finally said, "Alright. If you can pick two dishes of lentils out of the ashes for me in one hour, then you can go with us." The stepmother thought to herself, "Here is a task that Cinderella cannot possibly do again," and she emptied the two dishes of lentils into the ashes.

Then the maiden went out the backdoor and into the garden again, where she called, "All you tame pigeons, all you turtledoves, all you birds of the air, come and help me pick the lentils from the ashes:

> The good go in the dish.
> The others you may keep, if you wish."

Then, as before, two white pigeons came, then turtledoves, and finally all the birds under the sky. Then they began to pick, pick, pick, pick—gathering all the good lentils into the dish. And before a half hour had passed, they were done and flew away.

Cinderella was delighted because she believed now she might go to the ball. But the stepmother said, "Even so, you shall not go with us. You have no clothes and cannot dance. We would be ashamed of you." And turning her back, the stepmother hurried away to the ball with her two daughters.

All alone, Cinderella went to her mother's grave beneath the hazel tree and cried:

> Shiver and quiver, little tree.
> Silver and gold throw over me.

Then the bird threw a gold and silver dress down to her, and slippers embroidered with silk and silver. As fast as she could, Cinderella put on the dress and hurried to the ball.

When she arrived, her stepsisters and stepmother did not recognize her but thought she must be a foreign princess because she looked so beautiful in her golden dress. It never occurred to them that this beautiful maiden was Cinderella because they believed their kitchenmaid was sitting at home, picking lentils out of the ashes. Then the prince approached her and took her by the hand, and he danced with no other. When gentlemen would come to ask if they might dance with her, the prince told them, "This is my partner."

When night came on and the festivities were drawing to a close, Cinderella made preparation to return home. But the king's son said, "No, wait, I will accompany you" because he wanted to see where the beautiful maiden lived. But she managed to slip away from him and, since the prince was pursuing her, she finally hid in the family's pigeon-house. Then her father appeared and the prince told him that a mysterious maiden was hiding in his pigeon-house. The old man thought to himself, "Surely, it can't be Cinderella," and went and got an axe and other tools, and he tore down the pigeon-house. But no one was to be found inside.

When the others got home, they found Cinderella in her dirty clothes, lying in her customary place among the ashes near the fire. When she had been in danger of being discovered, Cinderella had jumped out the back of the pigeon-house and hurried to the hazel tree. There she took off her beautiful clothes and laid them on the grave, and the bird had taken them away. Then she had put on her old gray gown again and hurried to the kitchen.

The festival began again the next day and, when her parents and the stepsisters were gone once more, Cinderella went to the hazel tree and said:

> Shiver and quiver, little tree.
> Silver and gold throw over me.

Then the bird threw down a more beautiful dress than the one before. And when Cinderella appeared at the ball, everyone was astonished by her beauty.

The prince had waited for her and when she arrived, he took her by the hand and danced with no other; if gentlemen came and asked to dance with her, he told them, "This is my partner." When it grew dark and Cinderella made her departure, the prince followed her in order to see into which house she went. But she got ahead of him and slipped into the garden behind her family's house. There stood a magnificent pear tree, and Cinderella climbed into its branches and hid there.

The prince did not know where she had gone, so he waited until the father appeared and said, "The mysterious maiden has escaped from me again, but I believe she has climbed into your pear tree." The father thought to himself, "Surely, it can't be Cinderella" and got an axe and chopped the tree down. But no one was to be found there. And when the others came home and went into the kitchen, Cinderella lay among the ashes, as usual, for she had jumped down on the other side of the tree, taken the beautiful dress to the bird in the hazel tree, and put on her old grey gown again.

On the third day, when the parents and sisters had gone away, Cinderella went once more to her mother's grave and said to the little tree:

> Shiver and quiver, little tree.
> Silver and gold throw over me.

And now the bird threw down to her a dress that was more splendid and magnificent than any she had yet had, and she was provided with shoes that were golden. And when she went to the festival
in the dress, everyone was speechless in astonishment. The prince
danced only with her, and if anyone invited her to dance, he said,
"This is my partner."

When the festivities were over, Cinderella wished to leave but
the king's son was anxious to go with her. Still, she escaped from
him so quickly that he could not follow. But the prince was clever
and had made a plan. The whole staircase had been smeared with
pitch so that when Cinderella ran down, her left shoe got stuck and
remained there. The king's son picked it up and saw that it was
small and golden. Next morning, he went to his father and said,
"No one shall be my wife except the woman whose foot fits this
tiny golden shoe."

The two stepsisters were glad to hear this because they had small
feet. When it came to be her turn to try on the shoe, the eldest,
accompanied by her mother, took it into her room. But she could
not get her big toe into it because the shoe was too small for her.
Then her mother gave her a knife and said, "Cut the toe off. When
you are queen, you will have no more need to go about on foot."
Then the maiden cut the toe off, forced her foot into the shoe,
swallowed the pain, and went out to the king's son.

Taking the stepsister as his bride, the prince mounted his horse
with her and rode off. But they had to pass by the grave and there,
on the hazel tree, sat two pigeons who cried:

> Turn and peep, turn and peep.
> There's blood within the shoe.
> The shoe it is too small for her.
> The true bride still waits for you.

Then the prince looked at her foot and saw how blood was trick-
ling from it. So, he turned his horse round and took the false bride
home again, saying she was not the right one.

Then it was the chance for the younger stepsister. She went into her room and got her toes safely into the shoe, but her heel was too large. So, her mother gave her a knife and said, "Cut a bit off your heel. When you are queen, you will have no more need to go about on foot." So, the maiden cut a piece of her heel off, forced her foot into the shoe, swallowed the pain, and went out to the king's son.

Taking her as his bride, he rode away with her. But when they passed by the hazel tree, the two pigeons cried out:

> Turn and peep, turn and peep.
> There's blood within the shoe.
> The shoe it is too small for her.
> The true bride still waits for you.

He looked down at her foot and saw how the blood was running out of her shoe and staining her white stockings quite red. Then he turned his horse around and took the false bride home again. "This also is not the right one," he told the parents. "Have you no other daughter?"

"No," said the father, "there is only the little kitchenmaid, a daughter my late wife left behind, but she cannot possibly be the one." The king's son said that may be the case but she was still to be brought to him. But the stepmother protested, "No, that cannot be. She is far too dirty and dusty to be seen in polite company." But the prince absolutely insisted on it, and Cinderella had to be called.

Cinderella first washed her hands and face until they were quite clean, and then she went and bowed before the king's son, who gave her the golden shoe. Seating herself on a stool, she took her foot out of the old wooden shoe and put on the golden shoe. It fit perfectly. And then when she stood up, the prince looked in her face and recognized she was the beautiful maiden he had danced with. "This is the true bride!" he cried.

The stepmother and her two daughters were horrified and grew pale with rage, but the prince took Cinderella up onto his horse and rode away with her. And as they passed the hazel tree, two white doves called out:

> Turn and peep, turn and peep.
> No blood is in the shoe.

The shoe is not too small for her.
The true bride finally rides with you.

When they had said that, the two birds came flying down and perched on Cinderella's shoulders, one on the right and the other on the left.

On the day of the wedding, the two stepsisters came to the ceremony, hoping to curry favor with Cinderella and share in her good fortune. When the bridal procession went to church, the eldest walked on the right side and the younger on the left, and the pigeons pecked out one eye from each of them. Afterwards, as they came back from the church, the elder was on the left and the younger on the right, and then the pigeons pecked out the other eye from each. And so, for their wickedness, they were punished with blindness for the rest of their days.

"Cinderella" and "Beauty and the Beast"

Perhaps the first signal of a link between the Grimms' "Ashenputtel" and Beaumont's "Beauty and the Beast" occurs when the father is about to go on a journey and asks his children what he should bring back for them. Cinderella's stepsisters ask for jewels and fine dresses, while Beauty's sisters solicit dresses, ribbons, and other finery. Cinderella and Beauty differ in asking only for a modest and natural gift: a branch from a tree and a rose.

The heroine's relations with her siblings are also remarkably similar. Cinderella and Beauty do all the housework and function as servants, while their siblings live pampered lives and go out of their way to torment the heroine. Both sets of sisters are also deceptive: Grimms' sisters acting as amateur podiatrists and butchering their feet to fool the prince, and Beauty's sisters feigning affection to delay her return to the Beast in the hope he will be angry and take revenge on her. And both sets of sisters are punished in ocular ways: Cinderella's sisters have their eyes pecked out, and Beauty's sisters are changed into statues that still possess the power of sight so that they may constantly behold her happiness.

Publishing their version of the Cinderella story several decades after Beaumont wrote, the Grimm Brothers may have collected an oral version of the folktale that had come to be influenced by

Beaumont's story. In any event, the shared elements suggest their deep similarity. In fact, the Grimms' Cinderella story may be seen as a cross-gender version of Beaumont's "Beauty and the Beast" — one featuring a hidden bride, the other a hidden groom. And in this way, Cinderella is something of a female Beast.

In telling similar stories, the two tales differ slightly in their cross-gender emphases. For example, both speak of the value of attachment to a parent and, at the same time, the eventual need to outgrow that dependence. But in "Beauty and the Beast" the emphasis falls upon the maiden's attachment to her father, while in "Ashenputtel" the focus is upon her connection with her mother.

As we have already seen, Beauty's special connection to her father is prominent in Beaumont's tale. While her sisters live a busy social life and go to parties, Beauty prefers to remain at home with her father; twice she turns down suitors, saying she prefers to remain with her father and care for him. Her affection is also evident, of course, in her offer to take her father's place at the Beast's castle and, once she is there, in her constantly consulting a magic mirror to get news about him since (more than anything else) she is most troubled by her forced separation from him. As the story unfolds, we are presented with a competition between the father and the Beast, and the question of exogamy arises: whether Beauty can ever separate from her father and transfer her affection to her companion. She eventually does. Given the chance to return home for a visit, Beauty flies to her father's side; but on that visit, she also realizes her feelings for the Beast and chooses him and returns.

Grimms' Cinderella is likewise attached to a parent but, in this case, to her mother. Though her mother is dead, Cinderella keeps her memory vitally alive by visiting the mother's grave three times a day and spending time there. In return for that attention, the tree that grows on the grave and the birds that inhabit it become maternal forces that incarnate the mother's promise to always watch over her daughter. And they do — providing Cinderella with dresses and shoes, helping her sort the lentils from the ashes, advising the Prince when he is overlooking her, and getting revenge upon the stepsisters. As embodiments of the mother, the tree and the birds are significant symbols; and in looking out for the girl's interests, they function in very much the same way the maternal fairy godmother does in the more well-known version of "Cinderella" by Perrault.

But just as Beauty must eventually outgrow her attachment to her father if she is ever to transfer her affection to the prince, Cinderella must separate from her mother if she is ever to do the same. Beauty undergoes a trial separation from her father when she goes to live at the Beast's, and she returns home once before choosing her partner. Cinderella makes three trial forays at separation when she goes to the ball, but she returns home each time before that denouement occurs.

Given the symbolic connection between her mother and the birds and the tree, it is significant that Cinderella retreats first to the pigeon-house (which is destroyed in the search for her) and then to the pear tree (which is chopped down, also in hopes of finding her). In symbolic terms, Cinderella experiments in partnering but retreats each time to her mother. But just as Beauty must sever her tie to her father to enter into a true relationship with the prince, the destruction of the pigeon-house and the pear tree suggest the gradual dissolution of Cinderella's ties to her mother which will eventually permit her nuptials with the prince.

But neither story ends there. In their conclusions, both tales suggest a third phase. Beginning with an extraordinary attachment to parent, both stories move to a dilemma where the maiden needs to choose between parent and partner. In the end, however, the need for that choice is mooted when the maiden gets her cake and eats it too, when she both gets a spouse and is reunited with her parent: Beauty's father attends her wedding and is transported with the happy couple to the prince's kingdom; at Cinderella's wedding, she not only gains a husband but her avian companions now perch on her shoulders.

As cross-gender versions of each other, then, Beaumont's "Beauty and the Beast" and the Grimms' "Ashenputtel" differ only in emphasizing which parent is important. A similar transposition occurs in the relegation of the other parent to a minor but contributory role. While Beauty's relations with her father are conspicuous, the fairy in Beaumont's tale has a minor role and serves in a maternal way by offering counsel in Beauty's dreams that leads to her maturation and wise decision. Likewise, while Cinderella's mother has the major role in the Grimms' tale, her father plays a minor part in her maturation, assisting her by symbolically severing her bond to her mother when he chops down the pigeon-house and the pear tree.

A similar shift in emphasis can be seen in the relationship between the maiden and the prince. "Cinderella" is often seen as a tale that presents a "bride test" since the question about who can wear the tiny shoe looms so large. But "Cinderella" also presents a "groom test": the question is whether the prince can separate the true bride from the false brides or, more specifically, the question is whether the prince can recognize his dancing partner and wife-to-be in her dejected and fallen state when she is not dressed in her finery. The prince, we should note, is slow to do so, but eventually he turns his gaze from the shoe to her face and recognizes the woman he fell in love with. In other words, looking beyond appearances and couture, he discovers the truth and the object of his love. Beauty does something similar when she looks beyond the Beast's appearance, discovering his virtues and accepting him.

This same shift of emphasis can be seen in what amounts to the transformation scene in both tales. In "Beauty and the Beast," the major change for Beauty is in the Beast's looks, as he changes into a handsome prince; incidentally, there is also a change of status since Beauty and her middle-class family now enjoy the perquisites of having married into the aristocracy. In "Cinderella," however, these major and minor keys are reversed. Apart from her washing her face, there is really no dramatic change in Cinderella's looks; what is made more significant is her change in status and her elevation from kitchenmaid to royal consort.

In these ways, then, "Beauty and the Beast" and "Ashenputtel" might be seen as cross-gender and transposed versions of each other. And in these ways, Cinderella might be recognized as a female version of the Beast in a remarkably similar story that tells not of a disguised groom, but of a disguised bride.

"EAST OF THE SUN, WEST OF THE MOON"

"East of the Sun, West of the Moon" is a tale that was collected by Peter Christen Asbjørnsen and Jørgen Moe in their Norske Folkeeventtyr *(Norwegian Folktales) which was published in several editions during the 1840s. My version of the story below is based on a translation of the tale in Andrew Lang's* The Blue Fairy Book *(1889).*

Once upon a time, there was a poor man who had many children and little to give them in the way of food or clothing. They were all pretty, but the prettiest of all was the youngest daughter.

One dark autumn evening—when it was raining heavily and blowing so hard that the walls of the cottage shook—the family was sitting together around the fireside, each of them busy with their own chore. Then someone rapped three times against the window. The father went outside to see who it was, and he saw a great big white bear standing there.

"Good-evening to you," said the White Bear.

"Good-evening," said the man.

"Will you give me your youngest daughter?" said the White Bear. "If you will, you shall be as rich as you are now poor."

The man had no objection to being rich but he thought, "I'd better ask my daughter about this." So, he went inside and told them that there was a great white bear outside who had promised to make them all rich if he might have the youngest daughter. But the maiden, herself, said no and would not hear of it. So, the man went out again and told the White Bear that he should come again next week to get his answer.

Then the father talked so much to his daughter about the wealth that they would have, and what a good thing it would be for herself, that at last she made up her mind to accept the Bear's proposal. She washed and made herself as presentable as possible. And then she mended her pitiful clothes and tied them into a bundle, because she really had very little else to take away with her.

In a week's time, the White Bear came to fetch her. Carrying her little bundle, she seated herself on his back and they departed. After they had gone a great ways, the White Bear asked her, "Are you afraid?"

"No, I am not," she replied.

134

"Keep a tight hold on my fur, then," he said, "and there will be no danger."

So, she rode for miles and miles until they came to a great mountain. When the White Bear knocked on the mountainside, a door opened and they went inside into a beautiful castle. There were many brilliantly lit rooms which shone with gold and silver, and a large banquet hall with a table covered by delicious foods. In fact, that does not begin to describe all the magnificent things that could be found there.

The White Bear gave her a silver bell and told her that when she needed anything, all she had to do was ring this bell and whatever she wanted would appear. So, after she had eaten and night was drawing near, she grew sleepy and thought she would like to go to bed. She rang the bell and suddenly found herself in a chamber where a bed stood, as pretty as anyone could wish. It had pillows of silk and curtains fringed with gold, and everything in the room was of gold or silver.

When she lay down and put out the light, a man came and lay down beside her. She didn't know it, but he was the White Bear who cast off his animal skin at night. In fact, she never saw her companion because he always came after she had put out the light and went away before daylight appeared.

All went happily for awhile, but then she began to be sad because she was alone all day. She missed her father and mother and brothers and sisters. Then the White Bear asked what troubled her, and she told him how dull and lonely it was all day in the mountain, and how she longed for the company of her parents and brothers and sisters.

"There might be a cure for that," said the White Bear, "if you would promise me never to talk with your mother alone, but only when others are in the room. She will take you by the hand," he warned, "and want to lead you into a room to talk. But you must never do that or you will bring great misery to both of us."

One Sunday, the White Bear came and said that the time had come to set out to see her father and mother. She sat on his back and they traveled a long, long ways until they came to a large and beautiful farmhouse. "This is where your parents live now," the White Bear explained. Then he added, "Do not forget what I said or you will do harm to both of us."

"No, indeed," she promised, "I won't forget." Then she entered her parents' home, and the White Bear turned around and went back.

Everyone was so happy to see her again that it seemed there would be no end to their rejoicing. And everyone told her how grateful they were because now, thanks to her, they had everything they wanted and everything was as good as it could be. And when they asked how she was getting along, she told them that all was well with her, too, and she had everything she wanted. But she didn't give them any further details.

After their midday meal, events unfolded just as the White Bear had predicted. The mother wanted to talk with her daughter alone and called her aside. But she remembered what the White Bear had said and wouldn't go. "What we have to say," she told her mother, "can be said in front of the others."

But at last her mother persuaded her, and they went apart. Then she told her mother the whole story: how every night a man came and lay down beside her when the lights were put out, how she never saw him because he always went away before it grew light in the morning, and how she was sad and lonely but believed she could be happy if she could only have during the day the company of the man who visited her at night. "Oh!" cried the mother in horror, "you must be sleeping with a troll! But I will teach you a way to see him. Take a bit of one of my candles and hide it away in your breast. When he is asleep, light the candle and have a look. But be sure not to let any candlewax fall upon him."

So, she took the candle and hid it in her breast, and when evening drew near the White Bear came to get her. When they had gone some ways, the White Bear asked her if everything had not happened just as he had predicted, and she admitted that it had. "Then, if you have done what your mother wished," said he, "you have brought great misery to both of us."

"No," she said, "I have not done anything at all."

When she reached the castle and went to bed, it was just as it was before: a man came and lay down beside her. Late at night, however, when she could hear that he was sleeping, she got up and lit her candle. Letting her light shine on him, she saw that he was the handsomest Prince that anyone had ever laid eyes on. Full of love, she felt she would die if she did not kiss him at once. But, stooping to kiss him, three drops of candlewax fell on his shirt and he awoke.

"Now you have done it," he said. "You have brought misery to both of us. My stepmother has bewitched me, so that I am a white bear by day and a man by night. If you could only have been patient for a year, not wanting to see me, then I would have been set free from the spell. But now all chances for our happiness are at an end, and I must leave you and go to my stepmother who lives in a castle which lies east of the sun and west of the moon. There I must live and marry a princess with a nose twelve feet long."

The maiden wept and lamented her hard fate, but he had to go. When she asked if she might accompany him, he explained that could not be. "Tell me the way, then," she said, "and I will follow you. Surely, I can be allowed to do that."

"Yes, you may do that," he replied, "but there is no way there. I am going east of the sun and west of the moon, and you could never get to that place."

When she awoke the next morning, both the Prince and the castle were gone. She was lying on a small green patch in the midst of a dark, thick wood and by her side lay her original bundle of mended clothes which she had first brought with her when she left her parents' home. Finally, when she had rubbed the sleep out of her eyes and wept until she was weary, she set out and walked for many, many long days.

At last, she came to a great mountain. Outside it an aged woman was sitting, playing with a golden apple. The girl asked her if she knew the way to the Prince who lived with his stepmother in the castle which lay east of the sun and west of the moon and who was to marry a Princess with a nose which was twelve feet long. "How do you happen to know about him?" inquired the old woman. "Maybe you are the one who ought to have him."

"Yes, indeed, I am," she said.

"So it is you, then?" said the old woman. "I know nothing about this Prince except that he dwells in a castle which is east of the sun and west of the moon. And you will be a long time getting there, if you ever get there at all. But you shall have the loan of my horse. You can ride on it to an old woman who is a neighbor of mine. Perhaps she can tell you about him. And when you get to my neighbor's house, strike the horse beneath the left ear and tell it to go home again. But, here, take this golden apple with you."

So, the girl seated herself on the horse and rode for a long, long ways, and at last came to the mountain where another aged woman was sitting outside using a golden comb. The girl asked her if she knew the way to the castle which lay east of the sun and west of the moon, but this old woman repeated what the first old woman had said, "I know nothing about it, but that it is east of the sun and west of the moon, and that you will be a long time getting there, if you ever get there at all. But you shall have the loan of my horse to go to an old woman who lives nearby. Perhaps she knows where the castle is. And when you get to my neighbor's house, strike the horse beneath the left ear and tell it to go home again." Then she gave her the gold comb, saying it might be of use to her.

So, the girl seated herself on the horse and rode a long way again, finally coming to a great mountain where sat another aged woman who was spinning at a golden spinning-wheel. Once again she asked if this woman knew the way to the Prince and where to find the castle which lay east of the sun and west of the moon. But the answer was the same. "Maybe it was you who should have had the Prince," said the old woman.

"Yes, indeed, I should have been the one," said the girl.

But this old crone knew the way no better than the others except that the place was east of the sun and west of the moon. "You will be a long time getting there, if ever you get there at all," she said, "but you may have the loan of my horse, and I think you had better ride to the East Wind and ask him. Perhaps he knows where the castle is and will blow you there. But when you get to him, strike the horse beneath the left ear and tell it to come home again." Then she gave the girl her golden spinning-wheel, saying, "Perhaps you may find a use for this."

The girl had to ride for a great many days before she got there. Then she asked the East Wind if he could tell her the way to the Prince who now lived east of the sun and west of the moon. "Well," said the East Wind, "I have heard about such a Prince and the castle, but I do not know the way there for I have never blown that far. But if you like, I will go with you to my brother the West

Wind. He may know something because he is much stronger than I am. Sit on my back and I will carry you there."

So, she seated herself on his back and they traveled with amazing speed. When they got where they were going, the East Wind went in and said that the girl he had brought was the one who ought to have had the Prince who lived in the castle that lay east of the sun and west of the moon, and now she was traveling to find him again. They would like to know if the West Wind knew anything about the castle's whereabouts. "No," said the West Wind, "I have never blown that far. But if you like, I will take the girl and go with her to the South Wind. He is much stronger than either of us and has roamed far and wide. Perhaps he can tell her what she wants to know."

So, she seated herself on the back of the West Wind, and they traveled far and fast. When they got where they were going, the West Wind asked the way to the castle that lay east of the sun and west of the moon, for this was the girl who ought to marry the Prince who lived there. "Oh, indeed!" replied the South Wind, "so, you are the one! Well," said he, "I have wandered about a great deal in my time and in all kinds of places, but I have never blown so far as that. If you like, however, I will go with you to my brother, the North Wind. He is the oldest and strongest of us all. If he does not know where this castle is, no one in the whole world will be able to tell you. Sit on my back and I will carry you there."

So, she seated herself on his back, and off they went at great speed. When they came near where the North Wind lived, they could tell he was wild and irritable because they felt cold gusts a long time before they got there. "What do you want?" he roared from afar, and they froze when they heard his voice.

"It is your brother," said the South Wind, "and this is the girl who should have had the Prince who lives in the castle which lies east of the sun and west of the moon. She wants to know if you have ever been there and can tell her the way, because her happiness lies in finding him again."

"Yes," said the North Wind, "I know where it is. I once blew an aspen leaf there, but I was so tired that for many days afterward I was not able to blow at all. However, if you really are desperate to get there and are not afraid to go with me, I will take you on my back and we will see if I can blow you that far."

139

"I must get there," she replied, "and I am willing to go by any possible way. I am not afraid and will not be, no matter how fast you go."

"Very well, then," said the North Wind. "But you must sleep here tonight because if we are ever to get there, we must have the whole day before us."

The next morning, the North Wind woke her and puffed himself up, and made himself so big and so strong that it was frightening to see. Then away they went, high up through the air, as if they could not stop until they reached the very end of the world. Down below there was such a storm! Forests and houses were knocked down. Ships on the sea were wrecked by the hundreds.

They tore on in this way, long and hard, but after much time had passed they were still above the sea. Gradually, the North Wind grew tired and more tired, until at last he was so weary that he was hardly able to blow any longer. He sank and sank, lower and lower, until at last he was so low that the waves dashed against the heels of the poor girl he was carrying. "Are you afraid?" asked the North Wind.

"I have no fear," the girl said, and it was true. But when they were not very far from land, the North Wind had just enough strength left to throw her on to the shore, and she landed just under the windows of the castle which lay east of the sun and west of the moon. But then the North Wind was so weary and worn out that he had to rest for several days before he could go home again.

Next morning she sat down beneath the walls of the castle to play with the golden apple, and the first person she saw was the maiden with the long nose who was to have the Prince. "How much do you want for that golden apple of yours, girl?" the Princess asked from an open window.

"It can't be bought for either money or gold," answered the girl.

"If it cannot be bought for either money or gold, what will buy it? Tell me what is you wish, no matter what it may be," said the Princess.

"Well, if I may pass the night with the Prince who is here, you can have it," said the girl.

"You may do that," said the Princess, because she had already hatched a plan. So, the Princess got the golden apple. But when the girl went up to the Prince's apartment that night, he was fast asleep because the Princess had conspired to keep him in a deep sleep. Then the poor girl called to him and wept, and she shook him and wept, but still she could not wake him. In the morning, as soon as day dawned, in came the Princess with the long nose and drove the poor girl out.

In the daytime, she sat down once more beneath the windows of the castle and began to play with her golden comb. Then all happened as it had happened before. The Princess asked her what she wanted for it, and she replied that it was not for sale for either money or gold but that if she could pass the night with the Prince, the Princess could have the comb. But when she went to the Prince's room that night, he was asleep again; and no matter what the weeping girl did, calling to him or shaking him, he still slept on. And when daylight came in the morning, the Princess with the long nose came and once more drove her away.

In the daytime, the girl seated herself once more under the castle windows and began to spin with her golden spinning-wheel, and the Princess with the long nose wanted to have that as well. When she asked for it, the girl said what she had said before: that it was not for sale for either money or gold but if she could pass the night with the Prince, the Princess should have the spinning-wheel.

"Yes," said the Princess, "I will gladly agree to that."

But in that place there were some godfearing folk who had been carried off and made into slaves to serve the trolls. They had been sitting in the chamber next to that of the Prince and had heard a woman coming there at night, weeping and calling to him. And they told the Prince about this.

So that evening, when the Princess came once more with what the Prince suspected was a sleeping potion, he pretended to drink it but threw it away behind him. So, when the girl went into his room this time, the Prince was awake and she told him all she had gone through to come there.

"Well, you have arrived just in time," said the Prince, "for I am to be married tomorrow. But I will not have the long-nosed Princess. You alone can save me. Here is my idea. Tomorrow I will say that I want to see what my bride can do and ask her to wash the shirt which has the three drops of candlewax on it. My stepmother will agree to this because she does not know that it is you who let them fall on it. No one can wash out those stains except for someone born of godfearing folk; it cannot be done by anyone from the godless pack of trolls. Then I will say that no one will ever be my bride but the woman who can do this, because I know that you can." Then there was great joy and gladness between them all that night.

The next day, when the wedding was to take place, the Prince said, "I must see what my bride is capable of."

"That you may do," said the stepmother.

"I have a fine shirt which I want to wear as my wedding shirt, but three drops of candlewax have stained it. I vow to marry no one but the woman who is able wash them out. If she cannot do that, she is not worth having."

Well, that is a very small matter, they thought. The Princess with the long nose began to wash as well as she could but the more she washed and rubbed, the larger the spots grew. "Bah! you can't wash at all," said the old troll-hag who was her mother, "give it to me." But she too had not had the shirt very long before it looked even worse; the more she washed it and rubbed it, the larger and blacker the spots became. So, the other trolls had to come and wash; but the more they did, the blacker and uglier the shirt became until it was as black as if it had been stuffed up a chimney.

"Oh," cried the Prince, "none of you is good for anything! Here, there is a beggar-girl sitting outside the window. I'll bet she can wash better than any of you! You, girl, come in here!" he called. So, in she came. "Can you wash this shirt clean?" he asked.

"I don't know," she said, "but I will try." And no sooner had she taken the shirt and dipped it in the water than it was white as snow, and even whiter than that.

"I will marry you," said the Prince.

Then the old troll-hag flew into such a rage that she burst, and the Princess with the long nose and all the little trolls must have burst too because they have never been heard from since. Then the Prince and his bride set free all the godfearing folk who were enslaved there and took away all the gold and silver they could carry. And they moved far away, far away from the castle which lay east of the sun and west of the moon.

"EAST OF THE SUN, WEST OF THE MOON" AND "BEAUTY AND THE BEAST"

"East of the Sun, West of the Moon" seems to combine "Beauty and the Beast" with the myth of "Cupid and Psyche." Not just a tale of male courtship, Asbjørnsen and Moe's tale adds a second half to Beaumont's story with its account of a maiden's quest to recover her lost partner, a lengthy section that resembles what happens in Apuleius's myth. Moreover, in both parts, problems of exogamy arise and they are seen in terms of complications involving a mother-in-law. What is interesting about "East of the Sun, West of the Moon" is its suggestion of gender equity: the problems of exogamy are presented from both a female and male perspective.

Marriage, especially an arranged marriage, may present a test of where one's loyalty lies, as well as the ability to transfer it. From within the family, the appearance of a would-be suitor may seem like the arrival of a wholly different Other, an Outsider, even someone from an entirely different species—in this case, a white bear. In the Norwegian tale, during their initial time together, the youngest daughter and the White Bear are only half committed to each other. Despite their nocturnal intimacy, they remain strangers to each other and apart during the day. Moreover, this half-hearted maiden terribly misses her family.

Aware that their relationship amounts to a trial of where her loyalty lies, the White Bear warns his partner that her mother will try to come between them. That, in fact, occurs when the mother persuades her daughter to light the candle and spy on her companion. Doing so, the maiden does her mother's bidding and is disloyal. This act of betrayal leads to their separation.

If "East of the Sun, West of the Moon" was following the pattern of "Beauty and the Beast," the maiden would have thrown the candle away and returned to the White Bear, thereby effecting his transformation. Beaumont's Beauty essentially does this when she turns her back on her conspiring sisters and departs from her father to be with the Beast, then Prince. But the Norwegian tale goes further in suggesting that the bride must not only be separated from her family, but the groom must also be separated from his.

In the second half of "East of the Sun, West of the Moon," the heroine must demonstrate a wholehearted commitment to their

143

relationship in the lengths she will go to reacquire him. And, indeed, she does: traveling to the ends of the earth and suffering extraordinary trials before she arrives at the castle which lies east of the sun and west of the moon. Now she must become the suitor, and she positions herself beneath an open window like a Juliet wooing her Romeo.

In the first half of the story, the White Bear has mother-in-law problems that frustrate his relationship with his partner. In the second half, the maiden faces mother-in-law problems and needs to separate her partner from his family. The Prince is under his stepmother's thumb, and this villain has chosen her own daughter to be his bride and keeps him imprisoned in her household. Eventually, the maiden effects a separation; and instead of the vision of unlikeness that open the tale (where girl meets bear), the story concludes with a shift of loyalties and a vision of "us" versus "them" when "godfearing folk" oppose and triumph over "the pack of trolls."

"East of the Sun, West of the Moon," then, presents a vision of gender equity and a balanced picture of the problems of exogamy, combining Beauty's difficulties in separating from her father with Cupid's complications in separating from his mother Venus. Just as the White Bear fetches the maiden from her father's house, she must fetch him from his stepmother's house. Just as he has come as a suitor, she must become a suitor. Finally, their half-heartedness must become a wholehearted commitment to each other in a situation where exogamous problems are resolved and where a comprehensive loyalty between them redefines who is "other."

"THE FROG KING"

Most people misremember "The Frog King." In their wish-constructed versions, the frog is changed into a handsome prince when the princess gives him a kiss; according to a contemporary bumper sticker, "You have to kiss a lot of toads, before you find your handsome prince." But in the version of the tale the Grimm Brothers used at the start of their 1812 edition of Kinder und Hausmärchen (Children's and Household Tales), *an altogether different action brings about the denouement and the end of the prince's enchantment. My version below is based on a translation by Edgar Taylor who in the 1820s was the first English translator of the Grimms' tales.*

In olden times when wishing still helped one, there lived a king whose daughters were all beautiful. But the youngest was so beautiful that the sun itself, which has seen so much, was astonished whenever it shone on her. Close by the king's castle lay a great dark forest and under an old tree in the forest, was a well. On hot days, the king's daughter went out into the forest and sat down by the side of the well. And when she was bored, she took a golden ball and threw it up high and caught it. This ball was her favorite plaything.

On one occasion, however, the golden ball did not fall back into the hand of the princess but fell on to the ground some ways from her. Then it rolled into the well and disappeared because the well was so deep that the bottom could not be seen. When this happened, she began to cry. And hearing this, someone said to her, "What troubles you, Princess? You cry so that even a stone would show pity."

She looked to where the voice came from and saw a frog stretching forth its big, ugly head from the water. "Ah, it is you, old water-splasher," she said. "I am weeping because my golden ball has been lost in the well."

"Don't be sad," answered the frog. "Maybe I can help you. But what will you give me if I bring your plaything up again?"

"Whatever you wish, dear frog," said she, "My clothes, my pearls and jewels, and even the golden crown which I am wearing."

The frog answered, "I do not care for your clothes, your pearls or jewels, nor for your golden crown, but if you will let me be your companion and sit by you at your table, and eat from your golden plate, and drink out of your cup, and sleep in your bed—if you will promise me this, I will go down below and bring your golden ball up again."

"Oh yes," said she, "I promise you all that if you will only bring my ball back again." But she thought to herself, "How silly this frog is. All he does is sit in the water all day with the other frogs and croak. He can be no companion to a human."

Once he received this promise, the frog put his head into the water and sank down. In a short while, he came swimming up again with the ball in his mouth and threw it on the grass. The king's daughter was delighted to see her pretty plaything once more, picked it up, and ran away. "Wait, wait," said the frog. "Take me with you. I can't run as fast as you can." But shout as he may, all his croaking did no good. She did not listen but ran home. And soon she forgot about the poor frog, who was forced to go back to his well again.

The next day when she had seated herself at the table with the king and all the courtiers, something came creeping—splish splash, splish splash—up the marble staircase, and when it had got to the top, it knocked at the door and cried, "Princess, young princess, open the door for me." She ran to see who was outside but when she opened the door, there sat the frog. Then she slammed the door in a great hurry, sat down to dinner again, and was quite frightened.

The king saw plainly that her heart was beating violently and said, "My child, what are you so afraid of? Is there a giant outside who wants to carry you away?"

"Ah, no," replied she. "It is no giant but a disgusting frog."

"What does a frog want with you?" asked the King.

"Well, dear father, yesterday as I was in the forest sitting by the well, playing with my golden ball, it fell into the water. And because I cried so, the frog brought it out again for me. And for doing this, I promised him he should be my companion. But I never thought he would be able to come out of the water. Now he is outside there and wants to come inside to be with me."

In the meantime, the frog knocked a second time and cried, "Princess, young princess, open the door for me. Do you not remember what you promised me yesterday down by the cool waters of the well. Princess, young princess, open the door for me."

Then the king said, "Since you have given your word, you must keep it. Go and let him in."

She went and opened the door, and the frog hopped in and followed her, step by step, to her chair. There he sat and cried, "Lift me up beside you." She delayed, until at last the king commanded her to do it. Once the frog was on the chair, he wanted to be on the table; and when he was on the table, he insisted, "Now, push your little golden plate nearer to me so that we may eat together." She did this, but it was easy to see that she did not do it willingly. The frog enjoyed what he ate, but she seemed to choke at almost every bite she took from their shared plate. After awhile he said, "I have eaten and am satisfied. Now I am tired. Carry me into your little room and make your little silken bed ready, and we will both lie down and go to sleep."

The king's daughter began to cry because she did not wish to carry the cold and slimy frog who now wanted to sleep in her clean little bed. But the king grew angry and said, "He who has helped you in your hour of need ought not afterwards to be despised."

So, with great reluctance, she took hold of the frog by two fingers, carried him upstairs, and put him in a corner. But when she was in bed, he crept to her and said, "I am tired. I want to sleep as well as you. Lift me up or I will tell your father."

At this, she grew terribly angry and grabbed him and threw him against the wall with all her might. "Now, will you be quiet, you horrible frog," she said. But when the frog fell to the floor, he was no longer a frog but a prince with kind and beautiful eyes. Then, with her father's consent, he became her dear companion and husband. And the prince told her how he had been enchanted by a wicked witch, how no one could have delivered him from the well but herself, and how tomorrow they would go together to his kingdom.

Then they went to sleep. And the next morning when the sun awoke them, a carriage came driving up with eight white horses which had white ostrich feathers on their heads and harnesses of golden chains. Behind them stood the young king's servant Faithful Henry. He had been so unhappy when his master was changed into a frog that he arranged to have three iron bands strapped around his heart, so that it wouldn't burst with grief and sadness.

The carriage was to take them to the prince's kingdom, and Faithful Henry helped the happy couple inside. Then he took his place at the back of the carriage and was full of joy because his prince had been delivered from the spell. And when they had driven a little ways, the prince heard a cracking sound behind him as if something had broken. So he turned round and cried, "Henry, the carriage is breaking."

"No, master, it is not the carriage. It is a band from around my heart, which was put there in my great pain when you were changed into a frog." Again and once again, while they were on their way, something cracked and each time the king's son thought the carriage was breaking. But it was only the bands which were springing from around the heart of Faithful Henry because his master was now free and happy.

"The Frog King" and "Beauty and the Beast"

Though they both tell stories of an Animal Groom, "Beauty and the Beast" and "The Frog King" are strikingly different. Both maidens are the youngest and most beautiful daughter, but Beaumont's Beauty is selfless and amiable while the Grimms' princess is self-centered and petulant. They also meet their Disguised Husband in different ways: Beauty by getting what she does not have (a rose) and the Princess by having returned to her what was originally hers (the golden ball).

The male leads are also different. While unattractive, the Beast is otherwise a gentleman and a model of decorum who does everything to make Beauty feel comfortable, who makes sure she has come to his castle out of her own free will, and who patiently awaits her decision. The clammy frog, on the other hand, is repulsive in every way and importunes the Princess at every chance, pressing her to comply and keep her hasty promise.

The banquet scenes in "Beauty and the Beast" are occasions for increased contact between the two characters, and in these Beauty becomes more familiar with her companion and feels a growing ease in his presence. The banquet scenes in "The Frog King" present the opposite picture. As the dreadful amphibian pushes closer and still closer—sitting next to her at the table, eating from her plate, and finally demanding that he share her bed—the Princess's squeamishness and disgust increases to a fever pitch.

The resolution of the two stories dramatically differs as well. Given her amiable nature and prompted by feelings of compassion and gratitude, Beaumont's Beauty accepts the Beast and he is transformed. The Grimms' Princess heads in the opposite direction. Like the bands around the heart of the Prince's servant Faithful Henry, she snaps. In a fit of passion rather than compassion, motived more by anger than by amiability, she forcibly rejects her suitor and throws the frog against the wall with all her might. This, too, results in the Animal Groom changing into a handsome prince.

Noticing how the same result occurs from entirely opposite causes, Maria Tatar has observed that a lesson might be learned here about the danger of drawing morals from fairy tales. In the case of these tales, what is the moral? That women should be agreeable or defiant? That happy endings are brought about by tenderness or by violence? Except for its insistence that promises should be kept, Tatar suggests, "The Frog King" may be a folktale that escaped the Grimm Brothers' usual censorious editing since it would be more customary of them to condemn untoward behavior like that of the Princess.[1]

But even in regard to keeping promises, "The Frog King" escapes easy moralizing. After all, the Princess's faithlessness stands out in stark contrast to the faithfulness of the Prince's servant Faithful Henry; more importantly, it is when she dramatically breaks her promise (to admit the frog to her bed), that she is rewarded. "Beauty and the Beast," it should be added, likewise evades easy moralizing about keeping promises. Beauty does fulfill her father's promise when she travels to the Beast's castle and takes her father's place; but when she returns home and succumbs to her sisters' devious pleadings, she breaks her promise to the Beast to stay no longer than a week. This brings him to the point of death, prompts her contrition and acceptance of him, and happily results in transformation. Both these stories, in other words, present the nightmare of contract law: broken promises are rewarded.

If there is an explanation for why the Princess's petulant act brings about such beneficent results, it may be that this act of disobedience is also a declaration of independence. We have already observed how "Beauty and the Beast" can be seen as the story of a woman who must dissolve her bonds with her father so that she may transfer her affection to someone outside the family. And Beauty does this when she chooses to return to the Beast's side. The Princess in "The Frog King" must also become her own person before the same is possible for her.

When her amphibian amigo appears at the door, the youngest daughter turns to her father for relief. This Daddy's Girl has to be told what to do, and he insists that she let her green guest in; and he is equally adamant that she keep her promise to let him eat from

---

1 Maria Tatar, *The Hard Facts of the Grimm's Fairy Tales* (Princeton, NJ: Princeton University Press, 1987) 174-75 and *Off With Their Heads! Fairytales and the Culture of Childhood* (Princeton, NJ: Princeton University Press, 1992) 154.

her plate and drink from her cup. And when the tiresome toad wishes to retire to her bed, her father once more obliges her to do what she has promised but is loath to do.

In her chambers, when she is less than compliant in taking the frog into her bed, he threatens to "tell her father." This is the very point at which she explodes, hurling the tattle-tale toad against the wall. But this moment of self-assertion, this act of disobedience, might also be seen as a declaration of independence; having broken with her father, she is ready for a partner, and the frog changes into a prince.[1]

Besides a move toward independence, "The Frog King" might also be seen as recounting the familiar phenomenon of gender antipathy. Ask young girls at a certain age what they think of boys, and it is interesting to note that they respond with disgust and repulsion: "Boys? Yuck. Cooties!" Ask boys of a certain age what they think of girls, and they will respond in the same way. But, *mirabile dictu*, give them a few more years and these same youngsters often find the opposite sex attractive. Both "The Frog King" and "Beauty and the Beast" might be seen as recounting this striking but also familiar change of attitudes.

In this regard, it is significant that the locus of transformation in "The Frog King" is the marriage bed; though this is not the case in Beaumont's version, the bed and passing the night there play an important part in many other versions of the Beauty-and-the-Beast story. Of course, the implications are sexual but the particular emphasis in Animal Groom stories falls even more on the first half of the word "heterosexuality"—upon "hetero," in its signification of "otherness." Animal Groom stories present a potential partner who is Wholly Other. And such stories embody, Tatar suggests,

---

1   If the greatness of the fairy tales lies in their prismatic ability to reflect many meanings, then "The Frog King" might be seen in an entirely different way as presenting the Prince's maturation rather than that of the Princess. The title of the tale directs us in this way, and the story may present his learning to become a gentleman. From this perspective, the Grimm tale is an account of a bad date. He acts like an animal with her. He is too forward and pushy. He is the kind of date who is "all hands"—or, in this case, legs. He does not back off at her resistances. Finally, when she forcibly throws him across the room, he is given the "no" that means "no" and learns that his animal and aggressive manner is not the way to be with a woman. So, he changes into a gentleman.

"the metaphorical wisdom of old wives on sexuality" — that "men are beasts."[1]

But "The Frog King" goes quite a ways beyond "Beauty and the Beast" in emphasizing the Animal Groom's repulsiveness. The Frog is clammy, slimy, icky, and disgusting; and the Princess is revolted by this nauseating creature and even reluctant to carry the loathsome amphibian with two fingers. Behind this, Bettelheim suggests, is a child's notion of sex once they come to learn about its physical processes.[2] For them, the sex act seems likewise filthy and disgusting, repulsive and unthinkable. It is hard for them to imagine that adults might find pleasure in something so nauseating and revolting. And, indeed, the transformation of these attitudes about sex is as remarkable as the transformation of a frog into a prince.

Other stories in the "Beauty and the Beast" tradition and akin to "The Frog King" work this situation out further in their own combinations of repulsion and the marriage bed. For example, in the Italian story "The Pig King" by Straparola, the enchanted Prince is otherwise human except for a porcine snout and the pleasure he takes in wallowing in the mud and dirtying everyone he comes into contact with. He must find a wife who does not mind being soiled and passing the night in his stinking and filthy bed. Fortunately, he finds such a partner, someone who relishes a good wallow, who welcomes the caresses of her foul-smelling companion, and who returns his affection. The next morning the Prince's mother finds the bride covered with mud from head to toe and entirely content.

Seen in the context of its story cousins, then, Beaumont's "Beauty and the Beast" takes on deeper and richer meanings. Like an accomplished jazz performer, Beaumont has played her own variations upon a well-known tune.

1   Tatar, *Hard Facts* 177.
2   Bettelheim 289-91.

SIX

ILLUSTRATIONS

IT IS DIFFICULT TO IMAGINE another story that addresses the most fundamental issues of illustration as does "Beauty and the Beast." Can there be another story that presents, in such a direct way, the elemental responses of aesthetic experience: the attractive and the repellent?

What, for example, does a woman named "Beauty" look like? Even in their abstractness, most fairy tale heroines (e.g., Little Red Riding Hood or Snow White) have names that suggest some specificity, but that is not the case with "Beauty." Moreover, the text provides virtually no clues or directions to an illustrator, except terms that circle back to the original concepts: Beauty is said to be especially "pretty" and "agreeable." For illustrators, then, the story remains incredibly "open" and picturing "Beauty" means moving from the Platonic Ideal to the particular. For the artist, such an endeavor is also something like a Rorschach test in reverse, a revelation of personality in one's pictorial choices.

And what does the Beast look like? Again, the text provides no clues or directions. Instead, the would-be illustrator is provided with synonyms that circle back to the concept of "beastliness" since he is described as "frightful," "horrid," "hideous," "ugly," and "monstrous." "Beastliness" certainly implies animal-likeness, but what kind of animal(s) and to what degree? And "beastliness" also implies repulsiveness but, again, in what way(s) and to what degree—if, as is the case, Beauty is eventually able to overlook this and befriend him?

Consider the Beast. If he is part animal and part human, how should that proportionality be represented? Like Shakespeare's Bottom, does the Beast only have a beastly head? Or like a satyr, is he a beast from the waist down? (And in the latter case, what is an illustrator to do about the randy nature of satyrs—viz. the furry genitals?) And what is he at the core: is he an animal-like human or an anthropomorphized animal? Moreover, what kind of animal? A bear, a lion, a walrus? Is he lupine, simian, feline, porcine? Or some unprecedented creature of tusks and trunk and tail?

For the most part, illustrators have answered these questions in three ways (see Figures 1-4). Nearly all have clothed the Beast, putting their wolves and lions and bears in the regalia of noblemen. Next, they have made the Beast bipedal, converting four-footed creatures into standing animals and seated brutes. Finally, the hybridity of the Beast is conveyed by setting and accoutrements; for example, in a frequently illustrated scene from the story, Beauty and the Beast are seen dining together in luxurious yet logistical circumstances: utensils laid out for Beauty on her side of the table, the Beast's claws or hooves resting on the other side, a pitcher and goblets between them.

From this point on, illustrators differ in the meanings they give to the story. While these choices are revealed to some extent in the way Beauty and other characters are portrayed, as Stephen Canham has suggested, the way the Beast is presented is often the best index to an illustrator's "take" on the tale.[1] So, the Beast has been, for example, grotesque, romantic, cute, silly, repugnant, horrific, and comic. Where a particular illustrator's Beast lies on the spectrum — say, between werewolf and teddy bear — often depends on whether "Beauty and the Beast" is seen primarily as a romantic story or as a children's story.

Eleanor Vere Boyle, for example, in *Beauty and the Beast: An Old Tale New-Told* (1875), presents a haunting, romantic story (Figures 5 and 6). Her walrus-like Beast is a marine creature so devoid of human features that he is striking in his complete "otherness." Her Beauty, on the other hand, is a familiar type: a Pre-Raphaelite maiden given to theatrical postures of hopelessness. Indeed, with its Italian setting and remarkable gorgeousness, Boyle's pictorial version seems theatrical: simultaneously operatic and Kafka-esque, gothic and dream-like.

Edmund Dulac — in Arthur Quiller-Couch's *The Sleeping Beauty and Other Tales* (1910) — also presents "Beauty and the Beast" as a romantic story but more along the lines of

---

1 Stephen Canham, "What Manner of Beast? Illustrations of 'Beauty and the Beast,'" *Image and Maker*, ed. Harold Darling and Peter Neumeyer (La Jolla, CA: Green Tiger Press, 1984) 14.

Scheherazade. Here the setting is Orientalized. Dulac's simian Beast and his stylized Beauty seem "Moorish" in the way Victorian popular theater and fiction conceived this style: exotic and languorous amour, the Sheik and the harem girl (Figure 7). When Beauty strikes a mannered pose with her guitar in one of Dulac's beautiful pictures (Figure 8), we almost hear those famous lines from Fitzgerald's translation of *The Rubaiyat of Omar Khayyám*: "A Jug of Wine, a Loaf of Bread—and Thou / Beside me singing in the Wilderness— / O, Wilderness were Paradise!"

These romantic and stylized versions of "Beauty and the Beast" differ considerably from those where the tale is deliberately presented as a children's story—when the tale is included, for example, in a collection of stories intended for the juvenile market. In these, Beauty is sometimes made quite young (perhaps to draw in the young reader) and (correspondingly) the Beast does not seem horrific or frightening at all.

For example, Gordon Browne's Beauty is an ambiguously miniature person (either a child pretending to be an adult or a child-like adult), while his Beast is a comic figure, a well-dressed wolf and lupine dandy (Figure 9). Nowhere as ambiguous, Jessie Wilcox Smith pictures Beauty as a young girl sharing tea with her pet, a beribboned monkey, a most inoffensive Beast (Figure 10). And Margaret Evans Price, while she presents her own Beauty as a slightly older Gibson Girl, likewise offers a Beast that is neither repulsive nor scary, but another pet—in this case, a cuddly lion (Figure 11).

Whether imagined as a romantic story or as a tale intended for children, "Beauty and the Beast" has been a favorite subject for illustrators and an opportunity for them to present their personal visions of the pleasing and ideal (on the one hand) and the monstrous and repellent (on the other). There have been dozens and dozens of illustrated versions of the tale. Among these, if one were to choose, two versions show conspicuous genius.

WALTER CRANE

Walter Crane's series of "Toy Books" were highly colored, large-format picture books published in London by Routledge and Sons in the late 1800s. They sold for a shilling, and each book took up a particular fairy tale. Crane, by means of wood engravings, supplied colored illustrations for these books. His "Beauty and the Beast" appeared in 1875 and is a work of considerable cleverness, full of wit and *double entendres*.

Of all Crane's illustrations for the story, his central picture (a double-page spread of Beauty and the Beast on a divan) is the most significant and merits extended consideration (Figure 12). The decor reveals the setting: the Empire furniture and the neo-classical touches indicate these events are unfolding in the time of Beaumont, in eighteenth-century France. In fact, in another picture, Versailles can be seen in the background (Figure 13).

Beauty is presented as a court lady, with a long dress and gloves and a partially opened fan. Her ribboned hair is arranged in a neo-classical manner. Indeed, neo-classical references appear in the wallpaper's Cupid (*vide* Apuleius's "Cupid and Psyche") and in another picture with its statue of Neptune, another animal/human (Figure 13).

The Beast is a hairy boar dressed like a country squire. With frilled cuffs, shirt front, monocle, hat, and boots, he is the picture of the chevalier. But his cloven hooves suggest there is something dia-bolical about the gentleman. This upright swine, this seated pig, this porcine aristocrat at tea time—is, altogether, the oxymoronic Beast.

In this busy illustration, Crane also makes numerous references to animals. The corners of the divan feature lions' heads, and lions' claws appear where the divan meets the floor. The table between Beauty and her gentleman caller rests on bird-like creatures. At their feet lies a leopard skin.

What Beauty's role should be in this animal kingdom is suggest-ed by the frieze that decorates the harpsichord at the left. There we see how "music soothes the savage beast." Behind Beauty, then, is a stringed instrument. And behind that is stationed a small piece of furniture with a pattern that echoes the lyre seen on the frieze. On top of the harpsichord, holding up a book, is a music stand that also echoes the frieze.

But there is still more to this picture which reveals, ultimately, the sexual meaning that Crane has given to the story. In an impres-sive essay on Crane's work, Paola Pallottino points out that it is important to notice where the gaze of each of the characters is directed: that is, upon the other's genitals. Moreover, Pallottino observes:

> The ploy of hiding the sexual organs in order to give them immediate emphasis is used.... Here the Beast draws attention to his sex with his hat, which he holds fast between his legs, while attention is drawn to Beauty's by the lace cuff of one of her sleeves, dangling across her knee. Going one step further, the radials of Beauty's raised fan converge on the center of her desire, while the Beast's mandolin, resting on the ground, is exactly placed to catch the monster's piercing gaze as it passes through the maiden's lap.

Besides this crossfire of glances, Pallottino also notices the "event" of the picture and its counter-clockwise motion:

> The Beast's leaden silence is compromised by the placing of his rigid "paw" along the headboard of the divan sufficient to imply an act of aggression, while Beauty strikes an anticipatory pose, her legs outstretched down to the footrest, seemingly readying herself. The composition of the two moves in a circular direction, centered on the teacups.[1]

The eventual posture the two characters might assume, *vis à vis* the divan, is implied.

Once Crane's sexual "spin" on the story is recognized, that understanding makes sense of other pictures in his book which might otherwise seem ambiguous or innocent. For example, Crane's concluding illustration (Figure 15) shows the Beast near death and Beauty consoling him. But there is something puzzling about Beauty's posture: while one leg and foot are visible, it is unclear where Beauty's other leg is located. Once Crane's sexual rendering of the divan picture is acknowledged, it seems more plausible to assert she may be on top of the Beast rather than alongside him. Then, too, it seems more plausible to suggest that the Beast's rigidity (his thrown-back head and thrust-up snout)

---

1 Paola Pallottino, "Beauty's Beast," *Merveilles et Contes*, 3,1 (May 1989): 62–63, 66.

may be the result of something more than the early stages of *rigor mortis*. Finally, it seems more plausible to assert, as Pallottino does, that in the background the Beast's servants (which Crane portrays as monkeys) seem to have come upon the two *in flagrante*: "the raised torches reveal their expression of surprise, as if they caught the couple in an explicit sexual act."[1]

To be sure, Crane has largely left matters ambiguous because this provides him with the perfect defense of being able to claim himself innocent and to accuse the reader of finding sexual innuendo of their own making. Still, when the illustrations are understood in their depths, when they are taken altogether, a sexual reading of these pictures does not seem a stretch. Indeed, such an understanding explains numerous, otherwise idle objects: why, for example, the Beast's sword has a prominent place not alongside his legs but between his legs in so many pictures (cf. Figures 12 and 13) and why (in terms of gender parity) clamshells, flowers, and fruits are used so frequently in decorations (cf. Figures 12-15).

After the scene on the divan, Crane next shows a resplendent and blushing Beauty in a triumphant procession with her monkey pages (Figure 14). Something clearly has happened, but what? One answer is given in the mural behind her where Eve has consorted with the serpent. Another answer is suggested by her now opened fan. Still another answer is given by the monkey page who seems to be exchanging a knowing look with the reader, nearly winking. Given the monkeyshines of his own pictures, Crane seems to be doing the same.

MERCER MAYER

Among recent illustrated versions of the tale, Marianna and Mercer Mayer's picture book *Beauty and the Beast* (1978) is strikingly rich and complex. Marianna Mayer has "retold" the story, largely making use of and modifying Villeneuve's version with its multiple dream sequences. But she has also added two items, both of which were subsequently borrowed by Disney Studios when they came to make their film. The first is that the Beast's great problem is his uncontrollable anger. The other is an explanation of how and why

---

1 Pallottino 66.

the prince was changed into a beast: "One day an old hag came begging at my palace gate. I showed her no pity, she was so ugly. The sight of her did not move me and I sent her away without food or money. As she left, she warned that I would spend the rest of my life wandering in my palace without a friend till someone could find beauty in me."[1]

By means of his pictures, Mercer Mayer has interpreted "Beauty and the Beast" as a story about "seeing." In a number of illustrations, there is an abrupt distinction between foreground and background, and this shortening of distances calls attention to our customary way of seeing and understanding perspective. For example, in one scene Beauty's superficial sisters are so dramatically foregrounded as to be "in the face" of the viewer, while behind them the picture is so oddly proportioned that the flat sense of perspective recalls medieval woodcuts or works in the American Primitive tradition (Figure 16). On the other hand, many pictures feature multiple arches, recession, and endless vistas which create a powerful impression of visual depth and which seem to convey the story's notion that we must see beyond the surface of things (cf. Figure 17).

For inspiration for his pictures, Mercer Mayer has drawn to a considerable extent on Jean Cocteau's film *La Belle et la Bête*.[2] On his part, Cocteau explained that he modeled scenes featuring the merchant and his family on the work of Vermeer, and other scenes featuring the Beast and his castle on illustrations of fairy tales by Gustave Doré.[3] Mayer likewise distinguishes between the two locales. In those scenes associated with "reality" (and the home life of the merchant and his family), Mayer uses brown tones and a style and setting that might be described as Flemish and medieval. In scenes associated with "fantasy" (the Beast and his castle), Mayer uses blues and a style and setting that might be described as art nouveau and Oriental.

1   Marianna Mayer, *Beauty and the Beast,* illus. Mercer Mayer (New York: Four Winds Press, 1978) unpaged.
2   However, in his very first picture (of the merchant and his family lamenting the loss of his fortune), Mayer echoes Durer's engraving "St. Jerome" — notably, a saint conspicuously associated with a lion.
3   Jean Cocteau, *Beauty and the Beast: Diary of a Film,* trans. Ronald Duncan (New York: Dover Publications, 1972) 7.

This "Orientalism" is not only conveyed in the luxurious accoutrements of the Beast's surroundings, but in Mayer's frequent use of
Egyptian motifs. His Beauty not only sports a scarab at times, but
statues of Egyptian mythological figures appear throughout: Ba (the
bird), Anubis (the jackal), Isis (the cow), et al. The appearance of
these quasi-animal deities seems connected to the fact that Mayer's
Beast is a magi or magician, but their anthropomorphic nature—
like the Sphinx, half human and half animal—is also intimately
connected to issues of the story.

Besides mythological creatures, real animals appear throughout
the illustrations; among them are barnyard animals, a rat, numerous
horses (but especially a black horse which, or who, serves as a messenger for the Beast), and a red bird (with whom Beauty identifies
since, at the Beast's castle, she too is "a bird in a gilded cage"). And
just as the Egyptian deities present figures that are "liminal" (in the
way the border between animal and human is blurred), the bound-
aries between the inanimate and the animate are made fuzzy by the
appearance of so many animals in the Beast's furnishings—in, for
example, candelabra shaped like entwining snakes, a bed board
carved with creatures of various kinds, and the proscenium arch of
the Beast's theater which looks like a lion with a gaping mouth.

Besides reappearing animals, Mayer uses roses as a repeating
motif. After Beauty makes her request for a rose in the story, they
begin to lightly appear in the pictures: as decorations in the curtains, for example, or on the bushes just inside the Beast's castle
grounds. Once the merchant plucks the fateful rose in the garden
and the Beast confronts him, these flowers appear more obviously,
more frequently, and more dramatically. In this picture (Figure 18),
it is interesting to note that both red and white roses appear; in
subsequent pictures, Beauty will be associated with red roses and
the Beast with white ones.

At the dinner scene where Beauty and the Beast meet, roses are
everywhere. Red and white flowers can be seen on the table, but
the rose motif can also be detected in the design of the tablecloth,
the pitcher, the chair upholstery, and elsewhere (Figure 19). Indeed,
the ubiquitous flower continues to appear in subsequent illustrations right up to the symbolic picture where the angry Beast is
seen in a demanding posture while Beauty weeps. In that picture,
Mayer seems to lightly suggest the erotic nature of what is being

demanded of Beauty by a cut rose floating in a glass of water and by the nearby cut fruit (Figure 20).

Before the Beast can get what he wishes, of course, the two of them must grow to know each other and Beauty must fall in love. Subsequent pictures, consequently, show Beauty's red roses and the Beast's white roses growing together. Near the end, after the Beast's transformation into a prince, roses are rampant and in full bloom. Moreover, to suggest the progress of the story, this scene now includes flowers of a hybrid color—pink roses.

By means of his white and red and (eventually) pink roses, Mayer conveys change in the story. That same sense of progression is conveyed in the stationing of the Beast *vis à vis* Beauty. At the beginning he is often seen towering over her, then (in a significant illustration where Beauty looks into a mirror) they see eye-to-eye, and finally (before his transformation) the Beast's head lies cradled against her breast (Figure 22). But this sense of evolution is conveyed in still another manner in the way Mayer makes use of eyes.

Until Beauty's change of heart, no one makes eye contact in this book: eyes are always averted or downcast; the sisters cast sideways glances at each other; the merchant's eyes roll up when the Beast approaches him from behind; and, at her first meeting with the Beast, Beauty looks askance. The change comes in an important picture where Beauty looks in a mirror. At this moment, she makes eye contact and looks directly at the Beast's image reflected there (Figure 21).

This picture is also significant in that it shows the Beast crying. The text makes no mention of this, but Mayer pictures the Beast with tears running from his eyes. Here, Mayer may have taken a page from Hans Christian Andersen's "The Little Mermaid"—a story featuring another half-human, half-animal whose "humanity" is shown at the end of the tale by her shedding tears. In a similar way, Mayer "humanizes" his Beast for his Beauty.

But there is another interesting thing about this picture. Not only does the text not mention that the Beast is weeping, it also does not mention the Beast appearing in the mirror at all. Albeit, this is a magic mirror; still, when Beauty looks in the mirror, we would customarily expect her to see herself. Instead, she sees the Beast. There is only one way both statements can be true and that is that the Beast is a reflection of her, a part of her.

Figure 1. Anonymous, Old Fairy Tales, no date.

Figure 2. Anonymous, *The Ideal Fairy Tales*, 1897.
Figure 3 (facing page). Anonymous, *The Favourite Book of Nursery Tales*, 1893.

Figure 4. H.J. Ford, *The Blue Fairy Book*, 1889.

Figure 5. Eleanor Vere Boyle, *Beauty and the Beast: Old Tale New Told*, 1875.

Figure 6. Eleanor Vere Boyle, *Beauty and the Beast: Old Tale New Told*, 1875.

Figure 7. Edmund Dulac, *Sleeping Beauty and Other Fairy Tales*, 1910.

Figure 8. Edmund Dulac, *Sleeping Beauty and Other Fairy Tales*, 1910.

Figure 9. Gordon Brown, *The Queen of Hearts and Other Plays*, 1919.

Figure 10. Jessie Wilcox, *The Now-A-Days Fairy Book*, 1911.

Figure 11. Margaret Evans Price, *Once Upon A Time*, 1921.

Figure 12. Walter Crane, *Beauty and the Beast*, 1875.

Figure 13. Walter Crane, *Beauty and the Beast*, 1875.

Figure 14. Walter Crane, *Beauty and the Beast*, 1875.

Figure 15. Walter Crane, *Beauty and the Beast*, 1875.

Figure 16. Mercer Mayer, *Beauty and the Beast*, 1978.

Figure 17. Mercer Mayer, *Beauty and the Beast*, 1978.

Figure 18. Mercer Mayer, *Beauty and the Beast*, 1978.

Figure 19. Mercer Mayer, *Beauty and the Beast*, 1978.

Figure 20. Mercer Mayer, *Beauty and the Beast*, 1978.

Figure 21. Mercer Mayer, *Beauty and the Beast*, 1978.

Figure 22. Mercer Mayer, *Beauty and the Beast*, 1978.

Figure 23. Mercer Mayer, *Beauty and the Beast*, 1978.

Illustration is also interpretation, and Mayer's picture (where Beauty looks in the mirror and instead sees the Beast) suggests that the meaning Mayer finds in the story is similar to that of Jungian critics who argue that the Beast is really a part of Beauty's personality, a part that she has been rejecting but needs to accept. That understanding of the tale is even more strongly reinforced by one of Mayer's concluding pictures where, after the Beast has been transformed, Beauty and her Prince look lovingly into each others' eyes. What is striking about the picture is the strong resemblance between Beauty and her Prince (Figure 23). In fact, they would seem to be twins.

At a fundamental level, then, and as its title suggests, "Beauty and the Beast" is a story about "looks," good looks and their opposite. In his variations upon perspective, in the way he invites readers to hunt for roses in his decorations, in his picturing of how averted eyes eventually make contact, Mayer also makes the tale into a story about "looking." But the conclusion even goes a bit further in a Jungian direction. This story, which features an utterable Otherness between two characters, ends with them as lookalikes.

SEVEN

CONTEMPORARY VERSIONS

ONE MEASURE OF THE POWER and endurance of "Beauty and the Beast" is its omnipresence. Short stories, novels, illustrated books, plays, parodies, even a rap rendition—incarnations of the story seem to have appeared in every genre. Indeed, a search for "Beauty and the Beast" at internet bookstores produces more than three hundred titles.

The story's widespread appeal is also evident in its multiple audiences. Children, of course, have always been especially addressed in versions as old as Beaumont's classic tale of the eighteenth century and as recent as Disney's film. Given the story's concerns, it will not be surprising to learn that it has also been pitched to adolescents in, for example, Robin McKinley's remarkable young-adult novel *Beauty* (1974) and in her later work *Rose Daughter* (1997) in which Beauty is a tomboy concerned about her looks and uneasy about the idea of romance.[1] And adults have also been targeted in other variations of the story, including Susan Wilson's novel *Beauty* (1996) in which, as the blurb on the back cover suggests, "Beauty and the Beast" is re-imagined as something like a Harlequin romance:

> When Alexandra Miller takes off for a remote spot in New Hampshire to paint Leland Compton's portrait, nothing has prepared her for what's in store.... Lee himself is hideously disfigured by a rare genetic disease. But in their long hours together deep in the wintry woods, Alix discovers that beneath Lee's disturbing exterior lies a true prince. Gradually, she realizes that she loves him.[2]

---

1 Robin McKinley, *Beauty: A Retelling of the Story of Beauty and the Beast* (New York: HarperCollins, 1993) and *Rose Daughter* (New York: William Morrow, 1997).
2 Susan Wilson, *Beauty* (New York: Simon and Schuster, 1997).

Immensely attractive and infinitely adaptable, "Beauty and the Beast" seems to be, to borrow from Joseph Campbell, a Tale with a Thousand Faces. Among contemporary incarnations, however, two stand out.

ANGELA CARTER'S "THE TIGER'S BRIDE"

Known for her quirky style, Angela Carter (1940-92) was widely praised for her short stories. In The Bloody Chamber *(1979), she played extravagant variations on well-known fairy tales ("Bluebeard," "Snow White," and others). Two or three of the stories were later used as the basis of a script she wrote with Neil Jordan and that became the film "The Company of Wolves."*

Besides writing novels, Carter also translated Perrault's fairy tales and assembled collections of feminist fairy tales. About that feminism, others have observed that Carter wished to recover an earthy, almost pagan sexuality and female power that had been buried by later Christianity and patriarchal culture.

My father lost me to The Beast at cards.

There's a special madness strikes travellers from the North when they reach the lovely land where the lemon trees grow. We come from countries of cold weather; at home, we are at war with nature but here, ah! you think you've come to the blessed plot where the lion lies down with the lamb. Everything flowers; no harsh wind stirs the voluptuous air. The sun spills fruit for you. And the deathly, sensual lethargy of the sweet South infects the starved brain; it gasps: "Luxury! more luxury!" But then the snow comes, you cannot escape it, it followed us from Russia as if it ran behind our carriage, and in this dark, bitter city has caught up with us at last, flocking against the windowpanes to mock my father's expectations of perpetual pleasure as the veins in his forehead stand out and throb, his hands shake as he deals the Devil's picture books.

The candles dropped hot, acrid gouts of wax on my bare shoulders. I watched with the furious cynicism peculiar to women whom circumstances force mutely to witness folly, while my father, fired in his desperation by more and yet more draughts of the firewater they call "grappa," rids himself of the last scraps of my inheritance. When we left Russia, we owned black earth, blue forest with bear and wild boar, serfs, cornfields, farmyards, my beloved horses, white nights of cool summer, the fireworks of the northern lights. What a burden all those possessions must have been to him, because he laughs as if with glee as he beggars himself, he is in such a passion to donate all to The Beast.

Everyone who comes to this city must play a hand with the *grande seigneur,* few come. They did not warn us at Milan, or, if they did, we did not understand them—my limping Italian, the bewildering dialect of the region. Indeed, I myself spoke up in favour of this remote, provincial place, out of fashion two hundred years, because, oh irony, it boasted no casino. I did not know that the price of a stay in its Decembral solitude was a game with Milord.

The hour was late. The chill damp of this place creeps into the stones, into your bones, into the spongy pith of the lungs; it insinuated itself with a shiver into our parlour, where Milord came to play in the privacy essential to him. Who could refuse the invitation his valet brought to our lodging? Not my profligate father, certainly; the mirror above the table gave me back his frenzy, my impassivity, the withering candles, the emptying bottles, the coloured tide of the cards as they rose and fell, the still mask that concealed all the features of The Beast but for the yellow eyes that strayed, now and then, from his unfurled hand towards myself.

"*La Bestia!*" said our landlady, gingerly fingering an envelope with his huge crest of a tiger rampant on it, something of fear, something of wonder in her face. And I could not ask her why they called the master of the place, *La Bestia*—was it to do with the heraldic signature—because her tongue was so thickened by the phlegmy, bronchitic speech of the region I scarcely managed to make out a thing she said except, when she saw me: "*Che bella!*"

Since I could toddle, always the pretty one, with my glossy, nut-brown curls, my rosy cheeks. And born on Christmas Day—her "Christmas rose," my English nurse called me. The peasants said: "The living image of her mother," crossing themselves out of respect for the dead. My mother did not blossom long; bartered for her dowry to such a feckless sprig of the Russian nobility that she soon died of his gaming, his whoring, his agonizing repentances. And The Beast gave me the rose from his own impeccable if outmoded buttonhole when he arrived, the valet brushing the snow off his black cloak. This white rose, unnatural, out of season, that now my nervous fingers ripped, petal by petal, apart as my father magnificently concluded the career he had made of catastrophe.

This is a melancholy, introspective region; a sunless, featureless landscape, the sullen river sweating fog, the shorn, hunkering willows. And a cruel city; the sombre piazza, a place uniquely suited to public executions, under the beetling shadow of that malign barn of a church. They used to hang condemned men in cages from the city walls; unkindness comes naturally to them, their eyes are set so close together, they have thin lips. Poor food, pasta soaked in oil, boiled beef with sauce of bitter herbs. A funereal hush about the place, the inhabitants huddled up against the cold so you can hardly see their faces. And they lie to you and cheat you, innkeepers, coachmen, everybody. God, how they fleeced us.

The treacherous South, where you think there is no winter but forget you take it with you.

My senses were increasingly troubled by the fuddling perfume of Milord, far too potent a reek of purplish civet at such close quarters in so small a room. He must bathe himself in scent, soak his shirts and underlinen in it; what can he smell of, that needs so much camouflage?

I never saw a man so big look so two-dimensional, in spite of the quaint elegance of The Beast, in the old-fashioned tailcoat that might, from its looks, have been bought in those distant years before he imposed seclusion on himself; he does not feel he need keep up with the times. There is a crude clumsiness about his outlines, that are on the ungainly, giant side, and he has an odd air of self-imposed restraint, as if fighting a battle with himself to remain upright when he would far rather drop down on all fours. He throws our human aspirations to the godlike sadly awry, poor fellow; only from a distance would you think The Beast not much different from any other man, although he wears a mask with a man's face painted most beautifully on it. Oh, yes, a beautiful face, but one with too much formal symmetry of feature to be entirely human: one profile of his mask is the mirror image of the other, too perfect, uncanny. He wears a wig, too, false hair tied at the nape with a bow, a wig of the kind you see in old-fashioned portraits. A chaste silk stock stuck with a pearl hides his throat. And gloves of blond kid that are yet so huge and clumsy they do not seem to cover hands.

He is a carnival figure made of papier-mâché and crêpe hair; and yet he has the Devil's knack at cards.

His masked voice echoes as from a great distance as he stoops over his hand and he has such a growling impediment in his speech that only his valet, who understands him, can interpret for him, as if his master were the clumsy doll and he the ventriloquist.

The wick slumped in the eroded wax, the candles guttered. By the time my rose had lost all its petals, my father, too, was left with nothing.

"Except the girl."

Gambling is a sickness. My father said he loved me yet he staked his daughter on a hand of cards. He fanned them out; in the mirror, I saw wild hope light up his eyes. His collar was unfastened, his rumpled hair stood up on end, he had the anguish of a man in the last stages of debauchery. The draughts came out of the old walls and bit me, I was colder than I'd ever been in Russia, when nights are coldest there.

A queen, a king, an ace. I saw them in the mirror. Oh, I know he thought he could not lose me; besides, back with me would come all he had lost, the unravelled fortunes of our family at one blow restored. And would he not win, as well, The Beast's hereditary palazzo outside the city; his immense revenues; his lands around the river; his rents, his treasure chest, his Mantegnas, his Giulio Romanos, his Cellini salt-cellars, his titles ... the very city itself.

You must not think my father valued me at less than a king's ransom; but at *no more* than a king's ransom.

It was cold as hell in the parlour. And it seemed to me, child of the severe North, that it was not my flesh but, truly, my father's soul that was in peril.

My father, of course, believed in miracles; what gambler does not? In pursuit of just such a miracle as this, had we not travelled from the land of bears and shooting stars?

So we teetered on the brink.

The Beast bayed; laid down all three remaining aces.

The indifferent servants now glided smoothly forward as on wheels to douse the candles one by one. To look at them you would think that nothing of any moment had occurred. They yawned a little resentfully; it was almost morning. We had kept them out of bed. The Beast's man brought his cloak. My father sat amongst these preparations for departure, staring on at the betrayal of his cards upon the table.

The Beast's man informed me crisply that he, the valet, would call for me and my bags tomorrow, at ten, and conduct me forthwith to The Beast's palazzo. Capisco? So shocked was I that I scarcely did capisco; he repeated my orders patiently, he was a strange, thin, quick little man who walked with an irregular jolting rhythm upon splayed feet in curious, wedge-shaped shoes.

Where my father had been red as fire, now he was white as the snow that caked the windowpane. His eyes swam; soon he would cry.

"'Like the base Indian,'" he said, he loved rhetoric. "'One whose hand, /Like the base Indian, threw a pearl away/Richer than all his tribe ... ' I have lost my pearl, my pearl beyond price."

At that, The Beast made a sudden, dreadful noise, halfway between a growl and a roar; the candles flared. The quick valet, the prim hypocrite, interpreted unblinkingly: "My master says: If you are so careless of your treasures, you should expect them to be taken from you."

He gave us the bow and smile his master could not offer us and they departed.

I watched the snow until, just before dawn, it stopped falling; a hard frost settled, next morning there was a light like iron.

The Beast's carriage, of an elegant if antique design, was black as a hearse and it was drawn by a dashing black gelding who blew smoke from his nostrils and stamped upon the packed snow with enough sprightly appearance of life to give me some hope that not all the world was locked in ice, as I was. I had always held a little towards Gulliver's opinion, that horses are better than we are, and, that day, I would have been glad to depart with him to the kingdom of horses, if I'd been given the chance.

The valet sat up on the box in a natty black and gold livery, clasping, of all things, a bunch of his master's damned white roses as if a gift of flowers would reconcile a woman to any humiliation. He sprang down with preternatural agility to place them ceremoniously in my reluctant hand. My tear-beslobbered father wants a rose to show that I forgive him. When I break off a stem, I prick my finger and so he gets his rose all smeared with blood.

167

The valet crouched at my feet to tuck the rugs about me with a strange kind of unflattering obsequiousness yet he forgot his station sufficiently to scratch busily beneath his white periwig with an over-supple index finger as he offered me what my old nurse would have called an "oldfashioned look," ironic, sly, a smidgen of disdain in it. And pity? No pity. His eyes were moist and brown, his face seamed with the innocent cunning of an ancient baby. He had an irritating habit of chattering to himself under his breath all the time as he packed up his master's winnings. I drew the curtains to conceal the sight of my father's farewell; my spite was sharp as broken glass.

Lost to The Beast! And what, I wondered, might be the exact nature of his "beastliness"? My English nurse once told me about a tiger-man she saw in London, when she was a little girl, to scare me into good behaviour, for I was a wild wee thing and she could not tame me into submission with a frown or the bribe of a spoonful of jam. If you don't stop plaguing the nursemaids, my beauty, the tiger-man will come and take you away. They'd brought him from Sumatra, in the Indies, she said, his hinder parts were all hairy and only from the head downwards did he resemble a man.

And yet The Beast goes always masked; it cannot be his face that looks like mine.

But the tiger-man, in spite of his hairiness, could take a glass of ale in his hand like a good Christian and drink it down. Had she not seen him do so, at the sign of The George, by the steps of Upper Moor Fields when she was just as high as me and lisped and toddled, too. Then she would sigh for London, across the North Sea of the lapse of years. But, if this young lady was not a good little girl and did not eat her boiled beetroot, then the tiger-man would put on his big black travelling cloak lined with fur, just like your daddy's, and hire the Erl-King's galloper of wind and ride through the night straight to the nursery and—

Yes, my beauty! GOBBLE YOU UP!

How I'd squeal in delighted terror, half believing her, half knowing that she teased me. And there were things I knew that I must not tell her. In our lost farmyard, where the giggling nursemaids initiated me into the mysteries of what the bull did to the cows, I heard about the waggoner's daughter. Hush, hush, don't let on to your nursie we said so; the waggoner's lass, hare-lipped, squint-eyed, ugly as sin, who would have taken her? Yet, to her shame, her belly swelled amid the cruel mockery of the ostlers and her son was born of a bear, they whispered. Born with a full pelt and teeth; that proved it. But, when he grew up, he was a good shepherd, although he never married, lived in a hut outside the village and could make the wind blow any way he wanted to besides being able to tell which eggs would become cocks, which hens.

The wondering peasants once brought my father a skull with horns four inches long on either side of it and would not go back to the field where their poor plough disturbed it until the priest went with them; for this skull had the jaw-bone of a *man*, had it not?

Old wives' tales, nursery fears! I knew well enough the reason for the trepidation I cosily titillated with superstitious marvels of my childhood on the day my childhood ended. For now my own skin was my sole capital in the world and today I'd make my first investment.

We had left the city far behind us and were now traversing a wide, flat dish of snow where the mutilated stumps of the willows flourished their ciliate heads athwart frozen ditches; mist diminished the horizon, brought down the sky until it seemed no more than a few inches above us. As far as eye could see, not one thing living. How starveling, how bereft the dead season of this spurious Eden in which all the fruit was blighted by cold! And my frail roses, already faded. I opened the carriage door and tossed the defunct bouquet into the rucked, frost-stiff mud of the road. Suddenly a sharp, freezing wind arose and pelted my face with a dry rice of powdered snow. The mist lifted sufficiently to reveal before me an acreage of half-derelict façades of sheer red brick, the vast man-trap, the megalomaniac citadel of his palazzo.

It was a world in itself but a dead one, a burned-out planet. I saw The Beast bought solitude, not luxury, with his money.

The little black horse trotted smartly through the figured bronze doors that stood open to the weather like those of a barn and the valet handed me out of the carriage on to the scarred tiles of the great hall itself, into the odorous warmth of a stable, sweet with hay, acrid with horse dung. An equine chorus of neighings and soft drummings of hooves broke out beneath the tall roof, where the beams were scabbed with last summer's swallows' nests; a dozen gracile muzzles lifted from their mangers and turned towards us, ears erect. The Beast had given his horses the use of the dining room. The walls were painted, aptly enough, with a fresco of horses, dogs, and men in a wood where fruit and blossom grew on the bough together.

The valet tweaked politely at my sleeve. Milord is waiting.

Gaping doors and broken windows let the wind in everywhere. We mounted one staircase after another, our feet clopping on the marble. Through archways and open doors, I glimpsed suites of vaulted chambers opening one out of another like systems of Chinese boxes into the infinite complexity of the innards of the place. He and I and the wind were the only things stirring; and all the furniture was under dust sheets, the chandeliers bundled up in cloth, pictures taken from their hooks and propped with their faces to the walls as if their master could not bear to look at them. The palace was dismantled, as if its owner were about to move house or had never properly moved in; The Beast had chosen to live in an uninhabited place.

The valet darted me a reassuring glance from his brown, eloquent eyes, yet a glance with so much queer superciliousness in it that it did not comfort me, and went bounding ahead of me on his bandy legs, softly chattering to himself. I held my head high and followed him; but for all my pride, my heart was heavy.

Milord has his eyrie high above the house, a small, stifling, darkened room; he keeps his shutters locked at noon. I was out of breath by the time we reached it and returned to him the silence with which he greeted me. I will not smile. He cannot smile.

In his rarely disturbed privacy, The Beast wears a garment of Ottoman design, a loose, dull purple gown with gold embroidery round the neck that falls from his shoulders to conceal his feet. The feet of the chair he sits in are handsomely clawed. He hides his hands in his ample sleeves. The artificial masterpiece of his face appals me. A small fire in a small grate. A rushing wind rattles the shutters.

The valet coughed. To him fell the delicate task of transmitting to me his master's wishes.

"My master—"

A stick fell in the grate. It made a mighty clatter in that dreadful silence, the valet started, lost his place in his speech, began again.

"My master has but one desire."

The thick, rich, wild scent with which Milord had soaked himself the previous evening hangs all about us, ascends in cursive blue from the smoke hole of a precious Chinese pot.

"He wishes only —"

Now, in the face of my impassivity, the valet twittered, his ironic composure gone, for the desire of a master, however trivial, may yet sound unbearably insolent in the mouth of a servant and his role of go-between clearly caused him a good deal of embarrassment. He gulped; he swallowed, at last contrived to unleash an unpunctuated flood.

"My master's sole desire is to see the pretty young lady unclothed nude without her dress and that only for the one time after which she will be returned to her father undamaged with bankers' orders for the sum which he lost to my master at cards and also a number of fine presents such as furs, jewels and horses —"

I remained standing. During this interview, my eyes were level with those inside the mask that now evaded mine as if, to his credit, he was ashamed of his own request even as his mouthpiece made it for him. *Agitato, molto agitato*, the valet wrung his white-gloved hands.

"Desnuda —"

I could scarcely believe my ears. I let out a raucous guffaw; no young lady laughs like that! my old nurse used to remonstrate. But I did. And do. At the clamour of my heartless mirth, the valet danced backwards with peturbation, palpitating his fingers as if attempting to wrench them off, expostulating, wordlessly pleading. I felt that I owed it to him to make my reply in as exquisite a Tuscan as I could master.

"You may put me in a windowless room, sir, and I promise you I will pull my skirt up to my waist, ready for you. But there must be a sheet over my face, to hide it; though the sheet must be laid over me so lightly that it will not choke me. So I shall be covered completely from the waist upwards, and no lights. There you can visit me once, sir, and only the once. After that I must be driven directly to the city and deposited in the public square, in front of the church. If you wish to give me money, then I should be pleased to receive it. But I must stress that you should give me only the same amount of money that you would give to any other woman in such circumstances. However, if you choose not to give me a present, then that is your right."

How pleased I was to see I struck The Beast to the heart! For, after a baker's dozen heart-beats, one single tear swelled, glittering, at the corner of the masked eye. A tear! A tear, I hoped, of shame. The tear trembled for a moment on an edge of painted bone, then tumbled down the painted cheek to fall, with an abrupt tinkle, on the tiled floor.

The valet, ticking and clucking to himself, hastily ushered me out of the room. A mauve cloud of his master's perfume billowed out into the chill corridor with us and dissipated itself on the spinning winds.

A cell had been prepared for me, a veritable cell, windowless, airless, lightless, in the viscera of the palace. The valet lit a lamp for me; a narrow bed, a dark cupboard with fruit and flowers carved on it bulked out of the gloom.

"I shall twist a noose out of my bed linen and hang myself with it," I said.

"Oh, no," said the valet, fixing upon me wide and suddenly melancholy eyes. "Oh, no, you will not. You are a woman of honour."

And what was *he* doing in my bedroom, this jigging caricature of a man? Was he to be my warder until I submitted to The Beast's whim or he to mine? Am I in such reduced circumstances that I may not have a lady's maid? As if in reply to my unspoken demand, the valet clapped his hands.

"To assuage your loneliness, madame ..."

A knocking and clattering behind the door of the cupboard; the door swings open and out glides a soubrettte from an operetta, with glossy, nut-brown curls, rosy cheeks, blue, rolling eyes; it takes me a moment to recognise her, in her little cap, her white stockings, her frilled petticoats. She carries a looking glass in one hand and a powder puff in the other and there is a musical box where her heart should be; she tinkles as she rolls towards me on her tiny wheels.

"Nothing human lives here," said the valet.

My maid halted, bowed; from a split seam at the side of her bodice protrudes the handle of a key. She is a marvellous machine, the most delicately balanced system of cords and pulleys in the world.

"We have dispensed with servants," the valet said. "We surround ourselves instead, for utility and pleasure, with simulacra and find it no less convenient than do most gentlemen."

This clockwork twin of mine halted before me, her bowels churning out a settecento minuet, and offered me the bold carnation of her smile. Click, click—she raises her arm and busily dusts my cheeks with pink, powdered chalk that makes me cough, then thrusts towards me her little mirror.

I saw within it not my own face but that of my father, as if I had put on his face when I arrived at The Beast's palace as the discharge of his debt. What, you self-deluding fool, are you crying still? And drunk, too. He tossed back his grappa and hurled the tumbler away.

Seeing my astonished fright, the valet took the mirror away from me, breathed on it, polished it with the ham of his gloved fist, handed it back to me. Now all I saw was myself, haggard from a sleepless night, pale enough to need my maid's supply of rouge.

I heard the key turn in the heavy door and the valet's footsteps patter down the stone passage. Meanwhile, my double continued to powder the air, emitting her jangling tune but, as it turned out, she was not inexhaustible; soon she was powdering more and yet more languorously, her metal heart slowed in imitation of fatigue, her musical box ran down until the notes separated themselves out of the tune and plopped like single raindrops and, as if sleep had overtaken her, at last she moved no longer. As she succumbed to sleep, I had no option but to do so too. I dropped on the narrow bed as if felled.

Time passed but I do not know how much; then the valet woke me with rolls and honey. I gestured the tray away but he set it down firmly beside the lamp and took from it a little shagreen box, which he offered to me.

I turned away my head.

"Oh, my lady!" Such hurt cracked his high-pitched voice! He dextrously unfastened the gold clasp; on a bed of crimson velvet lay a single diamond earring, perfect as a tear.

I snapped the box shut and tossed it into a corner. This sudden, sharp movement must have disturbed the mechanism of the doll; she jerked her arm almost as if to reprimand me, letting out a rippling fart of gavotte. Then she was still again.

"Very well," said the valet, put out. And indicated it was time for me to visit my host again. He did not let me wash or comb my hair. There was so little natural light in the interior of the palace that I could not tell whether it was day or night.

You would not think the Beast had budged an inch since I last saw him; he sat in his huge chair, with his hands in his sleeves, and the heavy air never moved. I might have slept an hour, a night, or a month, but his sculptured calm, the stifling air remained just as it had been. The incense rose from the pot, still traced the same signature on the air. The same fire burned.

Take off my clothes for you, like a ballet girl? Is that all you want of me?

"The sight of a young lady's skin that no man has seen before —" stammered the valet.

I wished I'd rolled in the hay with every lad on my father's farm, to disqualify myself from this humiliating bargain. That he should want so little was the reason why I could not give it; I did not need to speak for The Beast to understand me.

A tear came from his other eye. And then he moved; he buried his cardboard carnival head with its ribboned weight of false hair in, I would say, his arms; he withdrew his, I might say, hands from his sleeves and I saw his furred pads, his excoriating claws.

The dropped tear caught upon his fur and shone. And in my room for hours I heard those paws pad back and forth outside my door.

When the valet arrived again with his silver salver, I had a pair of diamond earrings of the finest water in the world; I threw the other into the corner where the first one lay. The valet twittered with aggrieved regret but did not offer to lead me to The Beast again. Instead, he smiled ingratiatingly and confided: "My master, he say: invite the young lady to go riding."

"What's this?"

He briskly mimicked the action of a gallop and, to my amazement, tunelessly — croaked: "Tantivy! tantivy! a-hunting we will go!"

"I'll run away, I'll ride to the city."

"Oh, no," he said. "Are you not a woman of honour?"

He clapped his hands and my maidservant clicked and jangled into the imitation of life. She rolled towards the cupboard where

she had come from and reached inside it to fetch out over her synthetic arm my riding habit. Of all things. My very own riding
habit, that I'd left behind me in a trunk in a loft in the country
house outside Petersburg that we'd lost long ago, before, even, we
set out on this wild pilgrimage to the cruel South. Either the very
riding habit my old nurse had sewn for me or else a copy of it
perfect to the lost button on the right sleeve, the ripped hem held
up with a pin. I turned the worn cloth about in my hands, looking
for a clue. The wind that sprinted through the palace made the
door tremble in its frame; had the north wind blown my garments
across Europe to me? At home, the bear's son directed the winds at
his pleasure; what democracy of magic held this palace and the fir
forest in common? Or, should I be prepared to accept it as proof of
the axiom my father had drummed into me: that, if you have
enough money, anything is possible?

"Tantivy," suggested the now twinkling valet, evidently charmed
at the pleasure mixed with my bewilderment. The clockwork maid
held my jacket out to me and I allowed myself to shrug into it as if
reluctantly, although I was half mad to get out into the open air,
away from this deathly palace, even in such company.

The doors of the hall let the bright day in; I saw that it was
morning. Our horses, saddled and bridled, beasts in bondage, were
waiting for us, striking sparks from the tiles with their impatient
hooves while their stablemates lolled at ease among the straw,
conversing with one another in the mute speech of horses. A
pigeon or two, feathers puffed to keep out the cold, strutted about,
pecking at ears of corn. The little black gelding who had brought
me here greeted me with a ringing neigh that resonated inside the
mist roof as in a sounding box and I knew he was meant for me to
ride.

I always adored horses, noblest of creatures, such wounded sensi-
tivity in their wise eyes, such rational restraint of energy at their
high-strung hindquarters. I lirruped and hurrumphed to my shining black companion and he acknowledged my greeting with a kiss
on the forehead from his soft lips. There was a little shaggy pony
nuzzling away at the *trompe l'oeil* foliage beneath the hooves of the
painted horses on the wall, into whose saddle the valet sprang with
a flourish as of the circus. Then The Beast wrapped in a black fur-
lined cloak, came to heave himself aloft a grave grey mare. No

natural horseman he; he clung to her mane like a shipwrecked sailor to a spar.

Cold, that morning, yet dazzling with the sharp winter sunlight that wounds the retina. There was a scurrying wind about that seemed to go with us, as if the masked, immense one who did not speak carried it inside his cloak and let it out at his pleasure, for it stirred the horses' manes but did not lift the lowland mists.

A bereft landscape in the sad browns and sepias of winter lay all about us, the marshland drearily protracting itself towards the wide river. Those decapitated willows. Now and then, the swoop of a bird, its irreconcilable cry.

A profound sense of strangeness slowly began to possess me. I knew my two companions were not, in any way, as other men, the simian retainer and the master for whom he spoke, the one with clawed forepaws who was in a plot with the witches who let the winds out of their knotted handkerchiefs up towards the Finnish border. I knew they lived according to a different logic than I had done until my father abandoned me to the wild beasts by his human carelessness. This knowledge gave me a certain fearfulness still; but, I would say, not much ... I was a young girl, a virgin, and therefore men denied me rationality just as they denied it to all those who were not exactly like themselves, in all their unreason. If I could see not one single soul in that wilderness of desolation all around me, then the six of us—mounts and riders, both—could boast amongst us not one soul, either, since all the best religions in the world state categorically that not beasts nor women were equipped with the flimsy, insubstantial things when the good Lord opened the gates of Eden and let Eve and her familiars tumble out. Understand, then, that though I would not say I privately engaged in metaphysical speculation as we rode through the reedy approaches to the river, I certainly meditated on the nature of my own state, how I had been bought and sold, passed from hand to hand. That clockwork girl who powdered my cheeks for me; had I not been allotted only the same kind of imitative life amongst men that the doll-maker had given her?

Yet, as to the true nature of the being of this clawed magus who rode his pale horse in a style that made me recall how Kublai Khan's leopards went out hunting on horseback, of that I had no notion.

We came to the bank of the river that was so wide we could not see across it, so still with winter that it scarcely seemed to flow. The horses lowered their heads to drink. The valet cleared his throat, about to speak; we were in a place of perfect privacy, beyond a brake of winter-bare rushes, a hedge of reeds.

"If you will not let him see you without your clothes—"

I involuntarily shook my head—

"—you must, then, prepare yourself for the sight of my master, naked."

The river, broke on the pebbles with a diminishing sigh. My composure deserted me; all at once I was on the brink of panic. I did not think that I could bear the sight of him, whatever he was. The mare raised her dripping muzzle and looked at me keenly, as if urging me. The river broke again at my feet. I was far from home.

"You," said the valet, "must."

When I saw how scared he was I might refuse, I nodded.

The reed bowed down in a sudden snarl of wind that brought with it a gust of the heavy odour of his disguise. The valet held out his master's cloak to screen him from me as he removed the mask. The horses stirred.

The tiger will never lie down with the lamb; he acknowledges no pact that is not reciprocal. The lamb must learn to run with the tigers.

A great, feline, tawny shape whose pelt was barred with a savage geometry of bars the colour of burned wood. His domed, heavy head, so terrible he must hide it. How subtle the muscles, how profound the tread. The annihilating vehemence of his eyes, like twin suns.

I felt my breast ripped apart as if I suffered a marvellous wound.

The valet moved forward as if to cover up his master now the girl had acknowledged him, but I said: "No." The tiger sat still as a heraldic beast, in the pact he had made with his own ferocity to do me no harm. He was far larger than I could have imagined. From the poor, shabby things I'd seen once, in the Czar's menagerie at Petersburg, the golden fruit of their eyes dimming, withering in the far North of captivity. Nothing about him reminded me of humanity.

I therefore, shivering, now unfastened my jacket, to show him I would do him no harm. Yet I was clumsy and blushed a little, for no man had seen me naked and I was a proud girl. Pride it was, not shame, that thwarted my fingers so; and a certain trepidation lest this frail little article of human upholstery before him might not be, in itself, grand enough to satisfy his expectations of us, since those, for all I knew, might have grown infinite during the endless time he had been waiting. The wind clattered in the rushes, purled and eddied in the river.

I showed his grave silence my white skin, my red nipples, and the horses turned their heads to watch me, also, as if they, too, were courteously curious as to the fleshly nature of women. Then the Beast lowered his massive head; Enough! said the valet with a gesture. The wind died down. All was still again.

Then they went off together, the valet on his pony, the tiger running before him like a hound, and I walked along the river bank for a while. I felt I was at liberty for the first time in my life. Then the winter sun began to tarnish, a few flakes of snow drifted from the darkening sky and, when I returned to the horses, I found The Beast mounted again on his grey mare, cloaked and masked and once more, to all appearances, a man, while the valet had a fine catch of waterfowl dangling from his hand and the corpse of a young roebuck slung behind his saddle. I climbed up on the black gelding in silence and so we returned to the palace as the snow fell more and more heavily, obscuring the tracks that we had left behind us.

The valet did not return me to my cell but, instead, to an elegant, if old-fashioned boudoir with sofas of faded pink brocade, a jinn's treasury of Oriental carpets, tintinnabulation of cut-glass chandeliers. Candles in antlered holders struck rainbows from the prismatic hearts of my diamond earrings, that lay on my new dressing table at which my attentive maid stood ready with her powder puff and mirror. Intending to fix the ornaments in my ears, I took the looking glass from her hand, but it was in the midst of one of its magic fits again and I did not see my own face in it but that of my father; at first I thought he smiled at me. Then I saw he was smiling with pure gratification.

He sat, I saw, in the parlour of our lodgings, at the very table where he had lost me, but now he was busily engaged in counting out a tremendous pile of banknotes. My father's circumstances had changed already; well-shaven, neatly barbered, smart new clothes. A frosted glass of sparkling wine sat convenient to his hand beside an ice bucket. The Beast had clearly paid cash on the nail for his glimpse of my bosom and paid up promptly, as if it had not been a sight I might have died of showing. Then I saw my father's trunks were packed, ready for departure. Could he so easily leave me here?

There was a note on the table with the money, in a fine hand. I could read it quite clearly. "The young lady will arrive immediately." Some harlot with whom he'd briskly negotiated a liaison on the strength of his spoils? Not at all. For, at that moment, the valet knocked at my door to announce that I might leave the palace at any time hereafter, and he bore over his arm a handsome sable cloak, my very own little gratuity, The Beast's morning gift, in which he proposed to pack me up and send me off.

When I looked at the mirror again, my father had disappeared and all I saw was a pale, hollow-eyed girl whom I scarcely recognised. The valet asked politely when he should prepare the carriage, as if he did not doubt that I would leave with my booty at the first opportunity while my maid, whose face was no longer the spit of my own, continued bonnily to beam. I will dress her in my own clothes, wind her up, send her back to perform the part of my father's daughter.

"Leave me alone," I said to the valet.

He did not need to lock the door, now. I fixed the earrings in my ears. They were very heavy. Then I took off my riding habit, left it where it lay on the floor. But, when I got down to my shift, my arms dropped to my sides. I was unaccustomed to nakedness. I was so unused to my own skin that to take off all my clothes involved a kind of flaying. I thought The Beast had wanted a little thing compared with what I was prepared to give him; but it is not natural for humankind to go naked, not since first we hid our loins with fig leaves. He had demanded the abominable. I felt as much atrocious pain as if I was stripping off my own underpelt and the smiling girl stood poised in the oblivion of her balked simulation of life, watching me peel down to the cold, white meat of contract and, if she did not see me, then so much more like the market place, where the eyes that watch you take no account of your existence.

And it seemed my entire life, since I had left the North, had passed under the indifferent gaze of eyes like hers.

Then I was flinching stark, except for his irreproachable tears.

I huddled in the furs I must return to him, to keep me from the lacerating winds that raced along the corridors. I knew the way to his den without the valet to guide me.

No response to my tentative rap on his door.

Then the wind blew the valet whirling along the passage. He must have decided that, if one should go naked, then all should go naked; without his livery, he revealed himself, as I had suspected, a delicate creature, covered with silken moth-grey fur, brown fingers supple as leather, chocolate muzzle, the gentlest creature in the world. He gibbered a little to see my fine furs and jewels as if I were dressed up for the opera and, with a great deal of tender cere- mony, removed the sables from my shoulders. The sables thereupon resolved themselves into a pack of black squeaking rats that rattled immediately down the stairs on their hard little feet and were lost to sight.

The valet bowed me inside The Beast's room.

The purple dressing gown, the mask, the wig, were laid out on his chair; a glove was planted on each arm. The empty house of his appearance was ready for him but he had abandoned it. There was a reek of fur and piss; the incense pot lay broken in pieces on the floor. Half-burned sticks were scattered from the extinguished fire. A candle stuck by its own grease to the mantelpiece lit two narrow flames in the pupils of the tiger's eyes.

He was pacing backwards and forwards, backwards and forwards, the tip of his heavy tall twitching as he paced out the length and breadth of his imprisonment between the gnawed and bloody bones.

He will gobble you up.

Nursery fears made flesh and sinew; earliest and most archaic of fears, fear of devourment. The beast and his carnivorous bed of bone and I, white, shaking, raw, approaching him as if offering, in myself, the key to a peaceable kingdom in which his appetite need not be my extinction.

He went still as stone. He was far more frightened of me than I was of him.

I squatted on the wet straw and stretched out my hand. I was now within the field of force of his golden eyes. He growled at the back of his throat, lowered his head, sank on to his forepaws, snarled, showed me his red gullet, his yellow teeth. I never moved. He snuffled the air, as if to smell my fear; he could not.

Slowly, slowly he began to drag his heavy, gleaming weight across the floor towards me.

A tremendous throbbing, as of the engine that makes the earth turn, filled the little room; he had begun to purr.

The sweet thunder of this purr shook the old walls, made the shutters batter the windows until they burst apart and let in the white light of the snowy moon. Tiles came crashing down from the roof; I heard them fall into the courtyard far below. The reverberations of his purring rocked the foundations of the house, the walls began to dance. I thought: "It will all fall, everything will disintegrate."

He dragged himself closer and closer to me, until I felt the harsh velvet of his head against my hand, then a tongue, abrasive as sandpaper. "He will lick the skin off me!"

And each stroke of his tongue ripped off skin after successive skin, all the skins of a life in the world, and left behind a nascent patina of shiny hairs. My earrings turned back to water and trickled down my shoulders; I shrugged the drops off my beautiful fur.

"The Lamb Must Learn to Run with the Tiger"

In her retellings of fairy tales in the stories of *The Bloody Chamber*, Angela Carter employs a two-part methodology. The first is to take a familiar fairy tale and link it to its folk antecedents and related old wives' tales, restoring (to the mild version of the tale we are familiar with) its originally earthy, pagan, and sometimes gothic flavor. Having restored the tale's roots, Carter then turns to playing a variation upon the tradition, giving the tale a new spin in a feminist and erotic direction—creating, as it were, a new "old wives' tale."

In her story "The Company of Wolves," Carter repositions "Little Red Riding Hood" in terms of its antecedent tradition in stories of werewolves. Then she presents her heroine in an empowered way: this Maiden in Red is no simple victim of male rapaciousness but, instead, an equal partner to the wolf and eager explorer of sex. Neil Jordan worked with Carter to create his magnificent 1984 film that takes its title from that short story, and in that film a character delivers a single line that might be seen as a summary both of the story and the film, as a recapitulation of Carter's endeavor as a feminist writer, and as a motto for "Tiger's Bride": "*If there's a beast in men, it meets its match in women too.*"

In her short and long fiction, her Japanese-themed stories and revisions of the fairy tales, her fantasies and even her anthologies, Carter always pursued that theme so succinctly put by the character in the film. Moreover, as the very words of that line suggest, the *ur*-story that lies behind Carter's work is "Beauty and the Beast." Indeed, as Marina Warner has observed, "Carter returned to the theme of Beauty and the Beast again and again, turning it inside out and upside down; in a spirit of mischief."[1]

While "Beauty and the Beast" may lie behind much of Carter's writing, that story is only directly addressed in two stories in *The Bloody Chamber*: "The Courtship of Mr. Lyon" and "The Tiger's Bride." In these, Carter plays entirely different variations upon Beaumont's tale.

Originally written for the British edition of *Vogue*, "The Courtship of Mr. Lyon" relocates the story to the late twentieth century. Beauty's father comes to the Beast's palatial home not when his horse gets lost in the forest but when his car breaks down in a snowstorm. Carter's Beauty is not Beaumont's virtuous virgin but a lacquered ingenue who forgets the Beast when she settles in London's luxuries and is swaddled in furs. And when she comes to her senses and returns to her suitor, when the Beast transforms, he does not dramatically become a handsome prince; instead, this leonine creature becomes an ordinary man with an unruly mane of hair and a broken nose like that of a prizefighter—or a lion. In this variation, Carter largely removes fantasy and flattens Beaumont's story in a realistic way; the results are fairly bland.

"Tiger's Bride," on the other hand, is an over-the-top variation that genuinely plays mischief with Beaumont's tale. Along the way, in her familiar manner, Carter provides a compendium of associations and allusions to explore "Beauty and the Beast." There are references to:

---

1 Warner 308.

- Tarot, carnival masks, ancient beliefs that beasts and women have no souls, and the enduring European theme of North versus South (which Thomas Mann made so much of);

- drops of wax upon bare shoulders ("Cupid and Psyche"), the galloping of horses ("the Erl-King") and their intelligence (*Gulliver's Travels*), the winds gathered up and loosed on the Finnish Border ("East of the Sun, West of the Moon"), and roses that are white but turn red when bloodied ("Sleeping Beauty" and "Snow White");

- pictures of "Beauty and the Beast" by Eleanor Vere Boyle (who sets the story in Italy), Edmund Dulac (who imagines the Beast in an orientalized manner), Walter Crane (who provides the Beast with monkey servants and sits him in a clawed chair), and Edward Hick's painting "The Peaceable Kingdom."

Mention is also made of Kubla Khan, the Tiger-man of Sumatra, legends of wild children born of women and bears, and nursery stories of boogies that gobble children up. There are, no doubt, other allusions beyond those mentioned here.

Positioning "Beauty and the Beast" in this wider context, Carter then turns Beaumont's story on its head. First is a tonal shift. Set in France and with a governess-like and didactic manner, Beaumont's measured story is one thing; re-situating the story to Italy, Carter's version is extravagant and fantastical, and she employs a tone that is carnival-like and almost operatic. Replete with a monkey servant and a full-size clockwork maid, who might be an extra from "The Nutcracker," this *opera buffa* version of "Beauty and the Beast" is a story of an entirely different coloratura.

Gone is Beaumont's devoted daddy who values his daughter over all others and everything else. This father loses his wealth and then his child while playing cards with La Bestia. And he is scarcely concerned with getting her back.

Lost in this card game and delivered to the castle, Carter's Beauty passes no long probation of acquaintance that terminates in her acceptance of the Beast's marriage proposal. Instead, she is free to go if she grants La Bestia his one wish: to see her naked. But Carter's Beauty is not Beaumont's timid and self-sacrificial maiden;

instead, she greets the Beast's request with a "raucous guffaw" and turns the request back at him in an insult that stings him. Here is an altogether different kind of Beauty, self-assured, haughty, and defiant.

The Beast, as well, is not Beaumont's polished nobleman regrettably enchanted into an unpleasing form. Carter's La Bestia is animal-like and rank. This grand seigneur is a Tiger-man, swathed in capes and scarcely erect, wearing a carnival mask like some Phantom of the Opera to cover his beastly visage, bathed in cologne to disguise his foul smell of fur and piss, and living in a ruined palazzo inside of which horses are stabled, a palace odorous with the smell of dung.

Here, too, Beauty does not experience her change of heart when, as in Beaumont's story, she realizes she has overstayed her time with her family and hurt the Beast. In Carter's case, the two are out riding and, in the company of other (equine) beasts, La Bestia sheds his clothes and runs on all fours. It is this moment of nakedness that sparks her change of heart and epiphany: "*The tiger will never lay down with the lamb.... The lamb must learn to run with the tiger.*" It is as if the "The Peaceable Kingdom" were transformed into a saturnalian orgy of animals — and in this spirit, she sheds her clothes and runs wild as well.

But Carter's final turning of Beaumont's tale upon its head occurs in her striking conclusion. Returning to the castle, Carter's Beauty sheds her clothes again, dresses in sables, and comes to La Bestia in his room — a chamber no longer perfumed to disguise its animal rankness. There, to the amplified hum of his purring, he licks her pelt, removing layer after layer of skin, disclosing her own tiger skin beneath.

To anyone familiar with Beaumont's "Beauty and the Beast" and expecting the transformation of the Beast into a man, Carter presents the opposite: Beauty is revealed to be a beast herself.

It is a conclusion that recalls Carter's subversive and feminist manifesto in "Company of Wolves": "*If there's a beast in men, it meets its match in women too.*" And it is a reminder, once again, of the power of "Beauty and the Beast" that it can lend itself to such versatility.

Tanith Lee's "Beauty"

Born in 1947, British writer Tanith Lee resides in London and admits to a special interest in ancient civilizations, psychic powers, and music. Previously a librarian, she is now a recognized and prolific writer of fantasy, science fiction, and works for juveniles and young adults. She has more than fifty books in print, most of which have been published by Macmillan or DAW. Often noted for her strong female characters, Lee indicates on the title page of her Red as Blood *that her revisions of the fairy tales are the work of "the Sisters Grimmer"—suggesting that they offer an alternative to the Brothers Grimm and their somewhat tamer stories.*

Chapter 1

His hundred and fifty-first birthday dawned aboard the sleek ship from Cerulean, high above the white-capped ocean that was the Earth. By nightfall he would be at home, in his beautiful robot-run house. Beyond the tall windows a landscape of the western hemisphere would fall away, pure with snow, to a frozen glycerine river. Far from the weather control of the cities, the seasons came and went there with all the passion and flamboyance of young women. And in the house, the three young women came and went like the seasons.

Dark slender Lyra with her starry eyes and her music—well-named; Joya, much darker, ebony skinned and angel-eyed, full of laughter—well-named, too. And the youngest, his only born child, made with a woman from whom he had long since parted: Estár, with her green-brown hair the color of the summer oak woods, and her unrested turbulent spirit—ill-named for a distant planet, meaning the same as the Greek word *psyche*.

It seemed his seed made daughters, either mixed with the particles of unknown women in crystal tubes, or mingled in a human womb. They were his heirs, both to his mercantile fortune and to his treasures of art and science. He loved each of them, and was loved in turn. But sometimes Estár filled him with a peculiar fear. Her life would never be simple, and perhaps never happy. He did not like to think of her, maybe far from the shelter of the house, the shelter he could give her. In fifty, sixty more years, he might be dead. What then?

185

Tonight, there was the ceremonial dinner party to welcome him home, and to mark his birthday. A few charming guests would be there, delighting in the golden rooms. There would be the exchange of presents, for, with every birthday, gifts were given as well as received. This time, they had told him, those three, laughing, what they wanted. "Natural things!" they had cried. Lyra wished for pearls, real pearls, the kind only to be taken from oysters which had died, neither cultured nor killed for. And Joya had demanded a dress of silk, an old dress made before the ending of the silkworm trade. Estár, he guessed, had subconsciously put them up to it, and when her turn came he had waited, uneasy in some way he could not explain. "A rose," she said, "a grown rose. But something from a hothouse or a city cultivatory won't do."

"In all this snow —" exclaimed Joya. "I can send to the east," he said. "No," said Estár, all too quietly. "You must pluck it yourself."

"But then," said Lyra, "he would have to detour from Cerulean. He'll never be home in time for the dinner party to give you such a present."

Estár smiled. "It seems I've posed you a riddle, Papa."

"It seems you have," he said, wincing a little at the title "Papa" which she had adopted from some book. His other daughters called him by his name, graciously, allowing him to be a person, not merely an adjunctive relation. "Well, I'll keep my eyes wide for roses in the snow."

Yet how ominous it had seemed, and not until the ship landed at the huge western terminus did he discover why.

"Mercator Levin? Would you be good enough to step this way?" The attendant was human, a courteous formality that boded ill.

"Is anything wrong?" he asked. "My cargo?"

"Is quite in order, I assure you. The commissioner wishes to speak with you, on another matter."

Perplexed, he followed, and presently entered the circular office with its panoramic views of the landing fields. Dusk was imminent, and the miles of ground constellated by lights. Far away, little flaming motes, the ships sank slowly down or up.

He was offered wines, teas, coffees, and other social stimulants. He refused them all, his oppression growing. The commissioner, a few years his junior, was patently troubled, and paving the way — to something. At last he leaned back in his chair, folded his hands

186

and said,

"Depending on how you see your situation, Mercator Levin, it is my duty to inform you that either a great honor, or a great annoyance, is about to befall your family."

"What can you mean?"

"This, sir, has been placed in our care, for you."

He watched, he looked, he saw, and the control and poise of one and a half centuries deserted him. Risen from a recess in the desk, a slim crystal box stood transparent in the solarized light. A heap of soil lay on the floor of the box. Growing straight up from it was a translucent stem only faintly tinged with color, and leafless. At the head of the stem there blossomed a rose slender as a tulip, its petals a pale and singing green. There were no thorns, or rather only one and that metaphysical, if quite unbearably penetrating.

"I see it is not an honor," said the commissioner, so softly Levin was unsure if he were dealing with a sadist or a man of compassion. In any event, that made no odds. "I'm very sorry, Mercator. But I had no choice. And you, as you know, have none either. As you see, the name and code stamped into the crystal are your own."

"Yes," he said.

"So, if you would be so kind. I am to act as the witness, you understand, of your acceptance."

"But I don't accept," Levin said.

"You know, sir, that failure to comply —"

"I know. I'll do it. But *accept*? How could I?"

"No." And the commissioner lowered his eyes.

When he was within a foot of the desk and the box, the crystal opened for him. Levin reached in and took the smooth stem of the green rose in his fingers. The roots broke away with a crisp snap, like fresh lettuce, and a sweet aroma filled the air. It was the most disgusting, nauseating scent he had ever smelled.

Homecoming, normally so full of pleasure, was now resonant with dread. He dismissed the snow-car at the edge of the hill, and climbed, as he always did, toward the lovely, sprawling house. Most of it was of one-story construction in deference to the high winds that blew here in winter and often in the spring also, and all weatherproofed in a wonderful plasteel that made its walls seem to catch the prevailing light within themselves, glowing now a soft dull silver like the darkening sky. It had been turned into lace besides by the hundred golden windows—every illuminator was on to welcome him.

Inside, the house was warm and fragrant, old wood, fine synthetics. The robot servants had laid everything ready in his rooms, even to the selection of bedside books and music. His luggage was here ahead of him. He prepared himself, dressed for the party, went down. He had hurried to do so, but without eagerness. The glass of spirit he left untouched.

The main communal room of the house was some forty square meters, summer-heated from the floor, and also by the huge open central fire of natural coals, its suspended chimney like the glass pillar of a hallucination floating just above. How that chimney had fascinated Lyra and Joya as children. Something in its strength and exquisite airy unactuality—

For a while, the scene held in the room. They had not noticed him yet, though they expected him at any second. Lyra was playing the piano in a pool of light. What would it mean to her to be sent away? She was studying with two of the greatest musicians of the age, and already her compositions—three concertos, a symphony, song cycles, sonatas—were phenomenal and unique. She promised so much to herself, to her world. And she was, besides, in love. The young man who stood by the piano, watching her white hands, her face. Levin looked at him with a father's jealousy and a father's pride that the lover of his daughter should be both handsome and good. The Asiatic blood that showed in his amber skin, the carven features and slanting eyes, the violinist's hands, the talent of his calling—all these were charming and endearing things.

And then, standing listening by the fire, Joya, jet-black on the redness of the coals, no longer fascinated by the chimney, fascinating instead her two admirers, one male and one female. They were her friends, poets, a little eccentric as all Joya's friends turned out to be. It had alarmed him at first. He had feared she would be forced to change. But Joya had not altered, only extending her sunshine to others, giving them a steadiness they lacked, herself losing none. And she was now four months pregnant. She had told him her news the day he left, her eyes bright. It was splendid, enchanting. The thought of her as the mother of children filled him with painful happiness. She did not know who had fathered the child, which would be a son, nor did she care, had not bothered with the tests to discover. He had chided her gently, since the father had every right to know, and Joya laughed: "Later. For now he's only mine."

And to send Joya away, two lives now — No! No, no.

Seated between the fire and the piano, the other guests were also listening to the music, four contemporaries of Levin's, well-known, stimulating and restful people of experience, and, in one case, genius, and three well-liked others, mutual acquaintances of them all. And there, on the periphery of the group, alone, his third daughter, his born daughter, and he grew cold at the perfection of the omens. The apple tint she used upon her brown hair had been freshly enhanced. Her dress, of the fashion known as Second Renascence, was a pale and singing green. She played with a glass of wine in her left hand, twirling the stem between her fingers. The translucent stem. It was as if she had known. He had heard rumors of such things before. It was ironical, for just now he recalled, of course, that she had almost never *been* born, her mother's frenetic life-style having brought on the preliminaries of an accidental abortion — the child had been saved, and had continued to grow inside the woman's womb to a well coordinated seventh-month term. But how nearly —

Estár seemed to feel his eyes on her. She looked about, and, not speaking to anyone, got up and came noiselessly over to him in the doorway. She was tall and slim, and almost a stranger.

"Welcome home, Papa." She did not reach to kiss him as the others did, restrained, perhaps inhibited. He had noticed it with many born children. Those not carried in flesh seemed far easier with the emotional expressions of the flesh, a paradox. "Did you," said Estár, "find my rose?"

He looked at her in devastating sadness.

"At first, I thought I'd have to fail you," he said. "But in the end — look. Here it is."

And he held the green flower out to her in silence.

She gazed at it, and her pale face whitened. She knew it, and if by prescience she had foretold it, then that clearly had not been with her conscious mind. For a long while she did not take the rose, and then she reached out and drew it from his hand. The music was ending in the room. In another moment the others would become aware of his arrival, of this scene at the door.

"Yes," Estár said. "I see it must be me. *They* are your daughters. I'm only your guest."

"Estár," he said. "What are you saying?"

"No," she said, "I'm sorry. I meant only I have nothing to lose, or little—a nice home, a kind father—but they have everything to lose … love, children, brilliance—No, it has to be me, doesn't it?"

"I intend to petition," he began, and stopped.

"You know that everyone petitions. And it does no good at all. When do I have to leave?"

"The usual period is a month. Oh Estár—if there were anything at all—"

"You'd do it. I know. You're marvelous, but there are limits. It's not as if I'll never see you again. And, I respect your judgment. I do. To choose me."

The music ended. There was applause and laughter, and then the first cry of his name across the room.

"You fool," he said to his youngest daughter, "don't you know that I chose you—not because I consider you expendable—but because I love you the best?"

"Oh," she said. Her eyes filled with tears, and she lowered her head, not letting him see them.

"That is the decision this thing forces us to," he said. "To sacrifice in blood. Could I ask you the unforgivable thing not to tell the others until this wretched party is over?"

"Of course," she said. "I'll go to my rooms for a little, ten minutes, perhaps. Then I'll come back, bright as light. Watch me. You'll be proud. Tell them I went to put your—your gift in water."

Levin had been a child five years old when the planet of his birth received its first officially documented visit from the stars. The alien ships fell like a summer snow, a light snow; there were not many. The moon cities, Martian Marsha, and the starry satellite colonies that drifted between, these the aliens by-passed. They came to the home world and presented it with gifts, clean and faultless technologies, shining examples of intellect and industry, from a culture similar to, much advanced on, greatly differing from, the terrestrial. And later, like wise guests not outstaying their welcome, the ships, and most of the persons who came with the ships, went away. Their general purpose was oblique if altruistic. The purpose of those who remained less so, more so. At first they were seen in the capacity of prefects. To some extent, Earth had been conquered. Left free, no doubt she must still answer now and then to her benign superiors. But the remaining aliens required neither answers nor menials. It seemed they stayed only because they wished to, in love with Earth, tired of journeying … something of this sort. Perfectly tended by their own machineries, setting up their own modest estates far from the cities and the thoroughfares of popular life, they appropriated nothing and intruded not at all. They seemed content merely to be there. It was easy, for the most part, to forget them.

And then, about the time that Levin ended his adult education, around twenty-six or so, the first roses were sent. Immersed in a last fascinating study of something he had now quite forgotten, he missed the event. Only common outcry had alerted him. He remembered ever after the broodingly sinister concern that overcame him. It seemed the aliens in fact had decided to demand one thing. Or rather, they asked, courteously and undeniably. Somehow, without any threat, it was made clear that they could take *without* asking, that to ask was their good manners. The rose was a gracious summons, and with the first roses an explanation went of what the gracious summons entailed. Despite the outcry, despite petitionings, letters, speeches loudly made in the senates and councils of every nation and every ethnic alliance of the world, the summonses were obeyed. There was no other choice. I *will not* had been replied to, gently, illimitably: *You will.*

Without force, without threat, by unspoken undemonstrated implication only. The Earth was in fee to her friends. Stunned at the first, the only blow, there was, finally, no battle. The battles came later, seven years later, when the second wave of roses — those alien roses from gardens blooming with the seeds of another planet, roses purple, azure, green — was dashed across humanity's quietude. Some resorted to concealment, then, and some fought. Some simply refused, standing firm; alone. But once again the inexorable pressure, invisibly and decipherably applied, undid them. Men found themselves in conflict only with other men. The aliens did not attack them or seize from them. But they waited and were felt to be waiting. Roses thrown on fire were found not to burn. Roses flung among garbage were mysteriously returned, all burnished. The aliens made no other demand. The first demand was always enough. Without their gifts, humanity would not thrive quite as it did. Gradually, persuaded by their own kind, bamboozled, worn out with beating their heads on the hard walls of censure, those who had hidden and fought and stood alone, crumbled, gave in, let go.

And it was a fact, in all the first two waves of the sending of the roses, and in all the sporadic individual sendings that had followed in these fifty years after the two waves, nothing had ever been asked of those who could not spare the payment. It had a kind of mathematical soulless logic, hopelessly unhuman—*in*human.

Always the families to whom the roses went were rich—not prosperous, as almost all men were now prosperous—but something extra. Rich, and endowed with friends and kin, abilities of the mind and spirit: consolations for the inevitable loss. The loss of one child. A son, or a daughter, whichever of the household was best suited to be sent, could most easily be spared, was the most likely to find the prospect challenging or acceptable, or, endurable.

He remembered how at twenty-six it had suggested to him immolations to Moloch and to Jupiter, young children given to the god. But that was foolish, of course. They did not, when they went to the alien estates, go there to die, or even to worship, to extend service. They were neither sacrifices nor slaves. They had been quite often after, visiting their families, corresponding with them. Their lives continued on those little pieces of alien ground, much as they had always done. They were at liberty to move about the area, the buildings, the surrounding landscapes, at liberty to learn what they wished of the aliens' own world, and all its facets of science and poetry.

There was only discernible in them, those ones who went away, a distancing, and a dreadful sourceless silence, which grew.

The visits to their homes became less. Their letters and videoings ceased. They melted into the alien culture and were gone. The last glimpses of their faces were always burdened and sad, as if against advice they had opened some forbidden door and some terrible secret had overwhelmed them. The bereaved families knew that something had consumed their sons and daughters alive, and not even bones were left for them to bury.

It was feared, though seldom spoken of, that it was natural xenophobia, revulsion, which destroyed and maybe killed the hearts of humanity's children. They had grown with their own kind, and then were sent to dwell with another kind. Their free revisitings of family and friends would only serve to point the differences more terribly between human and alien. The aliens—and this was almost never spoken of—were ugly, were hideous. So much had been learned swiftly, at the very beginning. Out of deference to their new world, out of shame, perhaps, they covered their ugliness with elegant garments, gloves, masking draperies, hoods and visors. Yet, now and then, a sighting—enough. They were like men or women, a little taller, a slender, finely muscled race.... But their very likeness made their differences the more appalling, their loathsomeness more unbearable. And there were those things which now and then must be revealed, some inches of pelted hairy skin, the gauntleted over-fingered hands, the brilliant eyes empty of white, lensed by their yellow conjunctiva.

These, the senders of roses.

It seemed, without knowing, Levin always had known that one day the obscene sacrifice would be asked of him. To one of these creatures would now travel his youngest daughter Estár, who wore by choice the clothing of reborn history.

While she ordered the packing of her luggage, he wrote letters and prepared tapes of appeal and righteous anger.

Both knew it to be useless.

Somewhere in the house, Joya and Lyra wept.

On the first day of Midwinter, the snow-car stood beside the porch.

"Good-bye," she said.

"I will—" he began.

"I know you'll do everything you can." She looked at her sisters, who were restraining their frightened tears with skill and decorum so that she should not be distressed. "I shall see you in the spring. I'll make sure of that," she said. It was true, no doubt. Joya kissed her. Lyra could not risk the gesture, and only pressed her hand. "Goodbye," Estár said again, and went away.

The snow sprang in two curved wings from the car. In ten seconds it was a quarter of a mile away. The snow fell back. The sound of crying was loud. Levin took his two remaining daughters in his arms and they clung to him. Catching sight of them all in a long mirror, he wryly noted he and they were like a scene from an ancient play — Greek tragedy or Shakespeare: Oedipus and Antigone, Lear with Cordelia lost — *A Winter's Tale.*

He wondered if Estár cried, now that she was in private and unseen.

Chapter 2

Estár had not cried; she was sickened from fear and rage. Neither of these emotions had she expressed, even to herself, beyond the vaguest abstracts. She had always been beset by her feelings, finding no outlet. From the start, she had seen Lyra express herself through music, Joya through communication. But Estár had been born with no creative skills and had learned none. She could speak coherently and seemingly to the point, she could, if required to, write concise and quite interesting letters, essays and fragments of descriptive poetry. But she could not convey *herself* to others. And *for* herself, what she was aware of, suffered, longed for — these concepts had never come clear. She had no inkling as to what she wanted, and had often upbraided herself for her lack of content and pleasure in the riches fate had brought her, her charming family, the well-ordered beauty of her world. At fifteen, she had considered a voluntary term at Marsha, the Martian colonial belt, but had been dissuaded by physical circumstance. It seemed her lungs, healthy enough for Earth, were not of a type to do well for her in the thin half-built atmosphere of Mars. She had not grieved, she had not wanted to escape to another planet any more than she wanted anything else. There had simply been a small chance that on Mars she might have found a niche for herself, a *raison d'Estár.*

Now, this enforced event affected her in a way that surprised her. What did it matter after all if she were exiled? She was no ornament at home to herself or others and might just as well be placed with the ambiguous aliens. She could feel, surely, no more at a loss with this creature than with her own kind, her own kin.

The fear was instinctive, of course, she did not really question that. But her anger puzzled her. Was it the lack of choice? Or was it only that she had hoped eventually to make a bond between herself and those who loved her, perhaps to find some man or woman, one who would not think her tiresome and unfathomable and who, their novelty palling, she would not come to dislike. And now these dreams were gone. Those who must live with the aliens were finally estranged from all humanity — that was well known. So, she had lost her own chance at becoming human.

It was a day's journey. The car, equipped with all she might conceivably need, gave her hot water and perfumed soap, food, drink, played her music, offered her books and films. The blue-white winter day only gradually deepened into dusk. She raised the opaque blinds for the forward windows and looked where the vehicle was taking her.

They were crossing water, partly frozen. Ahead stood a low mountain. From its conical exaggerated shape, she took it to be man-made, one of the structured stoneworks that here and there augmented the Earth. Soon they reached a narrow shore, and as the dusk turned gentian, the car began to ascend.

A gentle voice spoke to her from the controls. It seemed that in ten minutes she would have arrived.

There was a tall steel gate at which the snow-car was exchanged for a small vehicle that ran on an aerial cable.

Forty feet above the ground, Estár looked from the window at the mile of cultivated land below, which was a garden. Before the twilight had quite dispersed, she saw a weather control existed, manipulating the seasons. It was autumn by the gate and yellow leaves dropped from the trees. Later, autumn trembled into summer, and heavy foliage swept against the sides of the car. It was completely dark when journey ended, but as the car settled on its platform, the mild darkness and wild scents of spring came in through its opening doors.

She left the car and was borne down a moving stair, a metal servant flying leisurely before with her luggage. Through wreaths of pale blossom she saw a building, a square containing a glowing orb of roof, and starred by external illuminators.

She reached the ground. Doors bloomed into light and opened.

A lobby, quite large, a larger room beyond. A room of seductive symmetry—she had expected nothing else. There was no reason why it should not be pleasant, even enough like other rooms she had seen as to appear familiar. Yet, too, there was something indefinably strange, a scent, perhaps, or some strain of subsonic noise. It was welcome, the strangeness. To find no alien thing at once could have disturbed her. And maybe, such psychology was understood, and catered to.

A luminous bead came to hover in the air like a tame bird.

"Estár Levina," it said, and it's voice was like that of a beautiful unearthly child. "I will be your guide. A suite has been prepared for you. Any questions you may wish—"

"Yes," she broke in, affronted by its sweetness, "when shall I meet—with your controller?"

"Whenever you desire, Estár Levina."

"When *I* desire? Suppose I have no desire *ever* to meet—him?"

"If such is to be your need, it will be respected, wherever possible."

"And eventually it will no longer be possible and I shall be briskly, escorted into his presence."

The bead shimmered in the air.

"There is no coercion. You are forced to do nothing which does not accord with your sense of autonomy."

"But I'm here against my will," she said flatly.

The bead shimmered, shimmered.

Presently she let it lead her silently across the symmetrical alien room, and into other symmetrical alien rooms.

Because of what the voice-bead had said to her, however, she kept to her allotted apartment, her private garden, for a month.

The suite was beautiful, and furnished with all she might require. She was, she discovered, even permitted access, via her own small console, to the library bank of the house. Anything she could not obtain through her screen, the voice-bead would have brought for her. In her garden, which had been designed in the manner of the Second Renascence, high summer held sway over the slender ten-foot topiary. When darkness fell, alabaster lamps lit themselves softly among the foliage and under the falling tails of water.

She wondered if she was spied on. She acted perversely and theatrically at times in case this might be so. At others she availed herself of much of what the technological dwelling could give her.

Doors whisked open, clothes were constructed and brought, baths run, tapes deposited as though by invisible hands. It was as if she were waited on by phantoms. The science of Earth had never quite achieved this fastidious level, or had not wanted to. The unseen mechanisms and energies in the air would even turn the pages of books for her, if requested.

She sent a letter to her father after two days. It read simply: *I am here and all is well.* Even to her the sparseness was disturbing. She added a postscript: *Joya must stop crying over me or her baby will be washed away.*

She wondered, as her letter was wafted out, if the alien would read it.

On the tenth day, moodily, she summoned from the library literature and spoken theses on the aliens' culture and their world.

"Curiosity," she said to the walls, "killed the cat."

She knew already, of course, what they most resembled—some species of huge feline, the hair thick as moss on every inch of them save lips, the nostrils, the eyes, and the private areas of the body. Though perhaps ashamed of their state, they had never hidden descriptions of themselves, only their actual selves, behind the visors and the draperies.

She noted that while there were many three-dimensional stills of their planet, and their deeds there and elsewhere, no moving videos were available, and this perhaps was universally so.

She looked at thin colossal mountain ranges, tiny figures in the foreground, or sporting activities in a blur of dust—the game clear, the figures less so. Tactfully, no stress was laid even here, in their own habitat, on their unpalatable differences. What Earth would see had been vetted. The sky of their planet was blue, like the sky of Earth. And yet utterly alien in some way that was indecipherable. The shape of the clouds, maybe, the depth of the horizon.... Like the impenetrable differences all about her. Not once did she wake from sleep disoriented, thinking herself in her father's house.

The garden appealed to her, however; she took aesthetic comfort from it. She ate out on a broad white terrace under the leaves and the stars in the hot summer night, dishes floating to her hands, wine and coffee into her goblet, her cup, and a rose-petal paper cigarette into her fingers.

Everywhere secrets, everywhere the concealed facts.

"If," she said to the walls, "I am observed, are you enjoying it, O Master?" She liked archaic terms, fashions, music, art, attitudes. They had always solaced her, and sometimes given her weapons against her own culture which she had not seemed to fit. Naturally, inevitably, she did not really feel uneasy here. As she had bitterly foreseen, she was no more un-at-home in the alien's domicile than in her father's.

But why was she here? The ultimate secret. Not a slave, not a pet. She was free as air. As presumably all the others were free. And the answers that had come from the lips and styluses of those others had never offered a satisfactory solution. Nor could she uncover the truth, folded in this privacy.

She was growing restless. The fear, the rage, had turned to a fearful angry ache to know—to seek her abductor, confront him, perhaps touch him, talk to him.

Curiosity…. If by any chance he did not spy on her, did not nightly read reports on her every action from the machines of the house, why then the Cat might be curious too.

"How patient you've been," she congratulated the walls, on the morning of the last day of the month. "Shall I invite you to my garden? Or shall I meet you in yours?" And then she closed her eyes and merely thought, in concise clipped words within her brain: *I will wait for you on the lawn before the house, under all that blossom. At sunset.*

And there at sunset she was, dressed in a version of Earth's fifteenth century, and material developed from Martian dust crystals.

Through the blossoming spring trees the light glittered red upon her dress and on her, and then a shadow came between her and the sun.

She looked up, and an extraordinary sensation filled her eyes, her head, her whole torso. It was not like fear at all, more like some other tremendous emotion. She almost burst into tears.

He was here. He had read her mind. And, since he had been able to do that, it was improbable he had ever merely spied on her at all.

"You admit it," she said. "Despite your respect for my—my privacy—how funny!—you admit I have *none!*"

He was taller than she, but not so much taller that she was unprepared for it. She herself was tall. He was covered, as the aliens always covered themselves, totally, entirely. A glint of oblique sun slithered on the darkened face-plate through which he saw her, and through which she could not see him at all. The trousers fit close to his body, and the fabric shone somewhat, distorting, so she could be sure of nothing. There was no chink. The garments adhered. Not a centimeter of body surface showed, only its planes, male and well-formed: familiar, alien — like the rooms, the skies of his world. His hands were cased in gauntlets, a foolish, inadvertent comple-ment to her own apparel. The fingers were long. There were six of them. She had seen a score of photographs and threedems of such beings.

But what had happened. That was new.

Then he spoke to her, and she realized with a vague shock that some mechanism was at work to distort even his voice so it should not offend her kind.

"That I read your thoughts was not an infringement of your pri-vacy, Estár Levina. Consider. You intended that they should be read. I admit, my mind is sensitive to another mind which signals to it. You signaled very strongly. Almost, I might say, with a razor's edge."

"*I*," she said, "am not a telepath."

"I'm receptive to any such intentional signal. Try to believe me when I tell you I don't, at this moment, know what you are think-ing. Although I could guess."

His voice had no accent, only the mechanical distortion. And yet it was — charming — in some way that was quite ab-human, quite unacceptable.

They walked awhile in the outer garden in the dusk. Illuminators ignited to reveal vines, orchids, trees — all of another planet, mutat-ing gently among the stands of terrestrial vegetation.

Three feet high, a flower like an iris with petals like dark blue flames allowed the moon to climb its stem out of the valley below.

They barely spoke. Now and then she asked a question, and he replied. Then, somewhere among a flood of Earthly sycamores, she suddenly found he was telling her a story, a myth of his own world. She listened, tranced. The weird voice, the twilight, the spring perfume and the words themselves made a sort of rhapsody. Later that night, alone, she discovered she could not remember the story and was forced to search it out among the intellectual curios of the library bank. Deprived of his voice, the garden and the dusk, it was a very minor thing, common to many cultures, and patently more than one planet. A quest, a series of tasks. It was the multitude of plants which had prompted the story, that and the rising of a particular star.

When they reentered the house, they went into an upper room, where a dinner was served. And where he also ate and drank. The area of the facial mask which corresponded with his lips incredibly somehow was not there as he raised goblet or fork toward them. And then, as he lowered the utensil, it *was* there once more, solid and unbreachable as ever. Not once, during these dissolves of seemingly impenetrable matter, did she catch a glimpse of what lay beyond. She stared, and her anger rose like oxygen, filling her, fading.

"I apologize for puzzling you," he said. "The visor is constructed of separable atoms and molecules, a process not yet in use generally on Earth. If this bothers you, I can forgo my meal."

"It bothers me. Don't forgo your meal. Why," she said, "are you able to eat Earth food? Why has this process of separable atoms not been given to Earth?" And, to her astonishment, her own fragile glass dropped from her hand in pieces that never struck the floor.

"Have you been cut?" his distorted voice asked her unemphatically.

Estár beheld she had not.

"I wasn't," she said, "holding it tightly enough for that to happen."

"The house is eager to serve you, unused to you, and so misunderstands at times. You perhaps wanted to crush something?"

"I should like," she said, "to return to my father's house."

"At any time, you may do so."

"But I want," she said, "to stay there. I mean that I don't want to come back here."

She waited. He would say she had to come back. Thus, she would have forced him to display his true and brutal omnipotence.

He said, "I'm not reading your mind, I assure you of that. But I can sense instantly whenever you lie."

"Lie? What am I lying about? I said, I want to go home."

"'Home' is a word which has no meaning for you, Estár Levina. This is as much your home as the house of your father."

"This is the house, of a beast," she said, daringly. She was very cold, as if winter had abruptly broken in. "A superior, wondrous monster." She sounded calm. "Perhaps I could kill it. What would happen then? A vengeance fleet dispatched from your galaxy to destroy the terrestrial solar system?"

"You would be unable to kill me. My skin is very thick and resilient. The same is true of my internal structure. You could, possibly, cause me considerable pain, but not death."

"No, of course not." She lowered her eyes from the blank shining mask. Her pulses beat from her skull to her soles. She was ashamed of her ineffectual tantrum. "I'm sorry. Sorry for my bad manners, and equally for my inability to murder you. I think I should go back to my own rooms."

"But why?" he said. "My impression is that you would prefer to stay here."

She sat and looked at him hopelessly.

"It's not," he said, "that I disallow your camouflage, but the very nature of camouflage is that it should successfully wed you to your surroundings. You are trying to lie to yourself, and not to me. This is the cause of your failure."

"Why was I brought here?" she said. "Other than to be played with and humiliated." To her surprise and discomfort, she found she was being humorous, and laughed shortly. He did not join in her laughter, but she sensed from him something that was also humorous, receptive. "Is it an experiment in adaptation; in tolerance?"

"To determine how much proximity a human can tolerate to one of us?"

"Or vice versa."

"No."

"Then what?"

There was a pause. Without warning, a torrent of nausea and fear swept over her. Could he read it from her? Her eyes blackened and she put one hand over them. Swiftly, almost choking, she said, "If there is an answer, don't, please don't tell me."

He was silent, and after a few moments she was better. She

201

sipped the cool wine from the new goblet which had swum to her place. Not looking at him at all, she said, "Have I implanted this barrier against knowledge of that type, or have you?"

"Estár," she heard him say, far away across the few yards of the table, "Estár, your race tends sometimes to demand too little or too much of itself. If there's an answer to your question, you will find it in your own time. You are afraid of the *idea* of the answer, not the answer itself. Wait until the fear goes."

"How can the fear go? You've condemned me to it, keeping me here."

But her words were lies, and now she knew it.

She had spoken more to him in a space of hours than to any of her own kind. She had been relaxed enough in his company almost to allow herself to faint, when, on the two other occasions of her life that she had almost fainted, in company with Levin, or with Lyra, Estár had clung to consciousness in horror, unreasonably terrified to let go.

The alien sat across the table. Not a table knife, not an angle of the room, but was subtly strange in ways she could not place or understand. And he, his ghastly nightmarish ugliness swathed in its disguise....

Again with no warning she began to cry. She wept for three minutes in front of him, dimly conscious of some dispassionate compassion that had nothing to do with involvement. Sobbing, she was aware after all he did not read her thoughts. Even the house did not, though it brought her a foam of tissues. After the three minutes she excused herself and left him. And now he did not detain her.

In her rooms, she found her bed blissfully prepared and lay down on it, letting the mechanisms, visible and invisible, undress her. She woke somewhere in the earliest morning and called the bead like a drop of rain and sent it to fetch the story he had told her.

She resolved she would not go near him again until he summoned her.

A day passed.

A night.

A day.

She thought about him. She wrote a brief essay on how she analyzed him, his physical aura, his few gestures, his inherent hideousness to which she must always be primed, even unknowingly. The distorted voice that nevertheless was so fascinating.

A night.

She could not sleep. He had not summoned her. She walked in her private garden under the stars and found a green rose growing there, softly lighted by a shallow lamp. She gazed on the glow seeping through the tensed and tender petals. She knew herself enveloped in such a glow, a light penetrating her resistence.

"The electric irresistible charisma," she wrote, "of the thing one has always yearned for. To be known, accepted, and so to be at peace. No longer unique, or shut in, or shut *out*, or alone."

A day.

She planned how she might run away. Escaping the garden, stumbling down the mountain, searching through the wilderness for some post of communications or transport. The plan became a daydream and he found her.

A night.

A day.

That day, she stopped pretending, and suddenly he was in her garden. She did not know how he had arrived, but she stepped between the topiary and he was there. He extended his hand in a formal greeting; gloved, six-fingered, not remotely unwieldy. She took his hand. They spoke. They talked all that day, and some of the night, and he played her music from his world and she did not understand it, but it touched some chord in her, over and over with all of its own fiery chords.

She had never comprehended what she needed of herself. She told him of things she had forgotten she knew. He taught her a board game from his world, and she taught him a game with dots of colored light from Earth.

One morning she woke up singing, singing in her sleep. She learned presently she herself had invented the fragment of melody and the handful of harmonies. She worked on it alone, forgetting she was alone, since the music was with her. She did not tell him about the music until he asked her, and then she played it to him.

She was only ashamed very occasionally, and then it was not a cerebral, rather a hormonal thing. A current of some fluid nervous element would pass through her, and she would recall Levin, Lyra, Joya. Eventually something must happen, for all that happened now was aside from life, unconnected to it.

She knew the Alien's name by then. It had no earthly equivalents, she could not write it, could not even say it; only, think it. So she thought it.

She loved him. She had done so from the first moment she had stood with him under the spring trees. She loved him with a sort of welcome, the way diurnal creatures welcome the coming of day.

He must know. If not from her mind, then from the manner in which, on finding him, she would hurry toward him along the garden walks. The way she was when with him. The flowering of her creativity, her happiness.

What ever would become of her?

She sent her family three short noncommittal soothing letters, nothing compared to the bulk of their own.

When the lawns near the house had altered to late summer, it was spring in the world and, as she had promised, Estár went to visit her father.

Chapter 3

Buds like emerald vapor clouded the boughs of the woods beyond the house. The river rushed beneath, heavy with melted snows. It was a windless day, and her family had come out to meet Estár. Lyra, a dark note of music, smiling, Joya, smiling, both looking at her, carefully, tactfully, assessing how she would prefer to be greeted, not knowing. How could they? Joya was slim again. Her child had been born two weeks ago, a medically forward seven-month baby, healthy and beauteous—they had told her in a tape, the most recent of the ten tapes they had sent her, along with Lyra's letters. Levin was standing by the house door, her father.

They all greeted, her, in fact, effusively. It was a show, meant to convey what they were afraid to convey with total sincerity.

They went in, talking continuously, telling her everything. Lyra displayed a wonderful chamber work she and Ekosun, her lover, were at work on—it was obvious he had been staying with her here, and had gone away out of deference to Estár's return, her need for solitary confinement with her family. Joya's son was brought, looking perfectly edible, the color of molasses, opening on a toothless strawberry mouth and two wide amber eyes. His hair was already thick, the color of corn. "You see," said Joya, "I know the father now, without a single test. This hair—the only good thing about *him*."

"She refuses even to let him know," said Levin.

"Oh, I will. Sometime. But the child will take my name, or yours, if you allow it."

They drank tea and ate cakes. Later there came wine, and later there came dinner. While there was food and drink, news to tell, the baby to marvel at, a new cat to play with—a white cat, with a long grey understripe from tail to chin-tip—a new picture to worship, Lyra's music to be heard—while there was all this, the tension was held at bay, almost unnoticeable. About midnight, there came a lull. The baby was gone, the cat slept, the music was done and the picture had faded beyond the friendly informal candlelight. Estár could plead tiredness and go to bed, but then would come tomorrow. It must be faced sometime.

"I haven't," she said, "really told you anything about where I've been."

Joya glanced aside. Lyra stared at her bravely. Levin said, "In fact, you have."

She had, he thought, told them a very great deal. She was strangely different. Not actually in any way he might have feared. Rather, she seemed more sure, quieter, more still, more absorbent, more favorably aware of them than ever in the past. One obvious thing, something that seemed the emblem of it all, the unexpected form of this change in her—her hair. Her hair now was a calm pale brown, untinted, no longer green.

"What have I told you then?" she said, and smiled, not intending to, in case it should be a smile of triumph.

"At least," he said, "that we needn't be afraid for you."

"No. Don't be. I'm really rather happy."

It was Lyra who burst out, unexpectedly, shockingly, with some incoherent protest.

Estár looked at her.

"He's—" she sought a word, selected one, "interesting. His world is interesting. I've started to compose music. Nothing like yours, not nearly as complex or as excellent, but it's fulfilling. I like doing it. I shall get better."

"I'm so sorry," said Lyra. "I didn't mean—it's simply—"

205

"That I shouldn't be happy because the situation is so unacceptable. Yes. But it isn't. I'd never have chosen to go there, because I didn't know what it would entail. But, in fact, it's exactly the sort of life I seem to need. You remember when I meant to go to Marsha? I don't think I would have done as much good there as I'm doing here, for myself. Perhaps I even help him in some way. I suppose they must study us, benignly. Perhaps I'm useful."

"Oh, Estár," Lyra said. She began to cry, begged their pardon and went out of the room, obviously disgusted at her own lack of finesse. Joya rose and explained she was going to look after Lyra. She too went out.

"Oh dear," said Estár.

"It's all right," Levin said. "Don't let it trouble you too much. Overexcitement. First a baby invades us, then you. But go on with what you were saying. What do you do on this mountain?"

He sat and listened as she told him. She seemed able to express herself far better than before, yet even so he was struck by the familiarity rather than the oddness of her life with the alien. Really, she did little there she might not have done here. Yet here she had never done it. He pressed her lightly, not trusting the ice to bear his weight, for details of the being with whom she dwelled.

He noticed instantly that, although she had spoken of him freely, indeed very often, in the course of relating other things, she could not seem to speak of him directly with any comfort. There was an embarrassment quite suddenly apparent in her. Her gestures became angular and her sentences dislocated.

Finally, he braced himself. He went to the mahogany cabinet that was five hundred years old, and standing before it pouring a brandy somewhat younger, he said, "Please don't answer this if you'd rather not. But I'm afraid I've always suspected that, despite all genetic, ethnic or social disparity, those they selected to live with them would ultimately become their lovers. Am I right, Estár?"

He stood above the two glasses and waited.

She said, "Nothing of that sort has ever been discussed."

"Do you have reason to think it will be?"

"I don't know."

"I'm not asking out of pure concern, nor out of any kind of prurient curiosity. One assumes, judging from what the others have said or indicated, that nobody has ever been raped or coerced. That implies some kind of willingness."

"You're asking me if I'd be willing to be his lover?"

"I'm asking if you are in love with him."

Levin turned with the glasses, and took her the brandy. She accepted and looked at it. Her face, even averted, had altered, and he felt a sort of horror. Written on her quite plainly was that look he had heard described—a deadly sorrow, a drawing inward and away. Then it was gone.

"I don't think I'm ready to consider that," she said.

"What is it," he said, "that gives you a look of such deep pain?"

"Let's talk about something else," she said.

Merchant and diplomat, he turned the conversation at once, wondering if he were wrong to do so.

They talked about something else.

It was only much later, when they parted for the night, that he said to her, "anything I *can* do to help you, you've only to tell me."

And she remembered when he brought the rose and gave it to her, how he had said he loved her the best. She wondered if one always loved, then, what was unlike, incompatible.

"This situation has been rather an astonishment to us all," he added now. She approved of him for that, somehow. She kissed him good night. She was so much easier with him, as if estrangement had made them closer, which it had not.

Two weeks passed. Lyra and Joya laughed and did not cry. There were picnics, boat rides, air trips. Lyra played in a live concert, and they went to rejoice in her. Things now seemed facile enough that Ekosun came back to the house, and after that a woman lover of Joya's. They breakfasted and dined in elegant restaurants. There were lazy days too, lying on cushions in the communal rooms listening to music tapes or watching video plays, or reading, or sleeping late, Estár in her old rooms among remembered things that no longer seemed anything to do with her. The green rose of her summons, which would not die but which had something to do with her, had been removed.

It was all like that now. A brightly colored interesting adventure in which she gladly participated, with which she had no link. The very fact that their life captivated her now was because of its—*ali-enness*. And her family, too. How she liked and respected them all at once, what affection she felt for them. And for the same reason.

She could not explain it to them, and would be ill-advised to do so even if she could. She lied to herself, too, keeping her awareness out of bounds as long as she might. But she sensed the lie. It needed another glass of wine, or another chapter of her book, or a peal of laughter, always something, and then another thing and then another, to hold it off.

At the end of two weeks her pretense was wearing thin and she was exhausted. She found she wanted to cry out at them: I know who you are! You are my dear friends, my dazzling idols—I delight in you, admire you, but I am sometimes uneasy with you. Now I need to rest and I want to go—

Now I want to go home.

And then the other question brushed her, as it must. The house on the mountain was her home because he (she wordlessly expressed his name) was there. And because she loved him. Yet in what way did she love him? As one loved an animal? A friend? A lord? A teacher? A brother? Or in the way Levin had postulated, with a lover's love? And darkness would fall down on her mind and she would close the door on it. It was unthinkable.

When she devised the first tentative move toward departure, there was no argument. They made it easy for her. She saw they had known longer than she that she wanted to leave.

"I almost forgot to give you these. I meant to the first day you came back. They're fawn topaz, just the color your hair is now."

On Joya's smoky palm, the stones shone as if softly alight.

"Put your hair back, the way you had it at the concert, and wear them then."

"Thank you," said Estár. "They're lovely."

She reached toward the earrings and found she and her sister were suddenly holding hands with complete naturalness. At once she felt the pulse under Joya's skin, and a strange energy seemed to pass between them, like a healing touch.

They laughed, and Estár said unthinkingly, "But when shall I wear them on the mountain?"

"Wear them for him," said Joya.

"For—"

"For him," said Joya again, very firmly.

"Oh," Estár said unthinkingly, and removed her hand.

"No, none of us have been debating it when you were out of the room," said Joya. "But we do know. Estár, listen to me, there's truly nothing wrong in feeling emotion for this—for him, or even wanting him sexually."

"Oh really, *Joya*."

"*Listen.* I know you're very innocent. Not ignorant, innocent. And there's nothing wrong in that either. But now —"

"Stop it, Joya." Estár turned away, but the machines packing her bag needed no supervision. She stared helplessly at the walls. Joya would not stop.

"There is only one obstacle. In your case, not culture or species. You know what it is. They way they *look*. I'm sorry, I'm sorry, Estár. But this is the root of all your trouble, isn't it?"

"How do I know?" She was exasperated.

"There is no way you can know. Unless you've seen him already, without that disguise they wear. Have you?"

Estár said nothing. Her silence, obviously, was eloquent enough.

"Go back then," said Joya, "go back and make him let you see him. Or find some way to see him when he doesn't realize you can. And then you will know."

"Perhaps I don't want to know."

"Perhaps not. But you've gone too far."

"You're trying to make me go too far. You don't understand."

"Oh, don't I?"

Estár rounded on her, and furiously saw only openness.

"You might possibly," said Estár, "want to spoil—something—"

"I might. But what does that matter? He—it—whatever the alien is, he's real and living and male and you're committed to him, and until you see him and know if you can bear it, how can you *dare* commit yourself?"

"But they're ugly," Estár said flatly. The words, she found, meant very little.

"Some humans are ugly. They can still be loved, loving."

"Suppose somehow I do see him—and I can't think how I would be able to—and suppose then I can't stand to look at him—"

"Then your feelings will undergo some kind of alternate chan-
neling, the way you are now is absurd."

"Oh prithee, sweet sister," Estár snarled, "let me be. Or, blameless
one, throw thou the first stone."

Joya looked bemused. Then she said, "I did, didn't I? Two of
them. You caught them, too."

And went out of the room, leaving the brown topaz earrings in
Estár's hand.

It was so simple to return in the end it was like being borne away
by a landslide.

All at once she was in a vehicle, the house flowing off behind
her to a minuscule dot, and so to nothing. Then she was alone and
sat down with her thoughts to consider everything—and abruptly,
before she was ready, the conical mountain loomed before her.

There was a ghost of winter frost in the garden by the gate.
Further on, the banana-yellow leaves were falling. She had seen
many places anachronized by a weather control, yet here it seemed
rather wonderful ... for no reason at all.

The blossom was gone from about the building, but roses had
opened everywhere. Alien roses, very tall, the colors of water and
sky, not the blood and blush, parchment, pallor and shadow shades
of Earth. She walked through a wheatfield of roses and in at the
doors.

She went straight through all the intervening rooms and arrived
in the suite the Alien called —— had given her. There, she looked
about her steadfastly. Even now, she was not entirely familiar with
the suite, and unfamiliar with large sections of the house and gar-
denland.

Under such circumstances, it was not possible to recognize this
place as her home. Even if, intellectually, she did so.

She wondered where he might be in the house. Surely he would
know she had returned. Of course he would know. If she went out
into her own garden, perhaps—

A word was spoken. It meant "yes." And although she did not
know the word she knew its meaning for it had been spoken inside
her head.

She waited, trembling. How close they were, then, if he could
speak to her in such a way. She had been probing, seeking for him,

her intuitive telepathy now quite strong, and she had touched him, and in turn been touched. There was no sense of intrusion. The word spoken in her head was like a caress, polite and very gentle.

So she went out into her garden, where it was beginning to be autumn now, and where the topiary craned black against the last of the day's sunlight. He stood just beyond the trees, by the stone basin with the colored fish. A heron made of blue steel balanced forever on the rim, peering downward, but the fish were sophisticated and unafraid of it, since it had never attacked them.

Suppose it was this way with herself? There he stood, swathed, masked, hidden. He had never given her cause to fear him. But was that any reason not to?

He took her hand; she gave her hand. She loved him, and was only frightened after all because he must know it. They began to talk, and soon she no longer cared that she loved him or that he knew.

They discussed much and nothing, and it was all she had needed. She felt every tense string of her body and her brain relaxing. All but one. What Levin, her father, had hinted, what Lyra had shied away from saying and Joya said. Could he perceive and sense this thing in her thoughts? Probably. And if she asked, in what way would he put her off? And could she ask? And would she ask?

When they dined that evening, high up in the orb of the roof, only the table lit, and the stars thickly clustered over the vanes above, she watched the molecules parting in his visor to accommodate cup or goblet or fork.

Later, when they listened to the music of his planet, she watched his long hands, cloaked in their gauntlets, resting so quiet yet so animate on the arms of a chair they were like sleeping cats.

Cat's eyes. If she saw them would she scream with horror? Yes, for weeks her sleep had been full of dreams of him, incoherent but sexual dreams, dreams of desire. And yet he was a shadow. She dreamed of coupling in the dark, blind, unseeing. She could hate Joya for being so right.

When the music ended, there came the slow turn of his head, and she beheld the graceful power of it, that concealed skull pivoted by that unseen neck. The cloaked hands flexed. The play of muscle ran down his whole body like a wave, and he had risen to his feet, in a miracle of coordinated movement.

"You're very tired, Estár," he said.

"But you know what I want to ask you."

"Perhaps only what you feel you should want to ask."

"To see you. As you are. It must happen, surely, if I live here with you."

"There's no need for it to happen now. Sometimes, with those others like yourself who are the companions of my kind, it only happens after many years. Do you comprehend, Estár? You're not bound to look at me as I am."

"But," she said, "you would allow it?"

"Yes."

She stared at him and said, "When?"

"Not tonight, I think. Tomorrow, then. You recall that I swim in the mornings. The mechanism that waits on you will bring you to my pool. Obviously, I swim without any of this. You can look at me, see me, and after that stay or go away, as you wish."

"Thank you," she said. Her head began to ache and she felt as if some part of her had died, burned out by the terror of what she had just agreed to.

"But you may change your mind," he said. "I won't expect you."

There was no clue in his distorted, expressive voice. She wondered if he, too, was afraid.

She made all the usual preparations for bed and lay down as if tonight were like any other, and did not sleep. And in the morning, she got up and bathed and dressed, as if it were any other morning. And when the machines had washed and brushed her hair, and enhanced her face with pastel cosmetics, she found she could not remember anything of the night or the routines of waking, bathing, dressing or anything at all. All she could remember was the thing to come, the moment when she saw him as he truly was. That moment had already happened to her maybe five thousand times, over and over, as she conjured it, fled from it, returned to it, in her mind.

And therefore, was he aware of all she had pictured? If he had not sensed her thoughts, he must deduce her thoughts.

She drank scalding tea, glad to be burned.

The voice-bead hovered, and she held out her hand. It came to perch on her fingers, something which she liked it to do, a silly affectionate ruse, her pretense, its complicity, that it was somehow creaturally alive.

"Estár, when shall I take you to the indoor pool?"

"Yes," she said. "Take me there now."

It was a part of the house she had not been in very much, and then, beyond a blank wall which dissolved as the molecules in his visor had done, a part of the house she had never entered. *His* rooms.

They opened one from another. Spare, almost sparse, but supple with subtle color, here and there highlighted by things which, at some other time, she would have paused to examine in fascinated interest — musical instruments from his world, the statue of a strange animal in stranger metal, an open book on whose surfaces he had written by hand in the letters of an alien alphabet. But then doors drew aside, and the bead glimmered before her out into a rectangular space, open above on the skies of Earth, open at its center on a dense blue water. Plants grew in pots along the edges of the pool, huge alien ferns and small alien trees, all leaning lovingly to the pool which had been minerally treated to resemble the liquids of their home. With a very little effort, Estár might imagine, it was his planet she saw before her, and that dark swift shape sheering through the water, just beneath its surface, that shape was the indigenous thing, not the *alien* thing at all. Indeed, she herself was the alien, at this instant.

And at this instant, the dark shape reached the pool's end, only some ten feet from her. There came a dazzle across the water as he broke from it. He climbed from the pool and moved between the pots of ferns and trees, and the foliage and the shadow left him, as the water had already done. It was as he had told her. She might see him, unmasked, naked, open-eyed.

She stared at him until she was no longer able to do so. And then she turned and walked quickly away. It was not until she reached the inner rooms that she began to run.

She reentered the suite he had given her, and stayed there only for an hour before she sent the voice-bead to him with her request. It returned with his answer inside five minutes. This time, there was no telepathic communion. She could not have borne it, and he had recognized as much.

Chapter 4

"Please don't question me," she said. "Please."

Her family who, not anticipating her arrival on this occasion, had not been waiting to meet her—scattered like blown leaves about the room—acquiesced in gracious troubled monosyllables.

They would realize, of course, what must have occurred. If any of them blamed themselves it was not apparent. Estár did not consider it, would consider nothing, least of all that she was bound, eventually, to return to the place she had fled.

She went to her apartment in Levin's house, glanced at its known unknown angles and objects, got into the remembered unremembered bed. "Bring me something to make me sleep," she said to the household robots. They brought it to her. She drank the cordial and sank thousands of miles beneath some sea. There were dreams, but they were tangled, distant, waking for brief moments she could not recall them, only their colors, vague swirlings of noise or query. They did not threaten her. When she woke completely, she had more of the opiate brought, and slept again.

Days and nights passed. Rousing, she would permit the machines to give her other things. She swallowed juices, vitamins and small fruits. She wandered to the bathroom, immersed herself in scented fluid, dried herself and returned to bed. And slept.

It would have to end, obviously. It was not a means of dying, merely of temporary oblivion, aping the release of death. The machineries maintained her physical equilibrium, she lost five pounds, that was all. No one disturbed her, came to plead or chide. Each morning, a small note or two would be delivered—Joya or Lyra—once or twice Levin. These notes were handwritten and full of quiet solicitude. They were being very kind, very patient. And she was not behaving well, to worry them, to throw her burden upon them second hand in this way. But she did not care very much about that. What galvanized her in the end, ousted her from her haven of faked death, was a simple and inevitable thing. Her dreams marshalled themselves and began to assume coherence. She began to dream of him. Of the instant when he had left the water and she had seen him as he was. So they condemned her to relive, over and over again, that instant, just as she had lived it over and over before it had happened. Once the dreams were able to do this to her, naturally, there was no point in sleeping any longer. She must wake up, and find a refuge in the alternative of insomnia.

Seven days had gone by. She emerged from the depths a vampire, eager to feed on each of the other living things in the house, to devour their lives, the world and everything, to cram her mind, her consciousness. Again, they humored her. None of them spoke of what must have caused this, but the strain on them was evident. Estár liked them more each second, and herself less. How could she inflict this on them? She inflicted it. Three days, three nights went by. She did not sleep at anytime.

Catching the atmosphere like a germ, Joya's son became fractious. The cat leapt, its fur electric, spitting at shadows. A terrible recurring headache, of which she did not speak but which was plain in her face, began to torment Lyra. Her lover was absent. Estár knew Ekosun would dislike her for consigning her sister to such pain. Finally Joya broke from restraint, and said to her, "I'm sorry. Do you believe that?" Estár ignored the reference, and Joya said, "Levin's in contact with the Mercantile Senate. They have a great deal of power. It may be possible to force the issue." "No one has ever been able to do anything of the sort." "What would you like me to do?" said Joya. "Throw myself from a great height into the river?" Estár laughed weakly. She took Joya in her arms. "It wasn't you. I would have had to — you were right. Right, right." "Yes," said Joya, "I was right. Perhaps one of the most heinous crimes known to humanity."

When Estár courteously excused herself and went away, Joya did not protest. Joya did not feel guilty, only regretful at the consequences of an inevitable act. Clean of conscience, she in turn set no further conflict working in Estár — the guilty are always the most prone to establish complementary guilt, and the most unforgiving thereafter.

And so Estár came to spend more and more time with Joya, but they did not speak of him once.

On the twelfth day Estár fell asleep. She dreamed and saw him, framed by the pool and the foliage of his planet, and she started awake with a cry of loud anger.

It seemed she could never forget the awfulness of the revelation, could not get away from it. And therefore she might as well return to the mountain. Probably he would leave her very much alone. Eventually, it might be possible for her to become reconciled. They might meet again on some level of communication. Eventually. Conceivably. Perhaps.

That evening she spent in one of the communal rooms of her family's house. She tried to repay their sweetness and their distress with her new calm, with gentle laughter, thanking them with these things, her reestablished sense of self, her resignation tinged by intimations of hope, however dull, and by humor coming back like a bright banner.

They drank cold champagne and vodka, and the great fire roared under the transparent column, for like the drinks still the nights were cold. Estár had grown in this house, and now, quite suddenly and unexpectedly, she remembered it. She smiled at her father who had said he loved her the best of his daughters. She knew it was untrue, and yet that he had said it to her had become a precious thing.

There was a movement, a flicker like light. For a moment she thought it came from the fire, or from some mote traveling across the air of the room, the surface of her eye. And then she knew it had moved within her brain. She knew that he had spoken to her, despite the miles between them, and the manner in which she had left him. There were no words at all. It was like a whisper, or the brush of a low breeze across the plateaux of her mind. She felt a wonderful slowness fill her, and a silence.

One hour later a message came for her, delivered to the house by a machinery only glimpsed in the gusty evening. She opened the synthetic wrapper. She had anticipated, nor was she wrong to have done so. There was one line of writing, which read: *Estár. Tomorrow, come back to the mountain.* And he had signed it with that name she could not read or speak, yet which she knew now as well, maybe better, than her own. She looked a long while at the beautiful unhuman letters. They watched her, and she said to them, "Tomorrow I am going back to the mountain. To him."

There was again that expression on her face; it had been there mostly, since she had reentered Levin's house on this last visit. (*Visit.* She did not belong to them anymore.) The expression of the children of Earth sacrificed to monsters or monstrous gods, given in their earthly perfection to dwell with beasts. That dreadful demoralizing sadness, that devouring fading in the face of the irreparable. And yet there was nothing in her voice, and as she left the room her step was untrammelled and swift. And Levin recollected, not wanting to, the story of lemmings rushing in blithe tumult toward the ocean to be drowned.

A peacock-green twilight enclosed the mountain garden and the building. Estár looked at it in wonder; it transformed everything. It seemed to her she was on some other planet, neither her own nor his.

A capsule had given her sleep throughout the journey. Drowsily serene she walked into the building and the voice-bead played about her, as if glad she had returned. They went to her suite and she said, "Where is he?" And opened her door to find him in the room.

She started back. In the blue-green resin of the dusk she saw at once that he was dressed in the garments of his own world, which concealed hardly anything of him.

She turned away and said coldly, "You're not being fair to me."

"It will soon be dark," he said. "If you leave the lamps unlit, you won't see me well. But you have seen me. The pretense is finished." There was no distortion to his voice. She had never really heard *him* speak before.

She came into the room and sat down beside a window. Beyond the glassy material, the tall topiary waved like seaweed in the sea of sky. She looked at this and did not look at him.

Yet she saw only him.

The water-sky dazzled as the pool had done, and he stepped out of the sky, the pool, and stood before her as in all her dreams, unmasked, naked, open-eyed. The nature of the pool was such, he was not even wet.

The hirsute pelt which covered his kind was a reality misinterpreted, mis-explained. It was most nearly like the fur of a short-haired cat, yet in actuality resembled nothing so much as the nap of velvet. He was black, like her sister Joya, yet the close black nap of fur must be tipped, each single hair, with amber; his color had changed second to second, as the light or dark found him, even as he breathed, from deepest black to sheerest gold. His well-made body was modeled from these two extremes of color, his fine mus-

217

culature, like that of a statue, inked with ebony shadows, and high-lighted by gilding. Where the velvet sheathing faded into pure skin, at the lips, nostrils, eyelids, genitals, the soles of the feet, palms of the hands, the flesh itself was a mingling of the two shades, a somber cinnamon, couth and subtle, sensual in its difference, but not shock-ing in any visual or aesthetic sense. The inside of his mouth, which he had also contrived to let her see, was a dark golden cave, in which conversely the humanness of the white teeth was in fact itself a shock. While at his loins the velvet flowed into a bearded blackness, long hair like unraveled silk; the same process occurred on the skull, a raying mane of hair, very black, very silken, its edges burning out through amber, ochre, into blondness — the sunburst of a black sun. The nails on his six long fingers, the six toes of his long and arched feet, were the tint of new dark bronze, translucent, bright as flames. His facial features were large and of a contrasting fineness, their sculptured quality at first obscured, save in profile, by the sequential ebb and flare of gold and black, and the domination of the extraordinary eyes. The long cinnamon lids, the thick lashes that were not black but startlingly flaxen — the color of the edges of the occipital hair — these might be mistaken for human. But the eyes themselves could have been made from two highly polished citrines, clear saffron, darkening around the outer lens almost to the cinnamon shade of the lids, and at the center by curiously blended charcoal stages to the ultimate black of the pupil. Analogously, they were like the eyes of a lion, and perhaps all of him lion-like, maybe, the powerful body, its skin unlike a man's, flawless as a beast's skin so often was, the pale-fire edged mane. Yet he was neither like a man nor an animal. He was like himself, his kind, and his eyes were their eyes, compelling, radiant of intellect and intelligence even in their strangeness, and even in their beauty. For he *was* beautiful. Utterly and dreadfully beautiful. Coming to the Earth in the eras of its savagery, he would have been worshipped in terror as a god. He and his would have been forced to hide what they were for fear the true sight of it would burn out the vision of those who looked at them. And possibly this was the reason, still, why they had hidden themselves, and the reason too for the misunderstanding and the falsehoods. To fear to gaze at their ugliness, that was a safe and sensible premise. To fear their grandeur and their marvel — that smacked of other emotions less wise or good.

And she herself, of course, had run from this very thing. Not his alien hideousness—his beauty, which had withered her. To condescend to give herself to one physically her inferior, that might be acceptable. But not to offer herself to the lightning-bolt, the solar flame. She had seen and she had been scorched, humiliated and made nothing, and she had run away, ashamed to love him. And now, ashamed, she had come back, determined to put away all she had felt for him or begun to feel or thought to feel. Determined to be no more than the companion of his mind, which itself was like a star, but, being an invisible, intangible thing, she might persuade herself to approach.

But now he was here in a room with her, undisguised, in the gracious garments of his own world and the searing glory of his world's race, and she did not know how she could bear to be here with him.

And she wondered if he were pleased by her suffering and her confusion. She wondered why, if he were not, he would not let her go forever. And she pictured such an event and wondered then if, having found him, she *could* live anywhere but here, where she could not live at all.

The sky went slowly out, and they had not spoken any more.

In the densening of the darkness, those distant suns, which for eons had given their light to the Earth, grew large and shining and sure.

When he said her name, she did not start, nor did she turn to him.

"There is something which I must tell you now," he said to her. "Are you prepared to listen?"

"Very well."

"You think that whatever I may say to you must be irrelevant to you, at this moment. That isn't the case."

She was too tired to weep, or to protest, or even to go away.

"I know," he said quietly, "And there's no need for you to do any of these things. Listen, and I shall tell you why not."

As it turned out, they had, after all, a purpose in coming to the Earth, and to that other handful of occupied planets they had visited, the bright ships drifting down, the jewels of their technology and culture given as a gift, the few of their species left behind,

219

males and females, dwellers in isolated mansions, who demanded nothing of their hosts until the first flowering of alien roses, the first tender kidnappings of those worlds' indigenous sons and daughters.

The purpose of it all was never generally revealed. But power, particularly benign power, is easily amalgamated and countenanced. They had got away with everything, always. And Earth was no exception.

They were, by the time their vessels had lifted from the other system, a perfect people, both of the body and the brain; and spiritually they were more nearly perfect than any other they encountered. The compassion of omnipotence was intrinsic to them now, and the generosity of wholeness. Yet that wholeness, that perfection had had a bizarre, unlooked-for side effect. For they had discovered that totality can, by its very nature, cancel out itself.

They had come to this awareness in the very decades they had come also to know that endless vistas of development lay before them, if not on the physical plane, then certainly on the cerebral and the psychic. They possessed the understanding, as all informed creatures do, that their knowledge was simply at its dawn. There was more for their race to accomplish than was thinkable, and they rejoiced in the genius of their infancy, and looked forward to the limitless horizons — and found that their own road was ended, that they were not to be allowed to proceed. Blessed by unassailable health, longevity, strength and beauty, their genes had rebelled within them, taking this peak as an absolute and therefore as a terminus.

Within a decade of their planetary years, they became less fertile, and then sterile. Their bodies could not form children, either within a female womb or externally, in an artificial one. Cells met, embraced, and died in that embrace. Those scarcity of embryos that were successfully grown in the crystalline generative placentae lived, in some cases, into the Third Phase, approximate to the fifth month of a human pregnancy — and then they also died, their little translucent corpses floating like broken silver flowers. To save them, a cryogenic program was instituted. Those that lived, on their entry to the Third Phase, were frozen into stasis. The dream persisted that at last there would be found some way to realize their life. But the dream did not come true. And soon even the greatest and most populous cities of that vast and blueskied planet must report that, in a year twice the length of a year of the Earth, only eight or nine children had been saved to enter even that cold limbo, which now was their only medium of survival.

The injustice of fate was terrible. It was not that they had become effete, or that they were weakened. It was their actual peerlessness which would kill the race. But being what they were, rather than curse God and die, they evolved another dream, and before long pursued it across the galaxies. Their natural faculties had remained vital as their procreative cells had not. They had conceived the notion that some other race might be discovered, sufficiently similar to their own that — while it was unlikely the two types could mingle physically to produce life — in the controlled environment of a breeding tube such a thing might be managed. The first world that offered them scope, in a system far beyond the star of Earth, was receptive and like enough that the first experiments were inaugurated. They failed.

And then, in one long night, somewhere in that planet's eastern hemisphere, a female of that race miscarrying and weeping bitterly at her loss, provided the lamp to lead them to their dream's solution.

With the sound and astounding anatomical science of the mother world, the aliens were able to transfer one of their own children, one of those embryos frozen in cryogenesis for fifty of their colossal years, into the vacated womb.

And, by their science too, this womb, filled and then despoiled, was repaired and sealed, brought in a matter of hours to the prime readiness it had already achieved and thought to abandon. The mother was monitored and cared for, for at no point was she to be endangered or allowed to suffer. But she thrived, and the transplanted child grew. In term, the approximate ten-month term normal to that planet, it was born, alive and whole. It had come to resemble the host race almost exactly; this was perhaps the first surprise. As it attained adulthood, there was a second surprise. Its essence resembled only the essence of its parental race. It was alien, and it pined away among the people of its womb-mother. Brought back to its true kind, then, and only then, it prospered and was happy and became great. It seemed, against all odds, their own were truly their own. Heredity had told, not in the physical, but in the ego. It appeared the soul of their kind would continue, unstoppable. And the limitless horizons opened again before them, away and away.

By the date in their travels when they reached Earth, their methods were faultless and their means secret and certain. Details had been added, refining details typical of that which the aliens were. The roses were one aspect of such refinements.

Like themselves, the plants of the mother world were incredibly long-lived. Nourished by treated soil and held in a vacuum—as the embryos were held in their vacuum of coldness—such flowers could thrive for half an Earth century, even when uprooted.

Earth had striven with her own bellicosity and won that last battle long before the aliens came. Yet some aggression, and some xenophobic self-protective pride remained. Earth was a planet where the truth of what the aliens intended was to be guarded more stringently than on any other world. A woman miscarrying her child in the fourth or fifth month, admitted to a medical center, and evincing psychological evidence of trauma—even now it happened. This planet was full of living beings, a teeming globe, prone still to accident and misjudgment. As the woman lay sedated, the process was accomplished. In the wake of the dead and banished earthly child, the extra-terrestrial embryo was inserted, and anchored like a star. Women woke, and burst into tears and tirades of relief—not knowing they had been duped. Some not even remembering, for the drugs of the aliens were excellent, that they had ever been close to miscarrying. A balance was maintained. Some recalled, some did not. A sinister link would never be established. Only the eager and willing were ever employed.

There was one other qualification. It was possible to predict logistically the child's eventual habitat, once born. Since the child would have to be removed from that habitat in later years, the adoptive family were chosen with skill. The rich—who indeed tended more often to bear their children bodily—the liberated, the open-minded, the unlonely. That there might be tribulation at the ultimate wrenching away was unavoidable, but it was avoided or lessened, wherever and however feasible. Nor was a child ever recalled until it had reached a level of prolonged yearning, blindly and intuitively begging to be rescued from its unfitted human situation.

Here the roses served.

They in their crystal boxes, the embryos frozen in their crystal wombs. With every potential child a flower had been partnered. The aura of a life imbued each rose. It was the aura, then, which relayed the emanations of the child and the adult which the child became. The aura which told, at last, this telepathically sensitive race, when the summons must be sent, the exile rescued.

The green rose now flourishing in her garden here was Estár's own rose, brought home.

The woman who had carried Estár inside her, due to her carelessness, had aborted Levin's child, and received the alien unaware.

The woman had needed to bear a child, but not to keep the child. Levin had gladly claimed what he took to be his own.

Estár, the daughter of her people, not Levin's daughter, not Lyra's sister or Joya's either. Estár had grown up and grown away, and the green rose which broadcast her aura began to cry soundlessly, a wild beacon. So they had released her from her unreal persona or let her release herself.

And here she was now, turning from the window of stars to the visible darkness of the room, and to his invisible darkness.

For a long while she said nothing, although she guessed — or telepathically she knew — he waited for her questions. At last one came to her.

"Marsha," she said. "They disqualified me from going there."

"A lie," he said. "It was arranged. In order that your transposition should be easier when it occurred."

"And I—" she said, and hesitated.

"And you are of my kind, although you resemble the genera which was your host. This is always the case. I know your true blood line, your true father and mother, and one day you may meet them. We are related, you and I. In the terminology of this world, cousins. There is one other thing."

She could not see him. She did not require to see him with her eyes. She now waited, for the beauty of his voice.

"The individual to whom you are summoned — this isn't a random process. You came to me, as all our kind return, to one with whom you would be entirely compatible. Not only as a companion, but as a lover, a bonded lover—a husband, a wife. You see, Estár, we've learned another marvel. The changes that alter our race in the womb of an alien species, enable us thereafter to make living children together, either bodily or matrically, whichever is the most desired."

Estár touched her finger to the topaz in her left ear.

"And so I love you spontaneously, but without any choice. Because we were chosen to be lovers?"

"Does it offend you?"

"If I were human," she said, "it might offend me. But then."

"And I, of course," he said, "also love you."

"And the way I am—my looks…. Do you find me ugly?"

"I find you beautiful. Strangely, alienly lovely. That's quite usual. Although for me, very curious, very exciting."

She shut her eyes then, and let him move to her across the dark. And she experienced in her own mind the glorious wonder he felt at the touch of her skin's smoothness like a cool leaf, just as he would experience her delirious joy in the touch of his velvet skin, the note of his dark and golden mouth discovering her own.

Seeing the devouring sadness in her face when she looked at them, unable to reveal her secret, Estár's earthly guardians would fear for her. They would not realize her sadness was all for them. And when she no longer moved among them, they would regret her, and mourn for her as if she had died. Disbelieving or forgetting that in any form of death, the soul—Psyche, Estár, (well-named)—refinds a freedom and a beauty lost with birth.

"WAIT UNTIL THE FEAR GOES"

"Beauty," it is often said, "lies in the eye of the beholder." Tanith Lee's story strongly suggests how beastliness resides there as well. In fact, the story is primarily concerned with the beholder's "contribution" and shows how the attributions of the attractive and the repellent arise from our anxieties and existential dis-ease. Lee makes this point by focusing almost exclusively on Estár and the gradual subsidence of her fears.

The first subtraction of causes for fear is made when the story opens and we are introduced to a futuristic Earth whose culture is extraordinarily accepting and non-judgmental. Sexual and racial open-mindedness are only some of the hallmarks of this Liberal Utopia of Right Thinking. For example, Estár and her sisters (one Caucasian and the other black) are the offspring of their father's liaisons with different women; and with their father's blessing, one sister has a live-in Asian male companion and the other sister has two lovers, one male and one female.

Even when Lee introduces information about the alien race that has come to Earth, she emphasizes there is little cause for alarm: worried that Earthlings might shudder at their otherworldly phys-iognomy, these aliens have donned masking devices and costumes so Earth's inhabitants *would not be startled*; and taking up residence on this planet, they settled in remote regions *out of deference* to the sensibilities of the natives. To be sure, these aliens have a worrisome custom of sending a summons (by means of a rose in a crystal box) to selected earthlings to join them as companions; but Lee stresses this was done *"without force, without threat"* and when those so invit-ed were reluctant to take up their invitations, their hosts simply *waited patiently* for them to come around. Moreover, when the cho-sen earthlings finally accepted their summonses, they came to *no harm* and, in fact, came to prefer the company of their otherworldly partners.

Nonetheless, when Estár receives her own rose and acquiesces to the summons, she is "sickened with fear and rage" because, as she perceives things, she is being forced to become the companion of an alien. When she comes to the Alien's home and meets her ser-vant, a luminous bead, she petulantly objects to being made a cap-tive and declares her irritable unwillingness to meet her other-worldly host. She is taken aback by the bead's reply: "There is no coercion. You are forced to do nothing which does not accord with your sense of autonomy." When she further protests, "But I am here against my will," the bead meets her comment with a silence meant to suggest that hers are mind-forged manacles. Indeed, as days pass, some of her fears begin to trickle away as she discovers she was "not a slave, not a pet. She was free as air."

Feeling more at ease in her new environment, Estár finally haz-ards a first meeting with the Alien. Again, what is remarkable about this encounter is the extraordinary lengths to which her other-worldly companion goes in order to remove any cause for anxiety in Estár, altering his otherworldly voice out of deference to her and donning a masking costume so she will not be startled by his appearance. Given these non-threatening efforts, Estár relaxes a little but recoils in panic when she realizes the Alien is telepathic and can read her thoughts. Again, he endeavors to calm her, reassuring her that she has no reason to be afraid of this form of communication.

Then occurs a significant interchange between the two, a conversation that redirects attention to Estár's own fears and resistances:

> "I should like," she said, "to return to my father's house."
> "At any time, you may do so."
> "But I want," she said, "to stay there. I mean that I don't want to come back here."
> She waited....
> He said, "I'm not reading your mind, I assure you of that. But I can sense instantly whenever you lie."
> "Lie? What am I lying about? I said, I want to go home.".....
> "You are trying to lie to yourself, and not to me.".....
> "Why was I brought here?" she said.... There was a pause. Without warning, a torrent, of nausea and fear swept over her. Could he read it from her? Her eyes blackened and she put one hand over them. Swiftly, almost choking, she said, "If there is an answer, don't, please don't tell me."

Estár resists. She is unwilling to go to the bottom of her fears. But she still has the presence of mind enough to wonder aloud, "Have I implanted this barrier against knowledge?" Having done nothing on his part to prompt her anxiety, in this harmless environment, the Alien advises Estár, "You are afraid of the *idea* of an answer, not the answer itself. Wait until the fear goes."

In the days that follow, Estár's fears begin to subside. She realizes she may come and go as she chooses, and though she occasionally toys with the idea of running away, there came a day when "she stopped pretending." Like a muscle once tensed in fear and now gradually relaxing, Estár's frightened anxieties slowly begin to evaporate.

On her first return home, Estár's family notices her new assurance, her new fearlessness. Still, she has not gone all the way in reckoning with her anxieties. Probing a little bit farther, "not trusting the ice to bear his weight," Estár's father ever so gently inquires whether she might consider becoming the Alien's lover.

Touching on a deeper level of her fear, Estár's father notices how his question prompts his daughter to turn away as a look of horror passes over her face: "What is it," he asks, "that gives you a look of such deep pain?" Estár resists. "I don't think I'm ready to consider that," she quickly replies, "Let's talk about something else." Even when Estár notes her own resistances and acknowledges her uneasiness and her unwillingness to even let these fears come into her conscious awareness, whenever the idea of accepting the Alien as her lover appears as a subject, a "darkness would fall down on her mind and she would close the door on it. It was unthinkable."

Before she returns to the Alien, Estár's sister Joya encourages her to go all the way and face her deep-seated fears. Observing that the stumbling block is Estár's apprehension about how the Alien might look, Joya encourages her sister to, once and for all, face this issue and ask to see the Alien naked, as he actually is and without disguising masks. In this way, Joya argues, Estár can decide for herself whether she can live and love her presumably monstrous companion. Still, Estár recoils, "You're trying to make me go too far."

Nonetheless, she returns and upon her return notices, as if for the first time, a metal sculpture of a heron poised above a fish pond and how the fish, never threatened, are unafraid and swim at ease. Estár realizes that the Alien "had never given her cause to fear him"; even when he telepathically communicates with her, "there was no sense of intrusion" but, instead, a kind of gentle politeness. Fearing only her growing love for him, Estár feels "every tense string of her body and her brain relaxing. All but one." It is her unconscious that first begins to grapple with this last fear, the fear of intimacy, and Estár's dreams start to fill with fantasies of lovemaking in the dark.

Finally, she asks to see him, naked, as he is — without the purdah of his cloaking costumes. Again, in consenting to her request, Lee stresses how her alien companion endeavors to remove any occasion for anxiety or any feelings of constraint; he provides her with numerous escape clauses: "There is no need for that to happen now. Sometimes, with others like yourself who are companions of my kind, it only happens after many years.... You are not bound to look at me as I am.... You can look at me, see me, and after that stay or go away, as you wish." Arranging a rendezvous for the next morning when he is swimming, he does not box her in but again leaves her with another escape clause. "You may change your mind," he says, "I won't expect you."

The next morning Estár comes to the swimming pool and sees the alien naked, as he is, without the comforting disguises he donned before out of deference to her fears. In a revelation that Lee withholds until later in the story, we understand that Estár has come expecting a ghastly glimpse of her horrific host but is, instead, undone by a vision of a handsome male of supernal beauty. What Estár thought would be a vision of Medusa's Gorgon head turns out, instead, to be a privileged glimpse of the Holy of Holies. In response now to her hierophantic encounter with startling beauty, Estár once more panics and runs away.

In this brilliant way, Lee harmonizes the apparent contradiction between "Beauty and the Beast" and the antecedent myth of "Cupid and Psyche"; indeed, Lee advises that Estár's name means "psyche," and other allusions to both the fairy tale and the myth appear throughout the story. Beaumont's story, it should be remembered, is about a repulsive Beast while Apuleius's myth concerns Cupid, the most beautiful of all males. By collapsing these two into each other, Lee indicates that aversion and attraction, beastliness and beauty, awfulness and awe-full-ness, are two sides of the very same coin.

When Estár felt herself *above* her presumably hideous companion, she could be condescending; now, after "the awfulness of that revelation," she feels *beneath* her astonishingly beautiful companion, and her condescension gives way to new fears about her unworthiness. Troubled by what she has seen, Estár retreats home a second time. Resisting still, she soaks herself in sleep-inducing drugs, then in petulant insomnia and quarrelsomeness. Finally, as time passes, her unconscious begins to reckon with what she has seen and with her fears, and finally her dreams achieve some coherence and she resolves to return to the Alien and their home.

Upon her return, Estár discovers the Alien in her sleeping quarters, and "she did not start" when he says her name. At this point, the Alien tells her the Story of his Race and reveals that Estár, herself, is of alien blood. To be sure, this account of godlike visitors from outer space and the implantation of embryos is something of a *deus ex machina*, but this plot contrivance explains many things: how, when Estár was younger and felt restless and out-of-place, these feelings were not just normal adolescent feelings of alienation but actually a hankering for her own tribe; how, when she finally gives her hand to her suitor and turns her back on her earthling family, the dilemma of exogamy is resolved since they were only her adoptive family; and finally why she is so powerfully drawn to her alien companion—he is her own kind.

With this conclusion, Lee offers what may be the most interesting ending of variants of "Beauty and the Beast." In Beaumont, the Beast changes into a handsome prince but we are left with unresolved issues: how Beauty, having developed an affection for the Beast, can fall so immediately in love with this new and handsome character who suddenly appears; and if, as the fairy suggests, Beauty has proved her virtue by recognizing the unimportance of looks, why good looks in her partner is the very way she is rewarded. In Carter's "Tiger's Bride," we are given another permutation; instead of the transformation of the Beast, as part of her own feminist and feral agenda, Carter has her Beauty change into a beast herself. But in Lee's story no change occurs in either character; instead, as Estár's fears gradually diminish, the notion of Otherness itself evaporates and is replaced by a recognition of fundamental sameness.

What is remarkable about Lee's story is how our attention is constantly brought back to Estár and her fears: it all comes down to her. Consistently and thoroughly, all external occasions for anxiety and apprehension are removed: her family is supportive, the Alien prepared to wait endlessly and patiently until she has worked through her issues. In no other story is our attention drawn so fixedly to the Beauty character and the processes she must go through. And in no other story is our attention drawn so fixedly to the beholder's contribution: to how the fundamental aesthetic reactions of attraction or repulsion, the attribution of beauty or beastliness, the feelings of humbled abashment or condescending rejection—how all these arise from our side and from existential disease.

It is significant, then, that what Estár essentially encounters is a strikingly handsome *black* male. To be sure, he is also animal-like and leonine in appearance. But these animal features only suggest the bestial otherness of his race, as they do in *Planet of the Apes*.

A racial allegory, *Planet of the Apes* was written by Pierre Boulle who was interned in a Japanese prisoner of war camp during World War II and who also wrote *The Bridge on the River Kwai*. Thinking of both his books, it is not difficult to imagine who is being represented in *Planet of the Apes*, in Boulle's simian overlords and their human slaves. Another science-fiction fantasy and racial allegory, Lee's story of intergalactic miscegenation might be imagined as the peaceful alternative to his book.

Racism, homophobia, and other forms of intolerance, Lee's story suggests, are based on fear — a fear of difference. When that fear is squarely faced, acknowledged, and deeply examined, anxiety can dissolve and the soul relax. In that calm, projections of Otherness disappear, sameness arises, and the story of "Beauty and the Beast" is undone.

EIGHT

FILMS

WHILE MANY THINK OF "Beauty and the Beast" as a classic heterosexual story, the two major film versions of the tale essentially present it as a gay version.[1] There is, of course, a certain logic to repositioning the story in this way. As Pat Calafia has observed, those who do not conform to the "mainstream's sexual mores are also seen as monsters."[2]

There have been several gay short stories based on the tale,[3] but perhaps the most accomplished is a lesbian retelling, "The Tale of the Rose" by celebrated Irish writer Emma Donoghue.[4] Following Beaumont's tale closely, Donoghue's own story differs slightly with the appearance of a masked Beast. Gradually, it is revealed that the Beast is a woman who has adopted the mask because others cannot accept her for who she is. Gradually, too, Beauty learns "that there was nothing monstrous about this woman" and "that beauty was infinitely various." As the story ends, we are told of opinions about the two lovers: "Some villagers told travelers of a beast and a beauty

1 Besides Jean Cocteau's and Disney Studios' films, one televised version has since appeared on videotape. First seen on Shelley Duvall's television series "Faerie Tale Theatre," "Beauty and the Beast" (1983; videotape, C and E Enterprises) stars Susan Sarandon, Klaus Kinski, Anjelica Huston, and Stephen Elliott; directed by Roger Vadim, the program mimics Cocteau's film. I am told that two other versions of the tale were also prepared for and broadcast on television: one an American production featuring George C. Scott as the Beast, the other written by the poet Ted Hughes and shown on British television. I have not seen either of these works and gather that they have not appeared on videotape and are difficult to obtain.

2 Pat Califia, "Saint George and the Dragon," *Once Upon a Time: Erotic Fairy Tales for Women*, ed. Michael Ford (New York: Masquerade Books, 1996) 123.

3 See Califia 123-45. Thomas S. Roche, "Beauty and the Beast," *Happily Ever After: Erotic Fairy Tales for Men*, ed. Michael Ford (New York: Masquerade Books, 1996) 69-80.

4 Emma Donoghue, "The Tale of the Rose," *Kissing the Witch: Old Tales in New Skins* (New York: HarperCollins, 1997) 27-40.

who lived in a castle and could be seen walking on the battlements, and others told of two beauties, and others, of two beasts."

But while Emma Donoghue has claimed the tale for lesbians and Angela Carter has claimed the tale for feminists, the gay males behind the Cocteau and Disney films have not only repositioned it in a homosexual context but shifted the story in a decidedly masculine direction. Instead of Beauty and her problems, these cinematic versions significantly change the focus to the other character referred to in the story's title. In these ways, the Cocteau and Disney films become a discourse on masculinity.

JEAN COCTEAU'S "BEAUTY AND THE BEAST"

La Belle et la Bête. 1946. 90 minutes. Black and white. Director: Jean Cocteau. Producer: Andre Paulve for Discina International Films. Screenplay by: Jean Cocteau, based on the fairy tale by Madame Beaumont. Cinematographer: Henri Alekan. Editor: Claude Ibéria. Art Direction: Christian Bérard. Technical Adviser: René Clément. Costume Design: Christian Bérard. Music: Georges Auric. Availability: with English subtitles, on videotape (Homevision) and DVD (Criterion).

After the horrors of World War II, French poet and film-maker Jean Cocteau stunned his contemporaries by insisting that the time was not right for realistic cinema. Instead, he called for films to take up fantastic and enchanting subjects. Cocteau, himself, turned to Beaumont's fairy tale to create his classic *La Belle et la Bête.*

In his *Beauty and the Beast: Diary of a Film*, Cocteau details the many problems he encountered in making it. Among other things, he hoped to shoot the film in color, but postwar shortages obliged him to make it in black and white. Moreover, during the filming of this story about the ugly Beast, Cocteau, himself, suffered from a number of painful and disfiguring skin problems, including boils, carbuncles, eczema, and impetigo.[1]

Set in eighteenth-century France, the film opens with a contrast between the hardworking and peasant-like Beauty (Josette Day)

---

1   See Cocteau's *Beauty and the Beast: Diary of a Film.*

and her sisters, Felicie (Nane Germon) and Adelaide (Mila Parely), who put on airs and act like aristocrats. The family is living in the country because their merchant father (Marcel André) lost his fortune when his ships went down in a storm. Undeterred, a friend of the family, Avenant (Jean Marais), asks Beauty to marry him; but she declines his offer in order to stay and help her father. When Avenant attempts to force his attentions on her, Beauty's brother, Ludovic (Michel Auclair), intervenes.

Word then arrives that one of the father's ships has safely arrived in port, and there is hope that the family will recover some of its wealth. As the father is about to depart, the two older sisters beg for expensive gifts; but, when asked, Beauty requests only a rose. When he arrives at the port, however, the father is disappointed to learn that his creditors have seized his ship; so, he heads home as impoverished as he came and gets lost in a forest during a storm. He spends the night at a mysteriously hospitable chateau where disembodied arms hold lighted candles and serve him dinner. When morning comes, he readies to depart but remembers Beauty's request for a rose. When he picks one in the garden, he is accosted by an angry Beast (Jean Marais) who threatens the father with death unless one of his daughters returns in his place. Taking Magnifique, the Beast's magical white stallion, the father returns home and tells his family all that transpired, and Beauty insists on taking his place with the Beast.

Riding Magnifique, Beauty returns to the Beast's luxurious palace where she is treated as a guest. Each night the Beast asks her if she will marry him, and each night she declines; nonetheless, their friendship and understanding of each other develops. Then, learning that her father is ill, Beauty begs for permission to visit him. The Beast reluctantly agrees to her departure and, as a token of his love, gives her the golden key to the pavilion that contains all of his wealth; he also adds that if she does not return soon, he will die.

When Beauty's sisters see her good fortune, they grow jealous and plot her downfall by having Ludovic and Avenant steal the Beast's fortune. When Beauty returns to the heartbroken Beast, she finds him dying and begs his forgiveness, saying she will be his wife. Simultaneously, Ludovic and Avenant arrive at the Beast's castle and force their way into the creature's treasure house; however, breaking into the glass pavilion, Avenant is shot with an arrow by a magical statue of the goddess Diana; dying, his looks change until he resembles the Beast. At the same time, the Beast, having learned of Beauty's love, changes into a fairy-tale prince who resembles Avenant. The Prince (Jean Marais) then explains that he was under a spell and could only be saved by the love of someone like Beauty, and they magically fly off to the Prince's kingdom.

COCTEAU AND THE HORROR OF HETEROSEXUALITY

Beauty-and-the-Beast tales traditionally present a rather rapid change of genres: what starts as a horror story soon changes into a romance. Apuleius's myth of "Cupid and Psyche" begins with what appears to be the sacrifice of a virgin to a monster as Psyche is readied for a "dark wedding" that seems more like a funeral: dressed in her bridal clothes, the lamenting maiden is accompanied by her weeping family to a mountaintop where she is to be sacrificed to a god who is said to be a monstrous snake. But the mood soon changes when Psyche's life is spared and she finds herself in luxurious circumstances, enjoying the nightly visits of her lover and falling in love with Cupid, the most beautiful of the gods. Beaumont's story also begins in a ghastly mode with Beauty anxious that she will be consumed by the monster; but events soon shift and she begins to enjoy the Beast's company, and that courtship ends with her marriage to the handsome prince.

What is conspicuously different about Cocteau's film, in comparison with prior treatments of the story, is the way he prolongs these horror motifs well beyond the point where they are customarily abandoned. In fact, Cocteau has essentially converted the story of "Beauty and the Beast" into a horror film; in one of the early scenes, for example, Beauty faints and in a manner reminiscent of the wedding night in "The Bride of Frankenstein," her monstrous bridegroom carries her across the threshold into her boudoir. We might wonder what lies behind Cocteau's conversion of "Beauty and the Beast" into a gothic story and film.

Psychologists have suggested that the motifs of horror in the early part of "Beauty and the Beast" reflect a maiden's anxiety about heterosexual intimacy, and the tale's termination of these motifs suggests a re-evaluation of those attitudes when an intimacy

234

that had first seemed disgusting is now considered desirable.[1] Cocteau's prolongation of these ghastly motifs in his film precludes such a rapid and easy revision of these attitudes; heterosexual intimacy remains horrific, repulsive, and animal-like. Offering a biographical explanation for this, critic Dennis DeNitto points out that "Cocteau, who freely admitted his homosexuality, often reveals in his creative writing an antipathy toward male-female sexuality."[2]

If the film reflects its maker's homosexual critique of heterosexual contact as horrific and repulsive, Cocteau is even more precise about identifying where the problem lies: in male heterosexual desire. Near the end, Cocteau's Prince offers the film's two-part moral: "Love can make a Beast of a man. It can also make an ugly man handsome." The second part of this statement (regarding the transformative power of love) is the conventional lesson we associate with Beaumont's story. But the first part of this statement ("Love can make a Beast of a man") is Cocteau's own contribution. In four of his additions to the story tradition, Cocteau indicates the beastly nature of male heterosexual desire.

Two of those additions are boudoir scenes; in fact, the boudoir is the locus of some of the most powerful moments in the film. On one occasion, Cocteau's Beauty spies the Beast outside her bedroom door after he has surrendered to his animal urges, gone on one of his nocturnal hunts, and slain an animal. Literally smoking with passion, the now sated Beast is full of self-disgust as he looks at his bloody hands. Absent-mindedly, he wanders into Beauty's boudoir whereupon she ejects him and makes apparent her revulsion at his animal ways. Still crazed but half-mindful of the gentleman within, the Beast shouts at Beauty to close her door, to lock him out of her boudoir when the fit is upon him.

On a similar occasion, the Beast appears at her bedroom door once more after another night of hunting, again smoking with passion and still bloody from the kill. She again turns him away, saying in disgust, "Aren't you ashamed of yourself? Go and clean yourself up."

1 Cf. Bettelheim 306.
2 Dennis DeNitto, "Jean Cocteau's 'Beauty and the Beast,'" *American Imago* 33 (1976): 153.

In Cocteau's frequent association of the Beast's animal urges with Beauty's boudoir, we soon understand his bloodlust and carnivorous desires in sexual terms. What is ugly and repulsive, disgusting and shameful, are male sexual desires and giving into them. As even the word "horny" suggests, such desires are seen as making a man animal-like.

Besides the two boudoir scenes, Cocteau's antipathy towards male heterosexuality is seen in a third way in his introduction of an entirely new character into the story tradition of "Beauty and the Beast." Avenant—played by Cocteau's lover, actor Jean Marais— is Beauty's handsome neighbor and would-be suitor. Avenant is phallically aggressive and sexually assertive; and Cocteau, a great admirer of Freud,[1] often pictures his character with bow and arrows. At the opening of the film, for example, Avenant shoots an arrow through the window of the house, and it pierces Beauty's reflection on the floor which she is washing. Shortly thereafter, he proposes to Beauty; and when she declines his marriage offer, Avenant tries to force his intentions upon her. Only the timely intervention of Beauty's brother saves her from events that seem headed in the direction of rape, events that again reflect unfavorably on male heterosexual desire.

The culmination of Avenant's masculine aggressiveness appears, however, near the end of the film in Cocteau's fourth addition to the story. Then Avenant travels to the Beast's castle and breaks into the "Temple of Diana," a locked jewel house guarded by Diana, the goddess of chastity. The Temple of Diana is something like the Temple of Virginity, and when Avenant breaks the glass of the skylight and forces his way into this place, this Freudian director wants us to understand this as the symbolic equivalent of rape. For his violation, Avenant is killed when the statue of Diana looses an arrow and strikes him. In a significant moment in the film, as Avenant is dying, his features change until he looks exactly like the Beast. In this way, Cocteau shows (quite literally) the ugliness of male heterosexual desire or how "Love can make a Beast of a man."

Having established for so long, and in various ways, his antipathy to heterosexuality, Cocteau, of course, runs into problems in the conclusion since a retelling of the story requires a romantic

1   DeNitto 124, 127.

denouement which ends with marriage. Here, let me suggest, Cocteau follows tradition but in a parodistic way.

Over the years, watching this film with various audiences, I can say that viewers react predictably to the conclusion. When Cocteau's Beast is transformed into the handsome prince, he appears as a fairy-tale dandy wearing leotards—and people laugh. Eventually that laughter subsides, and viewers attribute their initial amusement to a reaction to the corniness of old black-and-white films. My own feeling, however, is that Cocteau is on the side of the viewers and their patronizing reactions—that is, he deliberately and consciously evokes that amused and cynical response. In other words, Cocteau's "fairy tale" conclusion is a spoof, a parody, a deliberate send-up of the corny romantic endings of the films of his era.

First of all, the fairy-tale prince in leotards is a bit much. Other viewers have felt the same; at the première, when the sugar-cane dandy appeared on screen, Greta Garbo is reported to have loudly moaned, "Give me back my Beast!"[1] Moreover, there is a puzzling incongruity: this Prince (again played by Jean Marais) looks exactly like—as Beauty herself observes—Avenant. That Beauty would accept the lookalike of the suitor she so forcefully rejected at the start of the film is a bit much to believe.

Equally unconvincing, and just as "over the top," is Beauty's conversion from a self-possessed woman into a silly and flirtatious coquette. When the handsome Prince asks her if his looks displease her, she impishly says, "Yes," then (with much batting of the eyelashes) she coyly changes her response to "No." When he asks, "Are you happy?" she plays the ingenue and demurely replies, "I'll have to get used to this." And when he finally asks, "Are you afraid?" she delays her response, then finally melts on his shoulder, saying, "I'd like to be afraid … with you." It's enough to make a diabetic reach for the insulin.

But that seems to be Cocteau's intention. Throughout much of his film, Cocteau shows his own homosexual critique and personal distaste for heterosexuality. By reframing this romantic story as a gothic thriller, he lengthens the initial apprehension of heterosexual intimacy as horrific well beyond the point where that motif is cus-

1 These remarks are cited by critic Arthur Knight in a commentary on the film which appears on the Voyager DVD.

tomarily abandoned in most treatments of the story. Then he presents an unflattering vision of masculine sexual desire ("horniness") as animal-like and repulsive by adding various moments to the story that show his own additional theme that "Love can make a Beast of a man": in the boudoir scenes, and in the scenes that introduce the new and phallically aggressive character of Avenant. Finally, in his over-the-top confection of a conclusion, Cocteau pillories heterosexuality with parody.

If Cocteau's film presents a gay critique of heterosexuality, the Disney film proceeds in another manner. The later film subtly condemns homophobia and advocates a tolerance of "difference."

DISNEY'S Beauty and the Beast

1991. 85 minutes. Color. Director: Gary Trousdale and Kirk Wise. Producer: Don Hahn for Walt Disney Pictures, in association with Silver Screen Partners IV; released by Buena Vista. Screenplay by: Linda Woolverton, based on Beaumont's fairy tale. Editor: John Carnochan. Music: Howard Ashman (lyrics), Alan Menken (music). Availability: on videotape and DVD (Walt Disney Home Video).

The first animated film ever to have received a nomination for an Academy Award as Best Picture of the year, Disney Studios' "Beauty and the Beast" was an immense success that went on to win many honors. Of particular significance is the musical score by lyricist Howard Ashman and composer Alan Menken, which took Academy Awards and Golden Globe Awards in several categories.

While based on Beaumont's "Beauty and the Beast," the film takes considerable liberties with her story from the very beginning. While Beaumont's tale offers little explanation of how the prince first changed into the Beast, the film directly addresses this issue in a preamble. In a series of stained-glass-window images, a narrator (voice of David Ogden Stiers) tells of a spoiled and selfish prince. An old and ugly woman comes to his castle one night and begs for lodging in exchange for a rose. Despite being warned that "Beauty is found within," he rudely refuses her; the ugly woman, an enchantress in disguise, changes him into the Beast. He will remain in that hideous form, she advises him, unless he earns the love of a woman by his twenty-first birthday.

The scene then changes, and we are next provided with a musical introduction to Belle (voice of Paige O'Hara)—a beautiful, independent, young woman who loves books. Neighbors in her small French village find Belle a bit peculiar—with her dreamy far-off look, her head in the clouds, and her nose in a book. Moreover, Belle's reading has filled her with a desire for romance and adventure; she sings, "I want much more than this provincial life."

We are also introduced to Gaston (voice of Richard White), a handsome but conceited man about town. This vain, macho hunk is unconcerned about books and no environmentalist; in fact, in a moment of foreshadowing, we learn that he is best known as a hunter of animals. Most importantly, this brute has vowed to make Belle his wife. In fact, in a later scene, Gaston presses Belle to marry him and is turned away at the door.

Belle lives with her father Maurice (voice of Rex Everhart), an eccentric inventor. He leaves her to go to a distant fair to exhibit his inventions but, unfortunately, he and his horse get lost in the woods and are attacked by wolves. In this way, he is driven to seek refuge in a mysteriously hospitable castle populated by various animated objects: the charming candelabra named Lumière (voice of Jerry Orbach), the fussy butler mantel clock called Cogsworth (voice of David Ogden Stiers), the warm housekeeper teapot known as Mrs. Potts (voice of Angela Lansbury), her youthful son and teacup dubbed Chip (voice of Bradley Michael Pierce), and a wordless footstool that hops around like a lapdog. Enter, too, the Beast (voice of Robby Benson). He is angry at Maurice for trespassing in his home and locks the terrified old man in a dungeon.

When her father's horse returns without him, Belle goes in search and finds him imprisoned in the Beast's castle. When the Beast discovers yet another trespasser, he is furious. Nonetheless, he accepts Belle's offer that she take her father's place.

The household staff is delighted by this prospect, thinking Belle may be the one to break the prince's spell. Still, they worry, because, for this to succeed, the Beast will need to learn to control his temper. In fact, things do not go well from the start when the Beast hotly insists that Beauty come to dinner and she refuses, exhibiting her feisty and independent nature. Later she takes dinner in the kitchen with the animated utensils, who make her feel welcome with the song "Be Our Guest" and with a musical extravaganza that recalls similar numbers in Busby Berkeley's films.

Belle's independence is also evident when she goes one day to the West Wing, a ruined area of the castle that the Beast has declared "off limits" to her. There she sees a torn portrait of a handsome prince and also a rose under glass — the very rose the enchantress had given the prince, a flower that is slowly losing its petals as he approaches his twenty-first birthday. When the Beast finds her there, however, he is furious, and she runs away from him and outside the castle into a snowstorm. There she is attacked by wolves, but the Beast comes to her defense and is injured.

With the wounded Beast, the once feisty Belle becomes subdued, bandaging and nursing him. In succeeding scenes, it becomes apparent that "there's something there that wasn't there before" when the Beast presents Belle with his library and the two playfully throw snowballs at each other. They also dance in the ballroom to the title song ("Beauty and the Beast," sung by Angela Lansbury) and fall in love.

But by means of a magic mirror, Belle has seen that her father is ill and is worried about her, so she receives permission from the Beast to go visit him. Meanwhile, Gaston, thinking he can blackmail Beauty into marrying him, has arranged to have Belle's father carted off to an asylum. Once Gaston learns he has a rival, however, he changes tactics and organizes the villagers to attack the Beast. Carrying their burning torches, chanting their dislike of people who are different, the mob marches on the Beast's castle in an episode reminiscent of many similar ones in "Frankenstein" and other gothic movies.

While the animated bric-à-brac at the Beast's castle puts up a spirited defense against the invading mob, Gaston and the Beast fight mano-a-mano on the castle rooftop. Distracted by Belle's arrival, however, the Beast is stabbed in the back by Gaston, who then falls to his death. Dying as well, the Beast is told by Belle of her love and begins to transform.

Belle is confused about the identity of the handsome prince she sees next but, looking into his eyes, finally recognizes he is the same person as the Beast. Along with the Beast's transformation comes the transformation of the household paraphernalia who were equally under a spell, and they emerge now as housekeeper, butler, et al. In this upbeat atmosphere of reincarnation and reunion, the movie ends happily in a swirl of ballroom dancing.

DISNEY'S DISCOURSE ON MASCULINITY

From what we have been told, the story for the Disney film was composed in two phases. Scriptwriter Linda Woolverton first "read all the 'Beauty and the Beast' fairy tales," and then her job was to "convert them into a story that works for the [1990s]." In particular, Woolverton saw her goal as making Belle into a feminist heroine. That draft was then submitted to lyricist Howard Ashman who completely reworked the script.[1]

Ashman made two significant changes. First, he reoriented the focus of the film from Belle to the Beast, converting the story into a discussion of masculinity; as Don Hahn, the film's producer, recalled: "It was Ashman who realized, contrary to tradition, that this had to be the Beast's story. We didn't agree with him right away. But he was right. The Beast was the guy with the problem."[2] Ashman's second contribution (primarily by means of the lyrics of the film's songs) was a gay advocacy, a wish for social tolerance of "difference." In the final blending of Woolverton's and Ashman's scripts, Disney's "Beauty and the Beast" became, as Cynthia Erb suggests, a film where feminist and gay discourse overlap.[3] Of course, given the common impression that Disney Studios is a bastion of conservative values, this story-behind-the-story may come as a surprise.

Feminist enthusiasm for the film was short-lived. When the movie first appeared, critics were quick to praise Belle as an untypical Disney heroine: self-determined and feisty, and (most especially)

1 Bob Thomas, *Disney's Art of Animation: From Mickey Mouse to Beauty and the Beast* (New York: Hyperion, 1991) 143. Thomas's book provides a good overview of the production of Disney's "Beauty and the Beast."

2 David Ansen, "Just the Way Walt Made 'Em," *Newsweek* (18 November 1991): 80.

3 Cynthia Erb, "Another World or the World of an Other? The Space of Romance in Recent Versions of 'Beauty and the Beast,'" *Cinema Journal* (Summer 1995): 63.

a young woman who reads. Later critics were not so impressed. June Cummins, for example, pointed out that Belle is only shown reading for some fourteen seconds and what is suppose to be her feminist spunkiness slowly evaporates over the course of the film.[1]

Cummins complains that the film eventually descends into clichés. The other females in the film divide into two stereotypes: Mamas (Mrs. Potts and the Armoire who ministers to Belle) and Bimbos (the trio of vacuous blondes who swoon over Gaston and the feather duster who, in the conclusion, emerges from behind the curtain after a groping by Lumière and transforms into a scantily clad French maid who is an *oo-là-là* flirt). This leaves Disney's heroine few choices, and—*voilà!*—she finally falls into the first category, becoming a nurturer, not only in caring for her dotty dad, but in scolding the Beast for his temper tantrums and nursing him when she tends to his wounds after the wolf attack. In the end, in other words, Belle falls in line. The film capitulates to the conventional romance story, and the price of love seems to be Belle's sacrifice of all that originally made her a feisty heroine. As Marina Warner suggests, the film presents "Hollywood's cunning domestication of feminism."[2]

The character of Belle, however, does provide a bridge for the introduction of the film's gay subtext. Ashman's lyrics about her emphasize how she is "different"—because of her feminist desires, the pleasure she takes in reading, her unwillingness to settle and become Gaston's "little wife," and in her wanting something "more than this provincial life."[3] Indeed, the song about her amounts to an almost thesaurus-like list of synonyms for "queerness"; among other things, the townspeople describe Belle as "strange," "funny," "peculiar," "odd," and "very different from the rest of us." In this way, Ashman's lyrics link the film's feminist and gay agendas.

Ashman died of AIDS in March 1991, just before the release of the film; and, in retrospect, his lyrics for the film's songs amount to

1 June Cummins, "Romancing the Plot: The Real Beast of Disney's Beauty and the Beast," *Children's Literature Association Quarterly* (Spring 1995): 22–28.
2 Warner 313.
3 Opposite the townspeople's objection to Belle's "difference" is her great complaint about her "provincial" village for its "sameness": "Ev'ry day / Like the one before." She notes, for example, the arrival of the baker with this tray, "like always," with "the same old bread and rolls to sell."

a gay plea for open-mindedness. Just as Belle has a change of heart about the Beast, Ashman invites those intolerant of homosexuals to take up the great lesson of the film: "Finding you can change, learning you are wrong." There is in Disney's movie a special link between hostility towards the Beast and hostility toward homosexuals. Commenting on this after Ashman's death, Bill Lausch, Ashman's partner, observed in an interview: "Gay people will always identify with someone who's on the outside, who is feared and misunderstood.... We respond to being perceived as ugly, as a monster. People are afraid of what they don't understand—that's actually in the lyrics of one of the songs."[1]

Lausch is referring to the scene where a mob with burning torches attacks the Beast's castle and the Beast because he is "different"; the mob sings, "We don't like / What we don't under-stand. / In fact, it scares us." In light of Lausch's comments, that scene can now be recognized as an allegorized version of frenzied gay-bashing, as Gaston encourages the mob's homophobia and leads them to violence by suggesting that their children are in dan-ger because of the Beast's "monstrous appetite" and that they can't rest easy if they "let him wander free." In this allegorical way, then—and at a time when demagogues on the political right were championing their conservative views under the banner of "Family Values"—Ashman was pointing out (*sub rosa*) how homosexuals in the era of AIDS panic were being demonized and attacked.

As this scene suggests, Gaston is the villain. He is also the point at which the film's feminist and homosexual subtexts overlap because he is the nightmare of both: not only a gay-basher (as the mob scene intimates), but a chauvinist pig. When Gaston decides to marry Belle and presses his suit, he reveals himself to be the unreconstructed male of feminist thinking: unconcerned about Belle's reading and muddying her book, insisting she will be his "little wife" and that all their children will be boys. In perhaps too obvious a way, Gaston's nature is visually revealed when Belle rejects him, opening the door so that Gaston falls outside into a puddle of mud, and this chauvinist pig emerges from that puddle with a pig upon his head.

1 Michael Lassel, "'Beauty and the Beast' Genius Remembered," *The Advocate* (7 April 1992): 77.

By means of Gaston, the film also decidedly becomes a discourse on masculinity with Gaston representing everything that can go wrong in the heterosexual male. Gaston is a hyper-male: a cartoon-ish version of, say, Sylvester Stallone or Arnold Schwarznegger. As the song about him suggests, he is a hyperbole of masculinity, "burly and brawny," with a cleft chin and "biceps to spare"; more-over, "every last inch" of him is "covered with hair." He is also an over-the-top macho given to hunting and drinking with the boys. In short, he is a comic "paragon" and a laughable rendition of a "man among men."[1]

By means of Gaston, the story of the Beast also becomes clear. The Beast is—as Don Hahn, the film's producer, observed—a "guy with the problem." The problem is that he may become Gaston.

Gaston and the Beast are often linked in the film. They not only share an interest in Belle but also exaggerated musculature and aggressive natures (seen for example, in Gaston's trashing the tavern and regularly thumping his sidekick Le Fou, and in the Beast's destroying the West Wing and accosting Belle's father). Their relat-edness is also suggested in a visual way at one moment in the film when Gaston is in the tavern and sits in a chair decorated with fur and horns: seen from the back, he is the image of the Beast. They are also alter-egos where the inner/outer balance between appear-ance/virtue are counterposed: the one handsome but with a beastly nature, the other unpleasant to look at but essentially good beneath. Indeed, given the dramatic contrast between Gaston and the Beast, the title of the film may actually refer to them alone.

---

1   We might even consider the possibility that Gaston's emphatic masculinity amounts to a resistance to his own homosexuality. His aggressiveness, his machismo, his homophobia arise out of this resistance. In that regard, he resembles the marine in the film *American Beauty* who is the neighbor of Kevin Spacey's character Lester Burnham. That marine is emphatically macho, denouncing "faggots" and suspicious that Burnham is gay. In a late moment of frenzied self-abandon in the film, he kisses Burnham; finally, recoiling in revul-sion from what that kiss means and striking out, he slays Burnham. Gaston's attack on the Beast at the head of the mob and his homophobic antipathy towards "difference," as well as his gorgeous and emphatic masculinity, might be understood in the same way, then, as a reactive anxiety to his latent homo-sexuality.

At the beginning when the enchantress casts a spell on the conceited and selfish prince, she warns him that if he does not find someone to love him before his twenty-first birthday, he will remain a hideous beast forever. That potential future is represented by Gaston. Here is an explanation of the most significant link made between Gaston and the Beast. In the conclusion, two events are simultaneous and connected: the Prince cannot emerge from his beastly form until Gaston — and the form of masculinity he represents — is dead.

In this regard, the Disney film ought to be seen in the context of what were then current discussions about masculinity, especially those raised by Robert Bly in his bestselling *Iron John: A Book About Men*.[1] Musing on another fairy tale (the Grimms' "Iron John"), Bly identified an evolutionary progression between three kinds of males: the Macho Male of the 1950s — with his crewcut, a rough and sexist "man's man"; the Feminized or New Age Male of the 1960s and 1970s — the longhaired hippie who advocated peace in response to the Vietnam War and deferred to women by shunning the chauvinist attitudes criticized by the women's movement; and the New Male of the future — a man Bly imagined who could still be in touch with his feminine side but without forfeiting his masculinity. This schema essentially suggests the transformation of Disney's Beast: as he changes from an aggressive and threatening creature to a domesticated companion who, for example, helps Belle feed the birds without scaring them, to a promising prince. Woolverton and Ashman, in other words, translated this chronological notion of change between the decades into the life story of one character.

What, then, does the Disney film have to say about masculinity? In a very crude and reductive way, we can say that the message is that men, until they are twenty-one and if they are unmarried after that, can become beasts. As Cummins suggests, the Beast is a figure for the male adolescent: "Many of the characteristics that make the Beast ugly are exaggerations of normal male traits: his size, his hairiness, his gruffness, and his strength."[2] Indeed, the Beast —

---

1   Robert Bly, *Iron John: A Book About Men* (New York: Vintage Books, 1992). Bly's ideas were first rehearsed in a pamphlet, *The Pillow and the Key* (St. Paul, Minnesota: Ally Press, 1987).

2   Cummins 26.

moody and given to explosions of temper, muscle-bound and horny — seems the picture of the adolescent male trapped in a new and hairy body.

The danger is that he will become Gaston and adopt Gaston's retrograde form of masculinity — becoming a danger to women and to homosexuals, a chauvinist pig and a gay-basher. As the film's conclusion suggests, the prince can only emerge once Gaston (and his attitudes) are dead. It is worth noting that this same simultaneity occurs in the denouement of Cocteau's film: there, the death of the handsome and phallically aggressive Avenant is synchronous with the transformation of the troubled Beast into the handsome prince. Both these gay films, then, make use of "Beauty and the Beast" in a new way: as an occasion to discuss the complexities of masculinity.

DISNEY'S SUMMA

In his essay "Tradition and the Individual Talent,"[1] T.S. Eliot complains about our modern enthusiasm for originality, our prizing a literary work for its uniqueness and where it least resembles its predecessors. Instead, Eliot suggests, a new work is most interesting when it includes its predecessors and engages in a conversation with them. Prior to the appearance of a new work, Eliot proposes, its antecedents exist in a harmonious whole; what is interesting about a new work is how it slightly alters the already existing order, readjusting relations to create a new order.

Eliot's thinking is, of course, the nightmare of copyright lawyers; and Disney's attorneys, in legal circles, have an extraordinary reputation for zealously guarding their copyrights — basing their arguments, perforce, on the originality and uniqueness of their firm's productions. Fortunately, Disney's creative team is not so hamstrung. Part of the genius of their "Beauty and the Beast" is the way it echoes countless other works and plays with them in an intertextual way.

These echoes are so extensive that it is only possible to mention a few. When Belle first appears in her blue dress (singing "I want

1 T. S. Eliot, "Tradition and Individual Talent," *The Sacred Wood: Essays on Poetry and Criticism* (London: Methuen, 1920).

much more than this provincial life"), the filmmakers make a bow to "The Wizard of Oz," recalling Dorothy's wanting to leave grey Kansas to go "Somewhere over the rainbow." Later, in an unsuccessful attempt to groom the Beast for a dinner date with Belle, his curls and ribbons make him appear the counterpart of Bert Lahr's Cowardly Lion. The Beast, himself, recalls the similarly large, horned, bearded, snouted, hairy, and low-foreheaded monster in Maurice Sendak's *Where the Wild Things Are*, and the musical extravaganza ("Be Our Guest") when Belle eats in the kitchen with the dancing and animated utensils seems an echo of a similar scene in the film *Maurice Sendak's Really Rosie*; indeed, the Disney folks may make a sideways acknowledgment to Sendak by calling Belle's father "Maurice" and making him an inventor. The rooftop fight between Gaston and the Beast amidst gothic statuary is reminiscent of both the older "Hunchback of Notre Dame" and the more recent "Ghostbusters," while Lumière, the French-accented candelabra, has the manner of Maurice Chevalier, and the throaty voice of the Beast sometimes seems that of Star War's Darth Vader. Finally, recent Disney staff play with their own studio's traditions so that the film's ballroom scenes recall those from Disney's "Cinderella," the frightening woods (in which Belle's father gets lost) seem transplanted from "Snow White," and Belle's father the reincarnation of Geppetto in "Pinnochio."

But it is really in its addressing the story tradition of "Beauty and the Beast" that the Disney film shines. Linda Woolverton may have "read all the 'Beauty and the Beast' fairy tales" before she wrote her own script, but others involved with the film seem to have also done their homework. The genius of the film lies in the fact that it is a wonderful amalgam of prior versions of the story, a kind of *summa* that gathers together and echoes and responds to the story tradition.

Eliot said that the problem a new work faces is that its predecessors already exist in a harmonious whole; to be successful, a new work has to enter that tradition in such a way that a new harmonious whole is created. The way that Disney's "Beauty and the Beast" does this is worth considering; moreover, discussing the film in this way — noting how this new version alters, adjusts, borrows, and responds to its antecedents — provides a convenient way to revisit the subjects of this book.

Most frequently, we have observed, versions of the tale do not reveal how the Prince was originally changed into a beast. In the prelude to the Disney film, however, an explanation is offered: a beautiful fairy appears disguised as an old beggarwoman and asks for shelter but when the Prince is unable to see beyond appearances and refuses her, he is changed into the Beast and his castle put under a spell; this enchantment can only be broken if he can find a woman to love him before his twenty-first birthday. Here the Disney film seems to take a page from the picture book *Beauty and the Beast* by Marianna and Mercer Mayer, one of the few versions that offers an explanation of the Prince's transformation and which does so in a particular way: when he is no longer the Beast, the Prince tells Beauty, "Now at last I am free to tell you that the old woman was really a fairy in disguise sent to test me.... [She] put my whole palace in a magical spell till I could find you to redeem me."

In Disney's prelude, too, we are told about the enchanted rose the fairy gives the Beast; it is kept in a glass container and slowly loses its petals as he approaches the deadline of his twenty-first birthday. By associating the rose with the Beast, the Disney film differs considerably from the tale by Beaumont where it is associated with Beauty, since it is her fateful request for that flower which ultimately brings the two of them together. Instead, in the Disney film, the rose serves a plot function as a kind of "ticking clock" that adds urgency to this eighty-five-minute movie. In that regard, Disney's rose-under-glass resembles the rose-in-a-crystal-box that is sent by the aliens to Estár in the science-fiction short story "Beauty" by Tanith Lee—a blossom that likewise functions as an urgent reminder of a fate that cannot be avoided.

When Disney's Belle is introduced, those familiar with other versions of the tale might immediately notice the absence of her sisters. Gone is the sibling rivalry that plays so large a part in versions by Beaumont and others—though, perhaps, these superficial siblings who marry unworthy husbands may be reincarnated in the characters the Disney film calls "Bimbettes," the blonde maidens of the town who swoon over Gaston.

Gone, too, is the account of the merchant family's fall from wealth and forced retirement to the country where Beauty's sisters are so unhappy. Instead, Belle is already in the country when the

Disney film opens, and it is she who is unhappy and wants "more than this provincial life." In other words, this American film subtracts those issues which led Marxist critic Jack Zipes to see the subtext of Beaumont's "Beauty and the Beast" in terms of different social classes: the sisters (putting on airs and saying they will only marry a duke or an earl) as examples of *arrivistes* from the merchant class aspiring above their social station, the family's forced retirement to the country as an account of "putting the bourgeoisie in their place."

In Beaumont's tale, Beauty turns down several suitors, and her sisters marry obnoxious husbands. In the Disney film, these are collapsed into one character. Gaston is the obnoxious suitor and an addition to the story tradition, but the first addition of a character like this appears in Avenant in the film by Jean Cocteau. Like Avenant, Gaston is the handsome hunter and surly suitor. Early in Cocteau's film, when Beauty (called "Belle," of course, in this French film) declines Avenant's marriage proposal, he tries to press his attentions on her. In a distinct echo of that scene, the officious Gaston also presses his marriage proposal on Disney's Belle and is rebuffed.

The circumstances that bring Beauty into contact with the Beast are slightly different in the tale and the film. Beaumont's father is a merchant who makes a journey in hopes of recovering some of his wealth and gets lost, plucks the desired rose and offends the Beast, bargains with his captor and has his place taken by Beauty. Belle's father in the Disney film, on the other hand, is a dotty inventor who makes a journey to a fair to show off his wares and gets lost. In Beaumont's tale it may be a bit baffling why the Beast should be so offended by the merchant's taking such a small thing as a rose; the Disney film undoes that problem by indicating that the father occasions the Beast's anger not by an unknowing offense against hospitality but because he is guilty of trespassing. The other confusion undone by the Disney film is the moment in the tale when the merchant seems to bargain away his daughter in order to escape punishment by the Beast. In the Disney production, the father is not seen in so unflattering a light; instead, Belle learns her father is in trouble when his horse returns without him, goes searching for him, and finds him imprisoned at the Beast's castle. She is the one who proposes that she should take his place.

Both Belle and her father find the Beast's enchanted castle a place of magically animated hospitality. There is a long tradition of this. In the myth of "Cupid and Psyche" Apuleius tells how Psyche, when she comes to the mysterious palace, is ministered to by invisible servants and entertained by invisible musicians; the same is true for Beauty in Beaumont's tale. Perhaps the most striking vision of the animated castle, however, appears in Cocteau's film where human arms emerge from the wall to hold candelabras that move to accommodate their visitors and where human hands emerge from the table to hold a goblet and pitcher and pour out drinks for guests. In the Disney film, cartoonish objects function in the same way with Lumière (the candelabra) chatting away to his guests and Mrs. Potts (the teapot) and her son Chip (the cup) pouring out tea. In her own short story variants on "Beauty and the Beast," Angela Carter also features such animated creatures: in "The Tiger's Bride," Carter's Beauty is ministered to by a clockwork French maid who emerges from the cupboard; and in "The Courtship of Mr. Lyon," her Beauty character is entertained by a barking and whimpering spaniel. In Disney, Belle is ministered to by an animated armoire and entertained by an animated footstool that frisks about like a lapdog.

In her stay with the Beast, Bruno Bettelheim argues, Beauty has to deal with her "problem": her need to break her oedipal tie with her father so she can transfer her affection to her partner. This motif is largely absent from the Disney film partly because Belle's father is presented as a comic figure, a screwball inventor. While Belle does look out for her dotty dad, the pining for papa that is so much a part of Beaumont's story is largely absent here. Instead, the focus falls on the interaction between Belle and her monstrous companion.

In the Disney film, it is the Beast who has a "problem." And of all the problems he might have, the one he is given is that he is unable to control his temper. Here, again, the film seems to take a page from the Mayers' picture book. In Beaumont's tale, the Beast is a perfect gentleman who patiently waits for Beauty's change of heart; but the Mayers were the first to deviate from that tradition by presenting, in Marianna Mayer's text and Mercer Mayer's pictures, a Beast who explodes in anger and terrifies Beauty.

Marina Warner, it will be remembered, objected to Bettelheim's view of the story as an account of a woman with a problem. From her feminist perspective, Warner suggested that Beauty has no problem but is, instead, a plucky heroine who willingly encounters the monstrous and masculine. This is the line of thinking the Disney movie pursues in telling how Belle goes on her own to the Beast's castle and takes her father's place, and in presenting a woman who is feisty and outspoken. In this way, she resembles the willful princess in "The Frog King" who asserts herself when she throws her amphibian suitor against the wall. In the Disney film, Belle is equally assertive when she refuses the Beast's command that he dine with her and on other occasions when she does as she pleases despite his orders.

One of these occasions is when she travels to the West Wing, a part of the Beast's castle that he has forbidden her to enter. The forbidden place appears in Cocteau's glass pavilion which is the Beast's treasure house and in some folk versions of the Beauty-and-the-Beast story. Each of these corresponds with the moment in "Cupid and Psyche" or in "East of the Sun, West of the Moon" where the maiden breaks a taboo and lights a candle and discovers something about the secret identity of her companion. Violating a taboo by entering the West Wing, Belle sees a torn painting of the handsome prince before he was changed into a beast. It is a clue, and a clue very much like that given in the version of the story by Villeneuve when her Beauty enters a portrait gallery and also sees a painting of the handsome prince before his enchantment.

Typically, the violation of the taboo and the discovery of the secret identity leads to a separation of the maiden and the monster; Psyche has to go on a long journey and perform a series of tasks before she is reunited with Cupid, and the youngest daughter in "East of the Sun, West of the Moon" has to do the same before she is reunited with her prince. In the Disney film, this is abbreviated. When the Beast discovers Belle has entered the West Wing, he explodes in anger and she runs away, only to be attacked by wolves and then rescued by the Beast who is injured doing so. In the scenes where Belle nurses the injured Beast, we see that demonstration of the maiden's love which otherwise requires her sisterly counterparts to make long journeys, perform countless tasks, or weep buckets of tears.

In the various motifs in the background of his illustrations,

Walter Crane indicates that "Music soothes the savage beast." It may not be surprising, then, that this musical film ends in a swirl of ballroom dancing. Any mention of "balls" might, of course, summon up recollections of "Cinderella" and Belle is on this occasion equally transformed from the plain provincial maiden into the beautifully attired Belle of the Ball. Indeed, this ballroom scene echoes similar ones in the Disney film of this fairy tale.

Disney's "Beauty and the Beast," then, is playfully intertextual. This may not be so surprising. A clue is given early in the film when Belle tells the owner of the bookshop about the book she wishes to read again: "It's my favorite. Far off places, daring swordfights, magic spells, a prince in disguise ... [and here's] my fav'rite part ... where she meets Prince Charming / But she won't discover that it's him 'til chapter three." Belle's own story, in other words, is deliberately situated within the context of other traditional tales. Her story and this film is just the newest incarnation. As the title song indicates, "Beauty and the Beast" is a "tale as old as time."

Playing their own variation upon this old story, the folks at Disney, then, were doing nothing different than what other authors, illustrators, storytellers, and critics have done in their own short stories, myths, folktales, interpretations, pictures, and films. Each of these, this book has been suggesting, permits one more glimpse of the varied meanings that lie within this inexhaustibly rich fairy tale. "Beauty and the Beast" is a great work of literature and "what counts for us in a work of literature," Italo Calvino suggests, "is the possibility of being able to continue to unpeel it like a never-ending artichoke, discovering more and more new dimensions."

SELECTED BIBLIOGRAPHY

Adams, Jeff. *The Conspiracy of the Text: The Place of Narrative in the Development of Thought*. London: Routledge and Kegan Paul, 1986.

Ansen, David. "Just the Way Walt Made 'Em." *Newsweek* 18 November 1991: 74-80.

Baker, Ronald L. "Xenophobia in 'Beauty and the Beast' and Other Animal/Monster-Groom Tales." *Midwestern Folklore* 15,2 (Fall 1989): 71-77.

Barchilon, Jacques. "Beauty and the Beast." *Modern Language Review* 56 (1961): 81-82.

———. "'Beauty and the Beast': From Myth To Fairy Tale," *Psychoanalysis and the Psychoanalytic Review* 46,4 (Winter 1959): 19-29.

Bettelheim, Bruno. *The Uses of Enchantment*. New York: Vintage Books, 1977.

Bly, Robert. *Iron John: A Book About Men*. New York: Vintage Books, 1992.

———. *The Pillow and the Key*. St. Paul, MN: Ally Press, 1987.

Bottigheimer, Ruth B. "'Beauty and the Beast': Marriage and Money — Motif and Motivation." *Midwestern Folklore* 15,2 (Fall 1989): 79-88.

———. "Cupid and Psyche vs. Beauty and the Beast: The Milesian and the Modern." *Merveilles et Contes* 3,1 (May 1989): 4-14.

Bryant, Sylvia. "Re-Constructing Oedipus through 'Beauty and the Beast.'" *Criticism: A Quarterly for Literature and the Arts* 31,4 (Fall 1989): 439-453.

Burton, Anthony. "Beauty and the Beast: A Critique of Psychoanalytic Approaches to the Fairy Tale." *Psychocultural Review* 2 (1978): 241-58.

Califia, Pat. "Saint George and the Dragon." *Once Upon a Time: Erotic Fairy Tales for Women*. Ed. Michael Ford and Mike Ford. New York: Masquerade Books, 1996.

Campbell, Joseph. *The Hero with a Thousand Faces*. Princeton, NJ: Princeton University Press, 1973.

Canham, Stephen. "What Manner of Beast? Illustrations of 'Beauty and the Beast.'" *Image and Maker: An Annual Dedicated to the Consideration of Book Illustration*. Ed. Harold Darling and Peter Neumeyer. La Jolla, CA: Green Tiger Press, 1984.

Carter, Angela. *The Bloody Chamber*. New York: Penguin Books, 1993.

Cocteau, Jean. *Beauty and the Beast: Diary of a Film.* Trans. Ronald Duncan. New York: Dover Publications, 1972.

Cummins, June. "Romancing the Plot: The Real Beast of Disney's *Beauty and the Beast.*" *Children's Literature Association Quarterly* 20,1 (Spring 1995): 22-28.

Darnton, Robert. *The Great Cat Massacre and Other Episodes in French Cultural History.* New York: Basic Books, 1984.

DeNitto, Dennis. "Jean Cocteau's *Beauty and the Beast.*" *American Imago: A Psychoanalytic Journal for Culture, Science, and the Arts* 33 (1976): 123-54.

Donoghue, Emma. *Kissing the Witch: Old Tales in New Skins.* New York: HarperCollins, 1997.

Edens, Cooper. *Beauty and the Beast.* San Diego, CA: Green Tiger Press, 1989.

Ehrenstein, David. "As Long as Gays Play the Monster, We're Tolerable." *The Advocate* 576 (7 April 1991): 77.

Eliot, Thomas Stearns. "Tradition and Individual Talent." *The Sacred Wood: Essays on Poetry and Criticism.* London: Methuen, 1920.

Erb, Cynthia. "Another World or the World of an Other? The Space of Romance in Recent Versions of 'Beauty and the Beast.'" *Cinema Journal* 34,4 (Summer 1995): 50-70.

Estés, Clarissa Pinkola. *Women Who Run With the Wolves: Myths and Stories of the Wild Woman Archetype.* New York: Ballantine Books, 1992.

Fine, Gary Alan, and Julie Ford. "Magic Settings: The Reflection of Middle-Class Life in 'Beauty and the Beast.'" *Midwestern Folklore* 15,2 (Fall 1989): 89-100.

Gad, Irene. "Beauty and the Beast and The Wonderful Sheep — The Couple in Fairy Tales: When Father's Daughter Meets Mother's Son." *Psyche's Stories: Modern Jungian Interpretations of Fairy Tales.* Vol. I. Ed. Murray Stein and Lionel Corbett. Wilmette, IL: Chiron, 1991. 27-48.

Galef, David. "A Sense of Magic: Reality and Illusion in Cocteau's *Beauty and the Beast.*" *Literature-Film Quarterly* 12,2 (1984): 96-106.

Goble, Paul. *Buffalo Woman.* New York: Simon and Schuster, 1984.

Griswold, Jerry. "Wild at Heart." *Los Angeles Times Book Review,* 6 December 1992: 14, 34.

Hains, Maryellen. "Beauty and the Beast: 20th Century Romance?" *Merveilles et Contes* 3,1 (May 1989): 75-83.

Hammond, Robert M. "The Authenticity of the Filmscript: Cocteau's Beauty and the Beast." *Style* 9 (1975): 514-32.

Harrington, C. Lee, and Denise D. Bielby, "The Mythology of Modern Love: Representations of Romance in the 1980s." *Journal of Popular Culture* 24,4 (Spring 1991): 129-44.

Haries, Elizabeth Wanning. *Twice Upon a Time; Women Writers and the History of the Fairy Tale*. Princeton, NJ: Princeton University Press, 2001.

Hawkins, Harriet. "Maidens and Monsters in Modern Popular Culture: The Silence of the Lambs and Beauty and the Beast." *Textual Practice* 7,2 (Summer 1993): 258-66.

Hayward, Susan. "Gender Politics—Cocteau's Belle Is Not That Bête: Jean Cocteau's La Belle et La Bête." *French Film: Texts and Contexts*. Ed. Susan Hayward and Ginette Vincendeau. London: Routledge, 1990.

Hearne, Betsy. *Beauties and Beasts*. The Oryx Multicultural Folktale Series. Phoenix, AZ: The Oryx Press, 1993.

——. *Beauty and the Beast: Visions and Revisions of an Old Tale*. Chicago, IL: University of Chicago Press, 1989.

Henderson, Joseph. "Beauty and the Beast." *Man and his Symbols*. Ed. Carl G. Jung. Garden City, NJ: Doubleday, 1964.

Henein, Eglal. "Male and Female Ugliness Through the Ages." *Merveilles et Contes* 3,1 (May 1989): 45-56.

Hoggard, Lynn. "Writing with the Ink of Light: Jean Cocteau's Beauty and the Beast." *Film and Literature: A Comparative Approach to Adaptation*. Ed. Wendell Aycock and Michael Schoenecke. Lubbock, TX: Texas Tech University Press, 1988.

Hood, Gwyneth. "Husbands and Gods as Shadowbrutes: 'Beauty and the Beast' from Apuleius to C.S. Lewis." *Mythlore: A Journal of J.R.R. Tolkien, C.S. Lewis, Charles Williams, General Fantasy and Mythic Studies* 15 (Winter 1988): 33-43.

Jeffords, Susan. "The Curse of Masculinity: Disney's Beauty and the Beast." *From Mouse to Mermaid: The Politics of Film, Gender, and Culture*. Ed. Elizabeth Bell, Lynda Haas, and Laura Sells. Bloomington, IN: Indiana University Press, 1995.

Kolbenschlag, Maria. *Kiss Sleeping Beauty Good-Bye*. New York: Bantam Books, 1981.

Lassell, Michael. "Beauty and the Beast: Genius Remembered." *The Advocate* 600 (7 April 1992): 77.

Leavy, Barbara Fass. *In Search of the Swan Maiden.* New York: New York University Press, 1994.

Lee, Tanith. *Red as Blood or Tales from the Sisters Grimmer.* New York: Daw Books, 1983.

Lurie, Alison. "Winter's Tales." Rev. of *Burning Your Boats,* by Angela Carter. *New York Times Book Review,* 19 May 1996: 11.

Lüthi, Max. *Once Upon A Time: On the Nature of Fairy Tales.* New York: Frederick Unger, 1970.

Mayer, Marianna, *Beauty and the Beast.* Illus. Mercer Mayer. New York: Four Winds Press, 1978.

McGowan, Raymond. "Jean Cocteau and Beauty and the Beast." *New Orleans Review* 8,1 (Winter 1981): 106-08.

McKinley, Robin. *Beauty: A Retelling of the Story of Beauty and the Beast.* New York: HarperCollins, 1993.

———. *Rose Daughter.* New York: William Morrow, 1997.

Mintz, Thomas. "The Meaning of the Rose in 'Beauty and the Beast.'" *The Psychoanalytic Review* 56, 4 (1969-70): 615-20.

Neumann, Erich. *Amor and Psyche: The Psychic Development of the Feminine. A Commentary on the Tale by Apuleius.* Trans. Ralph Manheim. Princeton, NJ: Princeton University Press, 1956.

O'Brien, Dennis. "How CBS's Beauty and the Beast Adapts Consensus Reality to Shape Its Magical World." *Functions of the Fantastic: Selected Essays from the Thirteenth International Conference on the Fantastic in the Arts.* Ed. Joe Sanders. Westport, CT: Greenwood Press, 1995.

Opie, Iona, and Peter Opie. *The Classic Fairy Tales.* New York: Oxford University Press, 1974.

Pallottino, Paola. "Beauty's Beast." *Merveilles et Contes* 3,1 (May 1989): 57-74.

Pauly, Rebecca M. "Beauty and the Beast: From Fable to Film." *Literature-Film Quarterly* 17,2 (1989): 84-90.

Popkin, Michael. "Cocteau's Beauty and the Beast: The Poet as Monster." *Literature-Film Quarterly* 10,2 (1982): 100-09.

Propp, Vladimir. *Morphology of the Folktale.* 2nd ed. Ed. Louis A. Wagner. Austin, TX: University of Texas Press, 1968.

Ralston, W.R.S. "Beauty and the Beast." *The Nineteenth Century* (December 1878): 990-1012.